DETROIT

Sanders Pavilion of Sweets, at the corner of Michigan and Woodward, circa 1890.

AMERICAN URBAN RENAISSANCE

Tribes such as the Potawatomi and other Algonquian Indians were in Michigan for centuries before French explorers and missionaries arrived in the early 1600's. This scene is a village ca. 1500 A.D., from a painting by Robert Thom.

3

Detroit: American Urban Renaissance

a pictorial and entertaining commentary on the growth and development of Detroit, Michigan

Dedicated to Amy and Mark

Principal Author:

Arthur M. Woodford
Director
St. Clair Shores Public Library

Editors:
Larry P. Silvey
Douglas S. Drown

Art Director:
Rusty Johnson

Assistant Art Director:
James Michael Martin

Detroit: American Urban Renaissance is sponsored by The Greater Detroit Chamber of Commerce.

Copyright © 1979 by Continental Heritage, Inc.,
P.O. Box 1620, Tulsa, Oklahoma 74101.
All rights reserved.

Published in 1979 by Continental
Heritage, Inc.

Library of Congress Catalog Card
Number 78-68072

LSBN 0-932986-05-6

Detroit: American Urban Renaissance
is part of The American Portrait
Series of premium books published
by The Continental Heritage Press;
others include:
  The San Antonio Story
  Houston: a history of a giant
  Des Moines: Capital City
  The Saint Louis Portrait
  Cleveland
  San Diego
  Ft. Worth

A Detroit telephone construction crew in
1904: The foreman of the crew, which was
erecting one of the first long distance cables
leading out of Detroit, is on the left,
dressed for the photographer.

The fight for supremacy: It was 1913 at the intersections of Randolph, Monroe, Broadway and Gratiot, and just about every type of transportation of the time is seen. Fewer than 2 million motor vehicles were in use in the country at the time. From a painting by Robert Thom.

Fill'er up: In 1905, Detroiters purchased their gasoline from the back end of a horse-drawn tank wagon.

Contents

1. When beaver was king

The beaver would begin it all; a riot would cause its rebirth: Below, the interior of a fur trading store about 1750, a half century after Detroit's founding. Below right, the Detroit City Planning Commission at riot scene, 14th and Grand River, August 16, 1967. From left, Vice President Joseph Williams, Amadea Leone, Director Charles Blessing, Harold Smith, President Roland C. Foerster, and Victor P. Saran.

A fort in the wilderness

O n November 24, 1971, Henry Ford II presented a daring proposal to the Detroit City Council. At a time when many thought the city was dying, Ford showed his faith in its future by announcing plans for a $500 million riverfront development. Upon an area occupied by unsightly aging warehouses and unpaved parking lots, Ford detailed a positive scheme to build a complex that was to include a skyscraper hotel, four office towers, apartment buildings, theaters, exquisite shops and fine restaurants. Its name — Renaissance Center.

The choice of this name could not have been better, for this project was indeed to become the symbol of Detroit's rebirth.

In the summer of 1967 Detroit experienced a frightful riot. As a result of that civil disturbance, Detroiters, spearheaded by New Detroit, Inc., took stock of themselves and of their city. Working together they began to rebuild — constructing new office buildings and housing developments, renovating old neighborhoods, opening parks, expanding cultural activities, and providing more educational opportunities. The renaissance has not been limited to just the physical city, but has encompassed the very quality of life itself.

This rejuvenation of Detroit and of the spirit of the people who live here is one more example of the strength and resources of this great city. Since its founding nearly 300 years ago, Detroiters have faced several cycles of rebirth. The city has suffered famine, invasion by foreign troops, riot, pestilence, devastating economic depression, and fire. Each time its citizens have met disaster with courage and hope, rebuilding the city they love. This cycle has come once again, and once again Detroiters are meeting the challenge. Another rebirth is occurring. Detroit's greatest renaissance is underway.

Will it succeed? There is no doubt. We have only to look at our past to find the answer, a past that has shown the ability of Detroiters to struggle, to survive, and to grow.

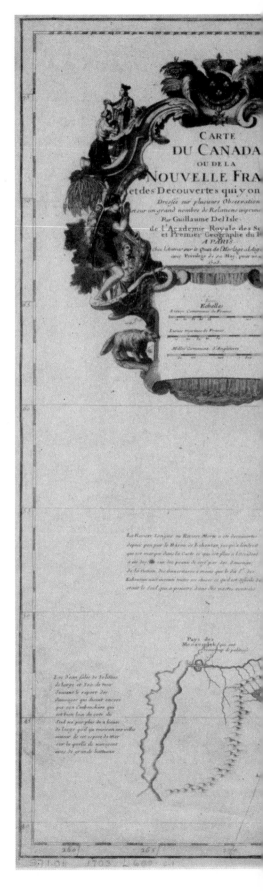

The founder: Antoine Laumet de Lamouthe Cadillac, whose bold plan for a French outpost began what would become one of the world's major cities, was memorialized with this statue by Julius Melchers. Right, the earliest known map of the Great Lakes region showing the location of Detroit. The map was published in 1703.

It began on the morning of July 24, 1701 when Antoine Laumet de Lamouthe Cadillac and a party of 50 soldiers, 50 traders and artisans, and two priests turned their 25 large canoes from midstream and headed toward the south bank of the river. The site Cadillac chose for his settlement was at a point where the river was most narrow and the high banks made it most defensible.

The river connected Lake St. Clair to the north with Lake Erie to the south. It was a frequently traveled waterway and the early French travelers had come to know the region well and had given it a name. They called it the Strait, or in their own tongue, *le Détroit.*

Cadillac and his men climbed the 20-foot bluff and surveyed the terrain. Deciding the location was a good one, he set his men to constructing a small fort. He would name it *Fort Pontchartrain du Détroit.*

Cadillac had great plans for his new French outpost, but never did he imagine that the site he had selected would one day be the center of one of the great metropolitan areas of the 20th century. The City of Detroit was born.

Fort Pontchartrain du Détroit was founded to control the rich fur trade in what is now Michigan and the Old Northwest and to prevent the British from encroaching upon the area. While the world trade in peltry is no small business today, it in no way exerts the powerful influence that it did in the 17th and 18th centuries. Furs were worn by French aristocrats and by the more affluent members of the middle class. Because France had become the fashion center of Europe under Louis XIV, the wearing of furs had spread to other European countries. Also of special importance in creating a demand was the vogue for the broad-brimmed beaver hat in the 17th century. For some time, Europe had been able to meet the demand for furs, but eventually the harvest of peltries ran short. Poland, which had been a chief source of beaver for the French market, became "trapped out." France turned to the New World and Canada.

However, the stage for the founding of Detroit in 1701 was set more than 165 years earlier.

12

13

French influence: Above, the French explorers Jolliet and Marquette at St. Ignace, Michigan, from a painting by Robert Thom. Below, a French voyageur, *a fur trade canoe boatman.*

France's claim to Canada dates back to 1535 when Jacques Cartier discovered the St. Lawrence River and sailed up it to the site of what was to become Montreal. In 1608 Samuel de Champlain arrived as governor and about that time the period of settlement began. Many of those first immigrants found the fur trade an easier, more profitable existence than the drudgery of farming. To control the trade, a string of outposts was established, some where missionaries had already settled. In fact, years before Detroit was founded, several of these forts or trading posts were flourishing in Michigan: Sault Ste. Marie as early as 1668, Fort de Baude at St. Ignace in 1686; Fort St. Joseph, where Port Huron is now located, in 1686; and others at or near the present-day cities of St. Joseph (1679) and Niles (1691).

Within a few years this system to control the fur trade through government outposts began to break down. More and more, the independent traders were dealing outside of government control. The result: a flood of furs went downstream to Montreal. The price of beaver dropped so far that the warehouses were full of skins that simply lay in storage and rotted because it did not pay to send them to France.

In addition, the Jesuit missionaries were pressuring the government to close the outposts because, in many cases, the Indians were being cheated out of their furs. The traders at the outposts were shamelessly and without restraint using brandy as their chief item of exchange.

As a result, in 1696, the government decreed that all furs had to be delivered by the Indians to Montreal. The forts strung around the Great Lakes were ordered closed and abandoned. Only the Jesuits were permitted to maintain mission settlements in Indian country.

Unfortunately for the French, this plan was equally unsuccessful, because the Indians, feeling no particular loyalty, turned to trade with the English. There was one man, though, who was developing a different plan. He was the former commandant at Fort de Baude at St. Ignace — Antoine Laumet de Lamouthe Cadillac. Cadillac felt so strongly that he returned to France to present his plan to Louis XIV.

Variations
of the
Beaver Hat

A clerical hat
(Eighteenth century)

The continental
cocked hat
(1776)

The Wellington
(1812)

The Paris beau
(1815)

The D'orsay
(1820)

The regent
(1825)

*Furry variety: Right, beaver fur found its
way around the heads of Europeans in
various forms, depending on the times and
the styles. Below, Count Louis
Pontchartrain. Bottom, Cadillac receives his
orders from Louis XIV. His plan had been
approved.*

Cadillac's plan was to stop treating the west as a mere outpost, and to plant a
genuine colony here; bring in farmers and artisans, develop towns, and urge the
Indians to establish their villages nearby. The farmers would make the towns
self-sustaining. The traders and Indians would bring in their furs and they would
make the towns financially stable. The king and his chief counselor, Count
Pontchartrain, whose jurisdiction extended over the colonies, were enthusiastic about
the plan and, early in 1701, Cadillac returned to Canada with the king's approval.

Cadillac immediately set about obtaining provisions and supplies for his expedition
and in early July, the flotilla of canoes pushed off from Montreal. They traveled up
the Ottawa River, through Lake Nipissing, and down the French River to Georgian
Bay. Once out of Georgian Bay and into Lake Huron, the expedition followed the
eastern shore south to the Detroit River. On the morning of the 24th they reached
the site of the new town. The landing point, as far as can be determined, was at the
foot of present-day Shelby Street, a few feet below Jefferson Avenue. Today the
Veterans' Memorial Building stands upon that spot.

Cadillac at once paced off the limits of his planned village between the Detroit
River and the small Savoyard River to the rear, marked the corners of his stockade,
and within two hours his men were in the nearby woods felling trees for
construction.

The next few weeks were spent clearing the land and building the fort. The
stockade consisted of a wall of 20-foot logs embedded 4 feet deep in the ground. A
blockhouse was set at each corner of the enclosure, and a moat was dug outside. At
least two gates provided access, one on the river side wide enough to allow large
loads to be brought in, and another in the east wall. There was really only one street
— Ste. Anne's — which paralleled the river along the top of the bluff. Another
shorter street above Ste. Anne's and two north-south streets were the only other
roads in the village.

Detroit's first major street was Ste. Anne's, right, which ran parallel to the river. Below, one of the earliest views of Fort Pontchartrain.

The first building erected was a church. It was completed in two days and the first Mass was sung on the feast of Ste. Anne, in whose honor it was dedicated and for whom it was named. The present-day Ste. Anne's church is located on the corner of Howard and Ste. Anne Streets on Detroit's near west side, not far from the Ambassador Bridge. Ste. Anne's is the second oldest continuous parish in the United States, the oldest being a parish in St. Augustine, Florida. After the church was completed, lots were marked out and houses were built. The original house lots were no larger than 25 feet wide and 25 feet deep. The houses were made of small oak logs chinked with grass and mud and

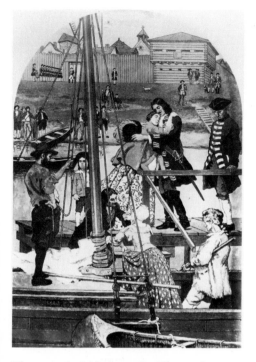

The arrival of Madame Cadillac and Madame Tonty brought the beginning of the feminine touch to Detroit in September 1701. Below, a French militiaman as he looked in 1752, and a playing card used as currency by the French government to pay soldiers at Detroit in 1711.

roofed with bark slabs. Next a large warehouse was built for storage of public property and furs and for use as a trade store. The total area of the new village would today be comprised of about one city block — Griswold, Jefferson, Shelby, and Larned.

In September 1701, Madame Cadillac and Madame Tonty, the wife of Alphonse de Tonty, Cadillac's second in command, arrived in Detroit. There had been no women in the original expedition and Cadillac wanted to convince the Indians that Detroit was intended to be a permanent settlement. In October, ground was broken near the fort, and about 15 acres of winter wheat were sown. There was a crop the following July, and although it was of rather poor quality, it demonstrated that the land could be cultivated and that the village could be reasonably self-sufficient.

As far as the fur trade was concerned, it went well from the first. A band of Hurons set up a village on the river where Third Street is today; the Ottawas settled across the river near the foot of Belle Isle; and the Potawatomis and Miamis set up their villages a short distance downriver. Before long, Cadillac reported 2,000 Indians in the area, and in the spring, distant tribes from as far away as Lake Superior and the Illinois country came in to trade their furs. The pelts that were shipped from *Fort Pontchartrain du Détroit* included bear, elk, deer, marten, racoon, mink, lynx, muskrat, opossum, wolf, fox, and beaver. Within a rather short time, Detroit was established as the center of the Great Lakes fur trade.

In 1706, Cadillac made one of his periodic trips to Montreal and Quebec. When he returned, he brought with him several families of settlers, and for the next few years the settlement prospered. In 1710, he was appointed governor of Louisiana Territory and in 1711 he left Detroit, never to return. In 1720, he returned to France and was given the governorship of Castelsarrasin, a small town near his birthplace. He filled that position until his death at age 72 on October 15, 1730.

At first, the farmers were granted house lots inside the fort while farming on the public domain outside the stockade walls. Beginning on March 10, 1707, the settlers, or *habitants* as they were then called, were awarded farms up and down both sides of the river. These farm grants, known as the private claims in today's land abstracts, consisted of river frontages of from one to four or five arpents (one arpent equals about 200 linear feet) and extended back two or three miles in some cases. In this manner each property owner had access to the river. This was extremely important as the river was a source for food and drinking water, and was the highway on which the farmer transported his goods to and from the marketplace. Eventually these grants became known as ribbon farms because of their long and narrow shape, and their boundaries are marked in modern Detroit by streets which bear the names of the original owners, such as Beaubien, Riopelle, St. Aubin, Chene, Campau, and Livernois.

For nearly 60 years after Cadillac's founding, the village remained French. And except for a siege of the fort by the Sauk and Fox Indians in 1712, and a few other occasional Indian troubles, life was quiet and uneventful.

The fertile soil yielded good crops of wheat, oats and corn. Most of what was raised was consumed by the families themselves, and the surplus was either sold or given for the support of the town, the garrison and the church. Almost every farm had cattle, pigs and chickens. The nearby forest teemed with deer and birds, and the river provided a never-ending supply of fish. Orchards of apple, peach and pear trees were to be found in abundance. From their fruit, cider and brandy were made.

The houses of the *habitants* were improved as time went on, although they were never pretentious. The early rough log structures eventually were clapboarded over; lofts or second floors, lighted by dormer windows, became common. Many of the houses were whitewashed and their Dutch doors were frequently painted apple-green. Their yards, enclosed by picket fences, contained the usual bake ovens and wells with long sweeps. Similar houses can still be seen along the St. Lawrence.

The *habitants* raised large families, and their sons and daughters married at an early age. While they were devoted to their church, they were also a merry lot, with their songs and dances. In warmer weather there was cart racing. In the winter months, horse racing and sleigh riding up and down the frozen river were the most common sports. Schools were not regularly kept, and most of the *habitants* were illiterate. Newspapers were unheard of and unneeded. When the occasional traveler brought news of the outside world or an official announcement was to be made, the town crier called it out from the steps of Ste. Anne's after Sunday morning Mass. Because there were no democratic institutions at this time, politics as we know it did not exist. Except for early day trials such as a smallpox threat in 1752, it was an isolated, and in many ways, idyllic life that Detroiters lived in this period.

The first printed plan of Detroit, below, was published in 1764 and was based on surveys made by Chaussegros De Lery from 1749 to 1755. Right, a fur trade canoe on the Mattawa River, Ontario.

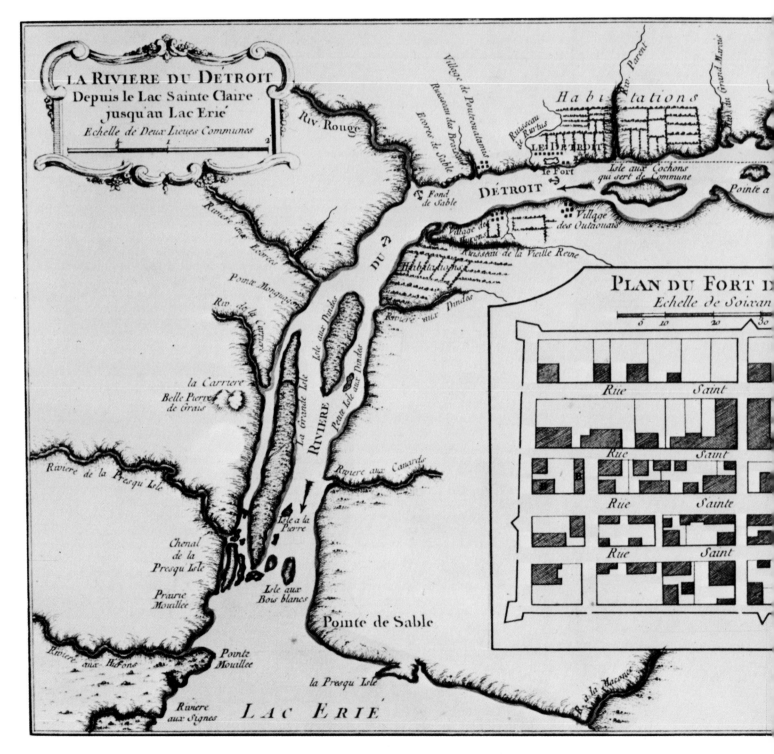

LA RIVIERE DU DÉTROIT
Depuis le Lac Sainte Claire jusqu'au Lac Erié
Echelle de Deux Lieues Communes

PLAN DU FORT D
Echelle de Soixan

British outpost

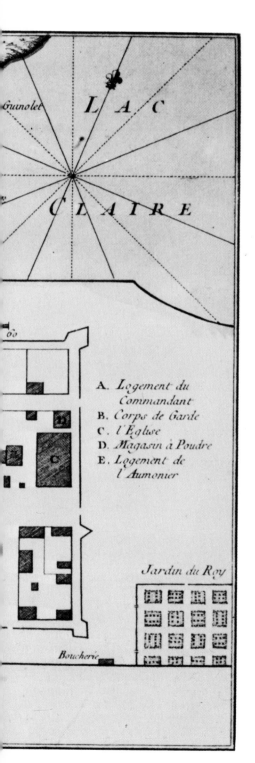

French rule came to an end in Detroit in 1760 when the village was given to the British as part of the spoils of the French and Indian War. While part of a long European power struggle, the conflict was almost entirely a North American war. It grew out of the desire of the English seaboard colonies to have a stake in the vast Ohio River and Great Lakes country.

The war lasted from 1754 until 1760, but Detroit was never directly involved. The conflict was settled on the Plains of Abraham just outside Quebec. On September 13, 1759, the army of General James Wolfe attacked and captured the city. A year later, on November 29, 1760, Montreal was surrendered to the British and Detroit was included in the terms.

Detroit was still more of an area than an actual village when it was taken over by the British. The entire population on both sides of the river numbered about 2,000, with only some 500 people living in the village proper or immediately nearby. The fort itself was considerably larger than the one Cadillac had built, extending about 100 yards in a north-south direction and 200 yards east and west.

Early in the spring of 1761, English traders began to arrive, thus affording the Indians an opportunity to dispose of their winter's catch of furs and to trade for needed goods. To satisfy the wants of the Indians, the traders stocked their stores with snowshoes, large brass locks, pewter plates, ink powder, burning glasses*, scalping knives, nightcaps, mounds of blankets, hair powder, candles, animal traps, Dutch ovens, tea, silver buckles, ear bobs, breast plates, powder, flints, shot, muskets, rolls of tobacco, mococks** of maple sugar, and barrels of rum.

As was the case under the French, large quantities of furs continued to be exported from Detroit. One such shipment consisted of the skins of 12,132 deer, 9,482 racoons, 682 wildcats and foxes, 413 bears and countless mink. Hard money, or specie, was scarce. In its place, the settlers used furs, slaves (usually Indians, but occasionally blacks and whites), tobacco, and clam and oyster shells manufactured by the New York Dutch and carried by the Indians as wampum.

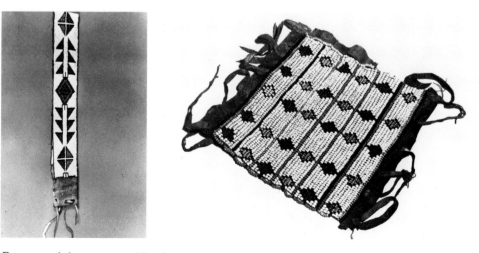

Because of the scarcity of hard money, various forms of wampum were traded, such as Indian wampum belts, left, and arm bands, right.

---

*Burning glasses were magnifying glasses which were used to start fires by concentrating the sun's rays.
**Mococks were Indian baskets designed to keep food.

PLAN
DETROIT
with its Environs.

A. The Town
B. Out Posts.
C. Pondiacs Encampment
D. Cap.t Dalyells defeat

A survey, above, was taken by Captain John Montresor, a British engineer who arrived in Detroit on October 3, 1763. The letter "C" (upper right on map) marks the camp of Pontiac. The Battle of Bloody Run began at the bridge over Parent's Creek (marked with "D" on map). From left Chippewa warrior, a private in the British 60th Foot-Royal Americans, ca. 1763, and Major Henry Gladwin of the 80th Armed Foot.

Unfortunately, the English traders proved to be an unscrupulous lot and hard bargainers as well. The Indians began to complain to Captain Donald Campbell, the fort's British commandant, about the high prices they had to pay. The English were not friendly as were the French, and the Indians, who at first had welcomed the British takeover of Detroit, were quickly disillusioned. As time went on, the dissatisfaction grew. The officers at the fort, with the possible exception of Captain Campbell, were disdainful and suspicious, and they treated the Indians with a frosty arrogance. When General Amherst issued orders limiting the distribution of ammunition, the Indians easily believed a rumor that the British were trying to starve them to death.

A popular legend has it that Major Gladwin, above, found out about Pontiac's plan from a beautiful Indian maiden, but facts would indicate that the plan was known by several people some time before its enactment. Below, Pontiac hands his belt of wampum to Gladwin, an act that would be followed by Gladwin's rebuke of the Indian.

I n the spring of 1763, the gathering tempest broke. Under a plan of confederation developed by Ottawa Chief Pontiac, the British forts from Niagara and Fort Pitt to Mackinac and St. Joseph were simultaneously attacked. For himself, Pontiac reserved the principal fort — Detroit.

Pontiac had a worthy foe, the British Commandant Major Henry Gladwin of the 80th Light Armed Foot, who had been sent to Detroit with a troop detachment in the fall of 1761. He superseded Campbell, who remained as second in command.

Pontiac made his first move in early May of 1763. He asked for a meeting with Gladwin. At the appointed time, Pontiac, with about 60 warriors, arrived at the fort's east gate, known thereafter as the Pontiac Gate. Today the location is marked by a plaque at the corner of Griswold and Jefferson. It was Pontiac's plan that once inside the fort, he would deliver a speech. Then if, in his opinion, conditions seemed favorable, he would signal his warriors to bring out the muskets that were hidden under their blankets and massacre the British troops. If conditions did not seem right, the attack was to be postponed.

The British, however, were well aware of the plan. For years, Detroiters have cherished the legend that Gladwin found out from a beautiful Indian maiden. Actually the "secret" was widely known. For weeks the Indians had been asking local blacksmiths for hacksaws and files. Several people had reported seeing Indians cutting down their musket barrels. Many of the French farmers knew of the plot; in fact Pontiac had actually tried to enlist their aid. There is also the story that a French girl warned her British fiance, and it was he who reported to Gladwin.

Whatever the facts, the British were ready and waiting. When the Indians entered the fort, they found the British troops in full battle dress. Pontiac asked why the soldiers were so heavily armed. Gladwin gave an evasive answer to the effect that he was merely drilling his troops. Then when Pontiac handed Gladwin a belt of wampum, Gladwin drew aside the Indian's blanket. He rebuked Pontiac fiercely for his treachery. Realizing all hope of surprise was gone, the Indians stalked out of the fort, their plan a complete failure.

Western artist Frederic Remington caught the romance of Detroit's conflicts with the Ottawas; left, he painted Pontiac and his warriors leaving the fort, and left below, Pontiac's siege of Detroit. Above, Maj. Robert Rogers, one of the luckier participants in the Battle of Bloody Run. Below, a view from the bridge that was over Bloody Run, on Jefferson Avenue, about a hundred years after the fateful event. Bloody Run is the stream in the center of the picture. The Detroit River is in the background.

So many dead and dying soldiers fell into Parent Creek that it became know thereafter as Bloody Run.

A few days later, Pontiac returned to the fort but was not allowed to enter. Enraged, he turned his warriors loose. They massacred the Turnbull family on a nearby farm, and proceeded to Belle Isle, where they killed several members of the James Fisher family.

On May 10, Captain Campbell and Lieutenant McDougall went with several Frenchmen to the home of Antoine Cuillerier to discuss a truce with Pontiac. The Chief's response was to hold the two officers as hostages for future bargaining.

The next two months were spent in a state of siege. The Indians and British fired upon each other intermittently, neither making any headway. On July 4, a party set out from the fort to retrieve some lead from the home of Jacques Baby. Enroute they met an Indian warrior whom they scalped and then decapitated. Lifting the bloody head, they shook it in the direction of the Indian camp. Unfortunately, the warrior was the nephew of the Chippewa Chief Wasson. In retaliation, Captain Campbell was cut to pieces and devoured. (McDougall had escaped two days earlier.) As was the custom with prisoners, Campbell's heart, still raw and dripping with blood, was consumed by Wasson. This act was not simple cannibalism to the Indians, but was symbolic of taking on the courage of the enemy.

One by one, the posts around the Great Lakes were attacked, and eventually every fort west of Niagara except Detroit was taken. Sandusky, St. Joseph, Fort Miamis, Presque Isle and Mackinac were all captured and their garrisons either massacred or held prisoner by the Indians.

At Detroit, the stalemate continued until July 28, when Captain James Dalzell and Major Robert Rogers arrived with some 300 reinforcements. Dalzell, an ambitious officer, persuaded Major Gladwin that a surprise attack on Pontiac's camp would defeat the Indians. Dalzell was urged to wait for more men, but he was determined to move at once. And so, one hour before daybreak on July 30, Dalzell led a column of 250 soldiers out of the fort and along River Road, present day East Jefferson Avenue.

When the soldiers reached Parent's Creek and began to cross the narrow foot bridge the waiting Indians, hidden in the bushes, opened fire. The lead troops were cut down before they could form a defense. One of those who fell was the overzealous Dalzell. Luckily, Major Rogers reached the nearby Campau house, from which he and his sharp-shooting rangers covered the retreat. Only 90 of the 250 men were saved. So many dead and dying soldiers fell into Parent's Creek, that its waters ran red. From that time on the battle and stream were known as Bloody Run.

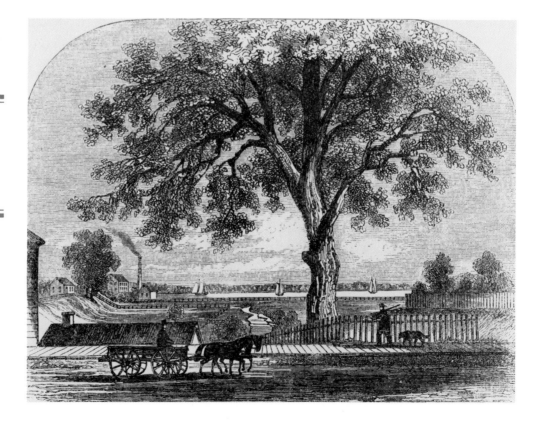

Pontiac's letter to Major Gladwin: dated October 30, 1763, it was written for him by a French sympathizer, proposing an end to the siege.

Lt. Gov. Henry Hamilton: he was the senior British officer in Detroit during the Revolution.

The siege continued through the summer months and into the early fall. But then it had to end, for the Indians needed to set out for their winter hunting. Despite Pontiac's protestations, the Chippewa, Potawatomi and Huron chiefs settled a weary peace with Gladwin and headed for home. Finally, on October 31, 1763, Pontiac sent a message to Gladwin offering to make peace. Without waiting for an official reply, Pontiac and his Ottawas left Detroit for their camp on the Maumee River. The siege was over and of all the western forts, only Detroit had survived.

Following Pontiac's War, life in Detroit settled down to a more peaceful pattern which continued more or less for about a dozen years.

The peace ended however, in 1775, when Britain's Atlantic seaboard colonies rose up in armed rebellion.

During the Revolutionary War, Detroit served as a base for Indian war parties which attacked American villages in Kentucky, Pennsylvania and New York. Led by white partisan raiders, these bands of Indians struck terror into the hearts of the American settlers, and with good reason. It has been estimated that more than 2,000 men, women, and children were killed and scalped by these Detroit-based Indian war parties.

At this time, Henry Hamilton was the senior British officer in Detroit. He had arrived here in November 1775 to assume his duties as lieutenant-governor. Although an army man, Hamilton's major responsibility was that of civil administrator, while the army garrison was under the command of Captain Richard B. Lernoult. Because he was ultimately responsible for planning and directing the raids, the Americans gave him the dubious title of "Hamilton the Hair-Buyer." Actually there is no real evidence that he paid for scalps; on the contrary, he frequently cautioned departing parties not to make war against women and children.

In 1778, the Americans organized an army under the command of Colonel George Rogers Clark to check these raiding parties and to capture the fort at Detroit. Clark began his campaign by capturing the posts at Kaskaskia and Cahokia near St.

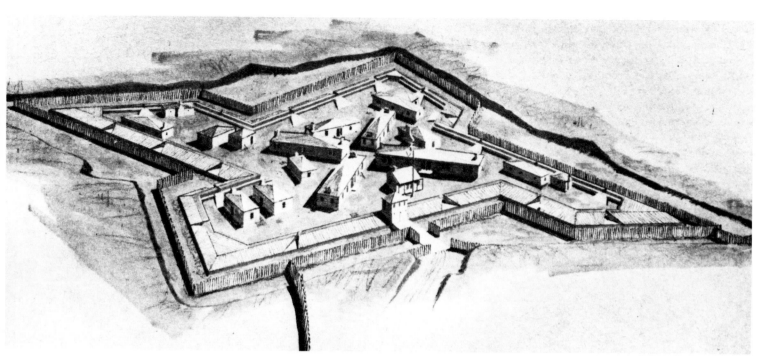

Capt. Richard B. Lernoult had a new fort built, top, as a defense against an American attack which never came. Completed in 1779, it would carry the names Fort Lernoult, Detroit and Shelby until it was finally torn down in 1827. Above, a private in the British King's 8th in 1775. Right, a map of Detroit in 1797, painted by Major Jacob Rivardi, a Frenchman serving in the Corps of Artillerists and Engineers of the U.S. Army. He was stationed in Detroit from 1796 to 1797.

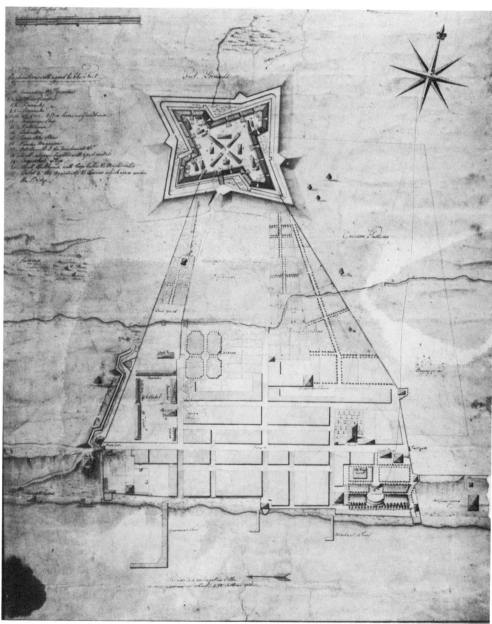

Above, a watercolor of Detroit in 1794, showing the southwest corner of the Citadel (now Congress and Jefferson), the small wooden houses of the town, sailboats, Indian canoes and the busy waterfront. Inset, a private of artillery, Wayne's Legion, 1796.

The final settlement: Gen. Anthony Wayne, far right, led the American troops which won the Battle of Fallen Timbers thereby ending the British hold on Detroit.

Louis. When it appeared that Clark might be ready to move against Detroit, Hamilton led a small force to Vincennes, Indiana, to block his advance. Thinking himself safe for the winter, Hamilton settled in at Vincennes. Clark, however, made an epic march across the flooded plains of southern Illinois and Indiana, and surprised the unsuspecting British. Outnumbered and unprepared, Hamilton surrendered.

In Hamilton's absence, Captain Lernoult, fearing an attack by the Americans, built a new fort at Detroit on the heights several hundred yards north of the town. Completed in April 1779, Fort Lernoult, named in honor of the captain, was ready for action. But the attack never came. Clark was never able to muster the forces necessary for such a campaign.

While the British remained in Detroit, the fort continued to be called Fort Lernoult. Following the arrival of the Americans, it was renamed Fort Detroit. After the War of 1812, it became Fort Shelby, in honor of the governor of Kentucky, who had led an army of Kentuckians to the relief of Detroit. In 1827, no longer needed, and in a sad state of disrepair the fort was torn down.

With the surrender of Cornwallis at Yorktown in 1781, the war came to an end; yet, it did not fully end for Detroit. In September 1783, the Treaty of Paris was signed, which placed the boundary of the United States at the middle of the Great Lakes. This meant that Detroit was to be relinquished to the Americans.

But the change of governments did not occur; the British refused to evacuate Detroit, claiming the American government had not lived up to some of its 1783

treaty obligations. So for some 10 years Detroit remained in British hands and continued as a center for the fur trade and as the chief western base for the British Indian Department.

Finally, President George Washington decided to force a settlement. He sent an army under the command of veteran General Anthony Wayne into the northwest, and in 1794, near present-day Toledo, Wayne's army soundly defeated a confederated Indian force at the Battle of Fallen Timbers. The British finally realized that their position was hopeless. When a new treaty was negotiated in the fall of 1794 with the British government, the Americans had no trouble in obtaining an article that provided for the evacuation of Detroit.

In the spring of 1796, the British garrison evacuated Detroit and moved across the river to Canada; their new base was Fort Malden in Amherstburg at the mouth of the Detroit River.

On July 11, 1796, a detachment of American soldiers, under the command of Captain Moses Porter, arrived in Detroit. The fort was turned over to them and the Stars and Stripes were hoisted.

Two days later, Lt. Colonel John Francis Hamtramck arrived with the remainder of the American force of 400 soldiers. Canadian born, but of Luxembourg and French ancestry, Colonel Hamtramck had served with distinction in the American army during the Revolutionary War. Hamtramck settled in Detroit, where he purchased a farm east of the city. Eventually the area grew into Hamtramck Township and later a northern section became the city of Hamtramck.

The Canadian view: A watercolor by Dr. Edward Walsh of the British 49th Regiment was performed on June 22, 1804. The Huron church in the foreground stood near the Canadian approach to the Ambassador Bridge. Left, the legendary Park House built in the 1790s by a British loyalist; it was dismantled when Americans arrived, and rebuilt in Amherstburg. Whether this is true or not is questionable. It is, however, the oldest standing house in the Detroit River region.

2. Heading west

"Woodward's Plan"

The arrival of the Americans at Detroit caused problems for some of the town's residents, especially those who were unwilling to give up their British citizenship. These included several of the more prosperous and influential merchants who wanted to retain their close trade alliances with Montreal. Some solved the dilemma by packing up their possessions and moving across the river to Canada where they were already large landowners. Among those who made this move were the families of John Askin and Angus MacIntosh.

Not all the merchants moved away, however. Families such as the Macombs, Campaus, Abbots and Mays accepted American citizenship and continued to be leaders in the community. In general, the change of government was accomplished with little difficulty, and for the next several years Detroit settled down to the life of a peaceful frontier community.

For the next decade, the population of the Northwest Territory, as this region came to be known, grew slowly. But grow it did and in 1805, the Territory of Michigan was established. To govern the new territory, President Thomas Jefferson appointed Revolutionary War veteran William Hull of Massachusetts as governor and Stanley Griswold of New Hampshire as secretary. The remainder of the new governing board, known as the Governor and Judges, was comprised of Judges Augustus B.

Territorial organization: Above, William Hull, Revolutionary War veteran, was appointed by Pres. Thomas Jefferson to be the first governor of the Territory of Michigan in 1805. Some merchants stayed in Detroit when the Americans took over; below left, James May stayed to become one of the town's leading citizens, as did merchant Joseph Campau, right.

The fire that gave birth to a motto: The fire of June 1805 which destroyed Detroit and which led Father Gabriel Richard, left, to say, "We hope for better things; it will arise from the ashes."

Woodward of Washington, D.C., Frederick Bates (who had been serving as Detroit's first postmaster since 1802) and John Griffin of Virginia.

On January 18, 1802, prior to these developments, an act had been adopted for the incorporation of Detroit. The act also called for a slate of municipal officers which included a board of five trustees, a secretary, an assessor, a tax collector and a marshall. The first meeting of the trustees was held in February 1802, in the tavern of John Dodemead on Jefferson Avenue near present-day Washington Boulevard. At this time, the town's population numbered about 500, not counting the soldiers at the fort. In all, the town contained about 300 buildings, including homes, sheds, stores, outhouses, barns and sites.

One of the first orders of business for the town's new board was the passage of fire protection ordinances. The threat of fire was a constant worry, for the buildings in the town were mostly of log or wood frame construction and were built close together.

The morning of June 11, 1805 dawned clear. It was a Catholic feast day as well as market day, so the French farmers had come to town early to attend Mass at Ste. Anne's before setting out their produce for sale. Elsewhere, the town was bustling as usual with people going about their business. One of the town's bakers, John Harvey, had set out to replenish his supply of flour. Climbing into his cart, he rapped his clay pipe against his boot. A live coal fell onto a pile of straw and set it afire. In a matter of seconds, the blaze engulfed Harvey's barn and spread rapidly to adjoining buildings.

The dreaded call of "Fire" was sounded and a bucket brigade was formed. The citizens carried buckets of water from the river and tried to dampen the flaming thatched roofs with swabs at the ends of long poles. The town's only fire engine was hauled out, but its suction hose was dropped into a vat next to a hatter's shop and became hopelessly plugged with bits of fur and felt. Householders and merchants scurried back and forth with armloads of possessions, trying to get them safely to the commons or onto canoes and bateaux.

The day was almost windless, but the fire created its own draft and it swept across the town in all directions. In less than three hours not a house was left standing. All that remained were one stone warehouse near the river, a blockhouse and a few fire blackened chimneys.

From the fort, which had remained untouched, observers gazed on a scene of indescribable desolation. People took refuge where they could find it: in the farm houses up and down the river, in the fort, in tents and in hastily constructed bowers of branches on the common. Father Gabriel Richard, the beloved priest of the town, set to work organizing relief, gathering food and finding clothing for the homeless. Fortunately, no one was seriously injured.

Surveying the scene, Father Richard was heard to murmur: "Speramus meliora; resurget cineribus." "We hope for better things; it will arise from the ashes."

Years later, these words would be incorporated into the city's seal, become its official motto, and preface a renaissance.

Father Richard had been at Ste. Anne's for the past seven years. An aristocratic Sulpician priest, he had barely escaped the Reign of Terror after refusing to take the oath of loyalty to the French Republic. From Paris, he had made his way to a seaport and had boarded ship for America. Soon he was in the wilds of Illinois and working with the Indians. In 1798, he arrived in Detroit.

For the first few days after the fire, little was done. The people were in a state of shock, despair and uncertainty. Left to themselves, Detroit's people would have rebuilt the town as before with its narrow streets and small clustered lots. Fortunately, wiser heads prevailed.

Governor Hull and the other newly appointed territorial officials arrived in Detroit on June 30 and immediately set to work. They rejected the idea of rebuilding the town within its former crowded area. Instead, they persuaded Congress to donate the commons east of the fort, plus an additional parcel known as the Ten Thousand Acre Tract to the north of the fort, so that the area of the town could be expanded. It was decided that one new lot would be given to each person 17 years of age or older who had been a resident of the town at the time of the fire. The location of each property was determined by a drawing and included in this drawing were 11 of the city's free blacks.

It was left to Judge Woodward to decide how the new town was to be laid out. Born in New York City in 1774, and a graduate of Columbia College, Woodward had lived and practiced law in Virginia and Washington, D.C. He had formed a close friendship with Thomas Jefferson, from whom he derived many of his ideas. These ideas, quite advanced for a fairly primitive frontier society, caused him to be

The Woodward Plan, as it
became known, called for a
system of interlocking
hexagons, bisected by broad
avenues and studded with
plazas.

Woodward's "Plan of the City of Detroit"
was drawn by surveyor Abijah Hull in
January 1807.

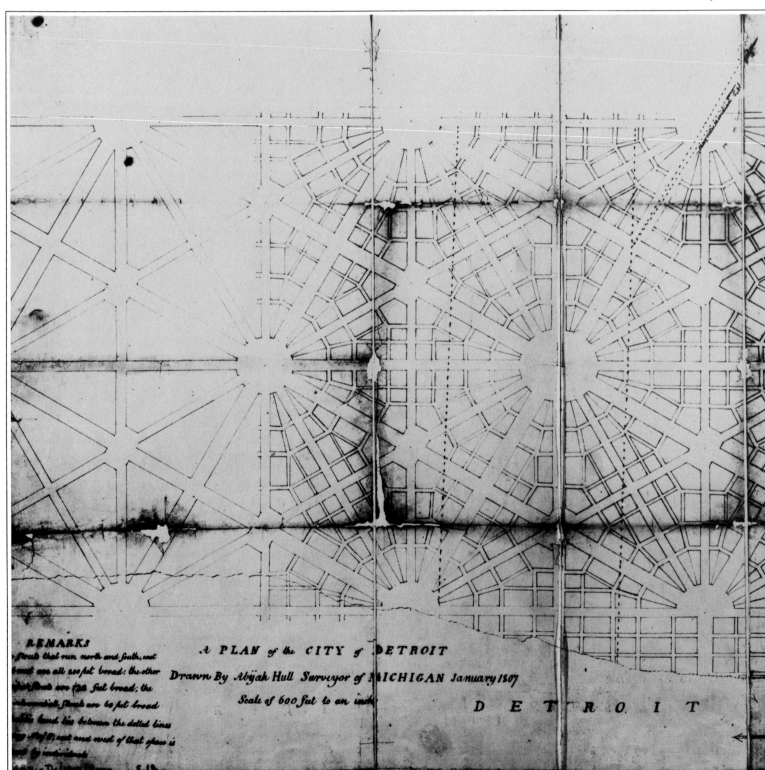

REMARKS

A PLAN of the CITY of DETROIT

Drawn By Abijah Hull Surveyor of MICHIGAN January 1807

Scale of 600 feet to an inch

DETROIT

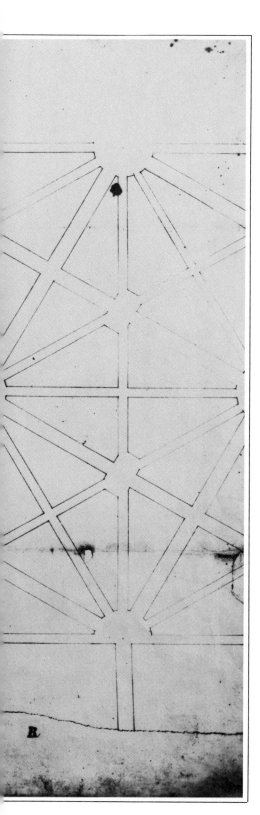

regarded by many Detroiters as an eccentric. While living in Washington, he had observed Major Charles L'Enfant lay out that capital city and adopted ideas for the new Detroit from L'Enfant's plans.

The Woodward Plan, as it came to be known, called for a system of interlocking hexagons, bisected by broad avenues and studded with plazas. Each hexagon was composed of twelve triangular units of eight blocks. In the center of each, one block — or one ninth of all the land — was to be reserved for public buildings, churches and schools. At the hub of each hexagon was a large, open, circular area — or circus — from which the avenues radiated like the spokes of a wheel. Each of these hexagonal units could be repeated and tied into others just like it, so that as the town grew in population, it could be expanded in any direction. Lots of no less than 5,000 square feet each would provide for spaciousness. Actually, these large lots established a traditional characteristic of Detroit; with plenty of land available, it became a city of single-family homes. For years, in fact, Detroit led the nation's major cities in the number of single owner-occupied houses. On the other hand, no row houses, which would have led to a greater concentration of population, were ever built.

Within a short time, Woodward's plan was adopted and several new streets were laid out according to his ideas, while some of the old streets were widened and renamed. Ste. Anne Street, Detroit's earliest street, became Jefferson Avenue.

The center of the town was now located between the river and Larned Street to the north. The major north-south streets being Wayne (now Washington Boulevard), Shelby, Griswold, Bates and Randolph. Construction west of Griswold was discouraged by the federal government, which wanted to keep a clear field of fire for the fort. A few families built their homes as far north as Grand Circus Park but in general, the area north of Campus Martius was largely unsettled open country.

It was Woodward's original plan that Washington Boulevard was to be the city's main street, but the location of the fort prevented its extension south to the river. The avenue that eventually did become the main street was named Woodward, not in his honor, the judge coyly observed, but because it ran "towards the wood, or woodward."

By 1818, the decision was made to abandon the Woodward Plan and to adopt the more familiar checkerboard pattern. Yet, in the central part of downtown, remnants of the Woodward Plan are still seen. Campus Martius, which marked a corner of the original hexagon, is one of the open plazas, with streets such as Woodward, Michigan, Cadillac Square, Fort, and Monroe radiating from it. Continuing up Woodward to Grand Circus Park, one can find a dramatic example of half of one of Woodward's projected circuses or large open spaces, and his radiating boulevards (Madison and Washington) and avenues are clearly discernible.

Tall and angular with piercing eyes, Judge Woodward continued to be one of Detroit's most influential citizens and the head of Michigan's judicial system until 1824, when he was appointed to a district judgeship in Florida by President Monroe. Some may question whether he was an eccentric or a genius years ahead of his time. But, there is no doubt that Augustus Brevoort Woodward was a remarkable man who left his mark on Detroit.

Following its rebuilding, the major mercantile interest of the town continued to be furs. Although the trade prospered, it did so in most cases at the expense of the Indians. Many independent traders were dishonest in their dealings with the Indians, and some of the government agents were little better.

Dissatisfaction with the government's fur trading policies and encroachment on their hunting lands by American settlers caused the Indians to look to the British for aid and comfort. Fort Malden, headquarters for the Canadian Indian Department, became a major center for Indian subsidies for tribes from all over Michigan and the Midwest. These Indian problems continued to grow and, while not the only causes, were major contributing factors to the War of 1812.

The War of 1812 marked a period of real suffering for the people of Detroit. In June 1812, Governor Hull reluctantly accepted command of a force of 2,500 U.S. Army regulars, Ohio volunteers and local militia. After an abortive assault on Fort Malden, Hull retreated to Detroit and prepared for an attack. He did not have to wait long. On August 13, General Isaac Brock, commander of British forces in Upper Canada and a most able military officer, sent Hull a demand for surrender. When Hull rejected the demand, Brock began a cannon bombardment of Detroit from the Canadian shore. Realizing that his supply lines were cut off and fearing Indian atrocities if he put up a fight, Hull decided to surrender.

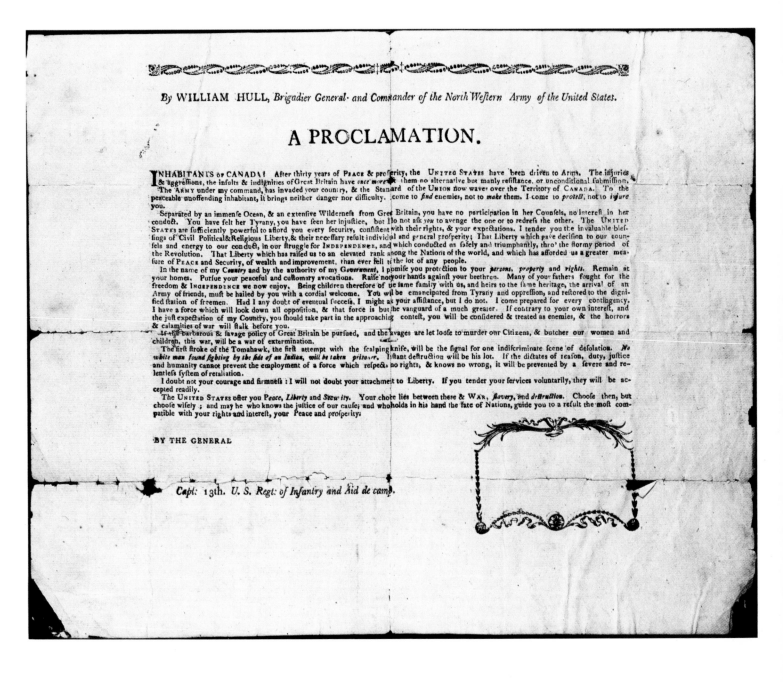

By WILLIAM HULL, *Brigadier General· and Commander of the North Western Army of the United States.*

A PROCLAMATION.

INHABITANTS of CANADA! After thirty years of Peace & profperity, the United States have been driven to Arms. The injuries & aggreffions, the infults & indignities of Great Britain have once more left them no alternative but manly refiftance, or unconditional fubmiffion. The Army under my command, has invaded your country, & the Standard of the Union now waves over the Territory of Canada. To the peaceable unoffending inhabitant, it brings neither danger nor difficulty. I come to *find* enemies, not to *make* them. I come to *protect*, not to *injure* you.

Separated by an immenfe Ocean, & an extenfive Wildernefs from Great Britain, you have no participation in her Counfels, no interest in her conduct. You have felt her Tyrany, you have feen her injuftice, but I do not afk *you* to avenge the one or to redrefs the other. The United States are fufficiently powerful to afford you every fecurity, confiftent with their rights, & your expectations. I tender you the invaluable bleffings of Civil Political & Religious Liberty, & their neceffary refult individual and general profperity; That Liberty which gave decifion to our counfels and energy to our conduct, in our ftruggle for Independence, and which conducted us fafely and triumphantly, thro' the ftormy period of the Revolution. That Liberty which has raifed us to an elevated rank among the Nations of the world, and which has afforded us a greater meafure of Peace and Security, of wealth and improvement, than ever fell to the lot of any people.

In the name of my Country and by the authority of my Government, I promife you protection to your *perfons, property* and *rights*. Remain at your homes. Purfue your peaceful and cuftomary avocations. Raife not your hands against your brethren. Many of your fathers fought for the freedom & Independence we now enjoy. Being children therefore of the fame family with us, and heirs to the fame heritage, the arrival of an Army of friends, muft be hailed by you with a cordial welcome. You will be emancipated from Tyrany and oppreffion, and reftored to the dignified ftation of freemen. Had I any doubt of eventual fuccefs, I might afk your affiftance, but I do not. I come prepared for every contingency. I have a force which will look down all oppofition, & that force is but the vanguard of a much greater. If contrary to your own interest, and the juft expectation of my Country, you fhould take part in the approaching conteft, you will be confidered & treated as enemies, & the horrors & calamities of war will ftalk before you.

If the barbarous & favage policy of Great Britain be purfued, and the favages are let loofe to murder our Citizens, & butcher our women and children, this war, will be a war of extermination.

The firft ftroke of the Tomahawk, the firft attempt with the fcalping knife, will be the fignal for one indifcriminate fcene of defolation. No white man found fighting by the fide of an Indian, will be taken prifoner. Inftant deftruction will be his lot. If the dictates of reafon, duty, juftice and humanity cannot prevent the employment of a force which refpects no rights, & knows no wrong, it will be prevented by a fevere and relentlefs fyftem of retaliation.

I doubt not your courage and firmnefs: I will not doubt your attachment to Liberty. If you tender your fervices voluntarily, they will be accepted readily.

The United States offer you *Peace, Liberty* and *Security.* Your chote lies between these & War, *flavery*, and *deftruction.* Choofe then, but choofe wifely ; and may he who knows the juftice of our caufe, and wholds in his hand the fate of Nations, guide you to a refult the moft compatible with your rights and interest, your Peace and profperity.

BY THE GENERAL

Capt: 13th. *U. S. Regt: of Infantry and Aid de camp.*

In this fashion, Detroit won the dubious distinction of being the only major American city ever occupied by a foreign foe. Altogether it was one of the most dreary military fiascoes ever suffered by American troops. It was made more so by the fact that with a numerically superior and well-armed force at Hull's command, not a single shot was fired in defense of Detroit. For his action, the aging Hull was court-martialed and sentenced to be shot for cowardice. At the last minute, however, President James Madison pardoned him in view of his Revolutionary War services, but Hull lived out his life in disgrace.

The British occupation that followed Hull's surrender lasted just over one year. During that time, the people of Detroit were forced to live under semi-martial law. Indians were allowed free access to the town and most of the merchants had their stores broken into and their merchandise carted away. Fearful of antagonizing his Indian allies, British commandant General Henry Proctor did nothing to prevent the plundering.

Following an American naval victory on Lake Erie on September 10, 1813, American troops invaded Upper Canada, and under the command of General William Henry Harrison, the Americans attacked the retreating British column. During the ensuing battle, Tecumseh, leader of the confederated Indian tribes, was killed, and on September 29, Detroit was reoccupied

A proclamation was issued by Gen. Hull in 1812 to Canadians, left, calling for volunteers to the American cause. It did little good, for Hull ended up surrendering Detroit to British Gen. Isaac Brock, below, without a shot being fired in defense of the city. Typical uniforms of the day for the soldiers of both sides: a private with the British 10th Royal Veteran Battalion, left, and a private with the American 1st Regiment of Artillery.

35

Shortly before the Americans recaptured Detroit in September 1813, Tecumseh, confederated Indian tribes leader, was killed during the Battle of the Thames, above. The American forces were led by Gen. William Henry Harrison, right. Far right, an engraving of Chief Tecumseh dressed in his uniform jacket as a British general.

by the Americans. Although the war was to continue for another year, Detroit was never again seriously threatened.

The year 1814, however, marked a low point in Detroit's history. The countryside had been ravaged by war. Indians, British and American troops had vied with each other in destroying fields, tearing down fences and barns for firewood, and in stealing livestock. In addition, the war had interrupted the planting of crops, and townspeople and soldiers were constantly hungry. The situation became so serious that in some outlying areas people were reduced to eating boiled hay. Judge Woodward wrote: "The desolation of this territory is beyond all conception (with) more than half of the population destitute..." Then, during the winter, an epidemic swept through the town and several hundred people died. No one was certain what the disease was and it was simply called a plague.

The war finally came to an end in late December 1814, with the signing of the Treaty of Ghent. The following February, word reached Detroit that the peace pact had been ratified by Congress. To celebrate the ending of the war, the leading citizens of the town gathered at the Woodworth's Hotel and staged an all night party billed as the Grand Pacification Ball. To show that there were no hard feelings, the Detroiters invited the British officers from Fort Malden to attend. The fiddles played late into the night, glasses were filled and emptied time after time, and huge quantities of food were consumed. It is reported that the party was a great success, and indeed did much to pacify the ill feelings of war.

Mercantile center

During the two decades that followed the War of 1812, Detroit was to experience its first dramatic growth. This prosperity can largely be attributed to one man — Lewis Cass. A man of extraordinary talents, he probably had a greater influence on the growth and development of Detroit and Michigan than did any other single individual.

Born in New Hampshire in 1782, Cass moved to Ohio as a young man. There he studied law and served in the Ohio legislature. He arrived in Detroit in 1812 as a colonel of Ohio Volunteers. After the city's capitulation, Cass was sent back to Ohio on parole. Later he was exchanged, and returned to Detroit in 1813 with General Harrison's army. Because of his services, both military and political, President Madison appointed Cass governor of the Michigan Territory on October 29, 1813.

Cass proved to be a most able administrator and served as governor of the

During the 1830s, the people of Detroit and Michigan suffered through a period of "land fever" as seen in this view of the Kalamazoo Land Office.

UNITED STATES LAND OFFICE

Walk-in-the-water ushered in a new era for Detroit transportation and its arrival was celebrated accordingly.

territory for 18 highly successful and progressive years. When he finally relinquished the position in 1831, he went on to become Secretary of War, minister to France, United States senator from Michigan, presidential nominee of the Democratic Party in 1848, and finally Secretary of State on the eve of the outbreak of the Civil War. Cass died in Detroit on June 17, 1866 at the age of 83.

Detroit had a population of 850 at war's end, with the Territory of Michigan at something less than 5,000. But with the war now over, and the threat of Indian attack no longer serious, a great migration to the West began. However, the rush of settlers by-passed Michigan. Instead, they poured into Ohio, Indiana and Illinois. One reason: Detroit and Michigan had gained a poor reputation from adverse government surveyors reports, one of which stated that Michigan was "an interminable swamp." Another basis for the lack of public enthusiasm for Michigan was its inaccessibility. To reach Detroit, one had to travel across Canada or across Ohio, a most difficult journey which included crossing the Black Swamp. The only other way to reach Michigan was by slow, uncertain and expensive passage across the lakes on a sailing vessel.

Thus, throughout the East, Michigan was given — however understandably — an undeservedly poor image. Governor Cass took note and action: visitors and tourists were invited to come and see Michigan for themselves. In 1817, President Monroe was persuaded to visit Detroit, and other distinguished citizens came from time to time. Their visits received considerable publicity in the East and helped change the unappealing image of Michigan.

Three national events also influenced this situation and were major elements in determining Detroit's growth. First was the development of the steamboat. In 1811, Robert Fulton sailed his *Clermont* up the Hudson River from New York and almost immediately people began to think in terms of steam navigation. At Black Rock, near Buffalo, ship-builders laid the keel of a 135-foot sidewheeler. Launched May 28, 1818, it was named, *Walk-in-the-Water.* As the first steamboat on the upper Great Lakes, she caused considerable enthusiasm in the West. Her maiden voyage was to be to Detroit.

The first: Its name was Walk-in-the-Water, and it was the first steamboat on the upper Great Lakes. Date of arrival at Detroit was August 27, 1818.

Steam navigation became big business in the 1820s and 1830s. Built at Detroit in 1833 by Oliver Newberry, the Michigan, above, was at the time the largest steamboat on the Great Lakes. Right, the Superior was one of the most popular of the early Great Lakes steamers. Built near Buffalo, she first arrived in Detroit on May 25, 1822.

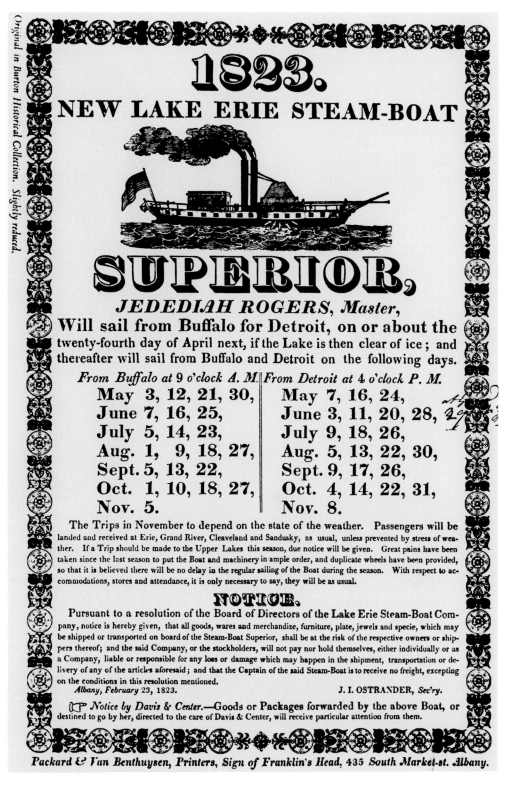

1823.

NEW LAKE ERIE STEAM-BOAT

SUPERIOR,

JEDEDIAH ROGERS, Master,

Will sail from Buffalo for Detroit, on or about the twenty-fourth day of April next, if the Lake is then clear of ice; and thereafter will sail from Buffalo and Detroit on the following days.

From Buffalo at 9 o'clock A.M.	*From Detroit at 4 o'clock P.M.*
May 3, 12, 21, 30,	May 7, 16, 24,
June 7, 16, 25,	June 3, 11, 20, 28,
July 5, 14, 23,	July 9, 18, 26,
Aug. 1, 9, 18, 27,	Aug. 5, 13, 22, 30,
Sept. 5, 13, 22,	Sept. 9, 17, 26,
Oct. 1, 10, 18, 27,	Oct. 4, 14, 22, 31,
Nov. 5.	Nov. 8.

The Trips in November to depend on the state of the weather. Passengers will be landed and received at Erie, Grand River, Cleaveland and Sandusky, as usual, unless prevented by stress of weather. If a Trip should be made to the Upper Lakes this season, due notice will be given. Great pains have been taken since the last season to put the Boat and machinery in ample order, and duplicate wheels have been provided, so that it is believed there will be no delay in the regular sailing of the Boat during the season. With respect to accommodations, stores and attendance, it is only necessary to say, they will be as usual.

NOTICE.

Pursuant to a resolution of the Board of Directors of the Lake Erie Steam-Boat Company, notice is hereby given, that all goods, wares and merchandize, furniture, plate, jewels and specie, which may be shipped or transported on board of the Steam-Boat Superior, shall be at the risk of the respective owners or shippers thereof; and the said Company, or the stockholders, will not pay nor hold themselves, either individually or as a Company, liable or responsible for any loss or damage which may happen in the shipment, transportation or delivery of any of the articles aforesaid; and that the Captain of the said Steam-Boat is to receive no freight, excepting on the conditions in this resolution mentioned.

Albany, February 23, 1823.   J. I. OSTRANDER, Sec'ry.

☞ *Notice by Davis & Center.*—Goods or Packages forwarded by the above Boat, or destined to go by her, directed to the care of Davis & Center, will receive particular attention from them.

Packard & Van Benthuysen, Printers, Sign of Franklin's Head, 435 South Market-st. Albany.

Walk-in-the-Water sailed from Buffalo on August 23, 1818, carrying 29 passengers. After a number of stops along the way, she arrived at the mouth of the Detroit River on the evening of August 26. The following morning, she picked up a welcoming delegation of distinguished Detroiters, at Fighting Island, including Judge Woodward, and headed upstream. Lacking a whistle, *Walk-in-the-Water* signaled her approach to Detroit by firing a small four-pounder cannon carried on her forward deck. Everybody in town turned out to greet her and there was wild cheering as she headed into her berth, with the not-so-dignified Judge Woodward astraddle her bowsprit, waving a bottle.

Although she was to continue in operation for only three years, *Walk-in-the-Water* ushered in a new era. Before long, other steamers were built and by 1831, they were arriving daily at Detroit's Bates Street wharf.

The combination of improved transportation and cheap land brought thousands of settlers to Michigan from the East.

The second factor affecting Detroit's growth was the sale to settlers of public land in Michigan. Again the important figure was Lewis Cass. As governor, one of the first things Cass did was to negotiate a series of treaties with the Indians, who called him "Big Belly" in friendly tribute to his ample girth. As a result of these negotiations, the Indians ceded most of the land in what is now Michigan to the federal government. A federal land office had been opened in Detroit as early as 1804, but at that time there just was not much land to sell. But after 1820, when the first treaties were signed, that all changed. In that same year, Congress passed a new land act permitting individuals to purchase a minimum of 80 acres for cash at $1.25 an acre; a settler with $100 could purchase a family-size farm. Sales of land at the Detroit office, in fact, became so brisk that on some days Jefferson Avenue was thronged with hundreds of men queued up waiting to file their claims. It is from such a situation that the expression, "a land office business," evolved.

The third factor to affect Detroit's growth was the Erie Canal. Opened in late 1825, this great inland waterway connected the eastern seaboard with the Great Lakes. Stretching 363 miles across New York State, the canal's eastern outlet was on the Hudson River between Albany and Troy; its western terminus was at Buffalo. It took eight long years to complete the canal at a cost of more than $725 million. So great was the traffic on the canal, however, that it proved profitable from its first day of operation. Huge barges, pulled by horses, carried passengers and cargo to Buffalo where they were transferred to lake steamers and sent on their way to Detroit. Hailing the canal's opening, the *Detroit Gazette* reported that: "We can now go from Detroit to New York in five and a half days. Before the war, it took at least two months more."

This combination of improved transportation and cheap land brought thousands of settlers to Michigan from New England and New York. And it was through Detroit that most of these settlers passed on their way to their new Michigan farms. In fact, during the 1820s and 1830s, the reception and outfitting of new settlers was Detroit's most important business.

Early tourism push: Circulated throughout the East, maps such as this one published in 1839 promoted Michigan. It was titled, Tourists' Pocket Map of Michigan Exhibiting its Internal Improvements, Road Distances, *etc.*

etroit's growth, at first not spectacular, was nonetheless steady. In 1819, the population was only 1,110, not much more than at the end of the war. By 1830, it had doubled to 2,222, and by 1840 it reached 9,124.

The new transportation and the Erie Canal affected Detroit and Michigan in another important way. The immigrants, mostly farmers, had produce to sell from their new farms, and the canal opened up a market for Michigan crops in the East. Even as the canal was being opened, newspapers reported the "singular fact" of the arrival in Detroit of a wagon load of flour from the mill in Pontiac. It was

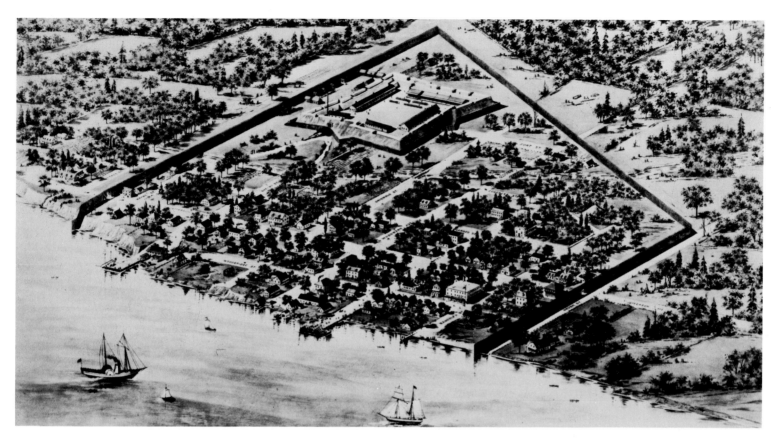

Detroit had only about a thousand inhabitants when the Walk-in-the-Water arrived in 1818. At the time that this bird's eye view was done, it was considered "historically correct in every detail."

Detroit's first public school building, top left, was on Woodbridge Street near Shelby. Occupied from 1838 to 1842, the school room was on the second floor, and the grocery store of N. Prouty was on the ground floor. The Rev. John Montieth, far left, had started a common school in 1816, but it ended when a teacher threw a knife at one of his students and was chased out of town. Left, the first University of Michigan building, constructed in 1817-18 on the west side of Bates Street near Congress.

the first ever from the interior. Two years later, the first bag of flour was loaded onto a boat for export. The next year it was followed by the first shipment of tobacco.

The vast fishing grounds of the Great Lakes could now also be commercially exploited. A typical catch might include pike, pickerel, perch, bass, bullheads, and sturgeon weighing up to 125 pounds. In a single day in the fall of 1824, 30,000 white fish were caught at the fishery on Grosse Ile just south of Detroit. By 1830, seven vessels were engaged in shipping salted fish to the East. Others carried products such as ice and cider, and returned with oysters and manufactured goods.

The New England families who settled in Detroit and Michigan brought with them their Yankee characteristics and colloquialisms, and their independence of mind. Along with household belongings and farm implements which the new transportation facilities permitted them to carry, they also brought their virtues of morality, thrift, religion and the desire for education.

Detroit had no schools during the French and British regimes. It was left to the Yankee settlers to introduce this somewhat revolutionary notion. In 1816, the Reverend John Monteith arrived from Princeton and immediately founded a common school. It came to an untimely end, however, when the teacher, a Mr. Danforth, hurled a knife at one of his obstreperous scholars, and was thereupon chased across the river by the vexed parents.

Father Richard had even less luck in trying to bring education to the community. In 1804, he had started a church school, and five years later he had imported the first printing press into the territory. The French citizens of the community showed little interest in either. He also had worked diligently to promote an Indian school to prepare Indian children for life in the rapidly changing culture. But this school also failed when its federal funding was withdrawn.

In 1817, Judge Woodward became actively engaged in the field of higher learning when he organized the *Catholepistemiad*, or University of Michigania. Thirteen *didaxiim* (professorships) were established. The Reverend Monteith was appointed to seven of these, Father Richard to six. Their combined annual salary was set at $181.25. In 1837, the school was moved to Ann Arbor, where it became and prospered as the world renowned University of Michigan.

Several other attempts were made at establishing public schools in Detroit, but they too met with little success. In 1842, however, a new law was passed which created a city-wide board of education. The act also gave the city the power to levy a school tax. To provide a place of learning for its new students, the Board of Education purchased its first schoolhouse the following year. Located at Park Place (now Times Square) near Grand River the building cost the grand sum of $540.

In 1819, the Territory of Michigan was permitted to elect a delegate to Congress; the first was William Woodbridge, above. Right, the first edition of Detroit's first newspaper.

During the formative years, Detroiters had almost as much trouble going to church as they had going to school.

MICHIGAN ESSAY;
OR, THE IMPARTIAL OBSERVER.

DETROIT, TERRITORY OF MICHIGAN:—PRINTED AND PUBLISHED BY JAMES M. MILLER.

VOL. I] THURSDAY, AUGUST 31, 1809 [NO. I.

A churchly view: the east side of Woodward between Congress and Larned in 1849, top; to the left is the Methodist Church, in the center is St. Paul's Episcopal Church, and on the right is the First Presbyterian Church. Above, the early 19th century Ste. Anne's Church on Larned between Bates and Randolph. It was completed in 1828.

Along with their lack of interest in books, the early French had little interest in newspapers. It was Father Richard who instigated the town's first newspaper. It was called the *Michigan Essay or The Impartial Observer,* a title almost as big as the paper itself. The first issue appeared August 31, 1809 with articles in both French and English. But this undertaking could hardly be called a success, for as far as is known there was never a second issue.

The next newspaper venture was fortunately better received. At the urging of Governor Cass, a new weekly called the *Detroit Gazette* began publication on July 25, 1817. Although crude when compared to today's journals, the *Gazette* was a lively and informative paper. As the city's first real newspaper, it continued publication until 1830.

During the next several years, a number of other papers began publication. By far the most successful of these published its first issue on May 5, 1831 as the *Democratic Free Press and Michigan Intelligencer,* a name that was soon shortened to the *Detroit Free Press.*

During the formative years of Michigan, Detroiters had almost as much trouble going to church as they had going to school. Except for the Catholics, they were well provided for by Ste. Anne's and by new parishes as the city grew. The British garrisons usually had chaplains, but there was no settled Protestant minister in Detroit until Reverend Montieth arrived in 1816. The following year, the Protestants banded together and formed the First Evangelical Soceity. In 1821, its name was changed to the First Protestant Society. As the Society grew, the various Protestant denominations broke away to form their own churches: the Methodists in 1823 and the Episcopalians in 1824. In 1825, the remaining members of the Society formed the First Presbyterian Church. During the next decade, other Protestant churches were formed. The first Baptist Church was organized in 1830, and the Second Baptist Church, Detroit's first black church, was established in 1836. The Congregationalists moved into their first church in 1844.

The city's first Lutheran church was established in 1833 following the initial wave of German immigrants into Detroit. It was also at this time that Detroit's Jewish community began to grow. Within a few short years, there were enough members to form Congregation Beth El, organized in 1850.

The New England settlers who poured into the Michigan Territory quickly found that they had little liking for the autocratic rule of the Governor and Judges, a form of government in whose affairs they had no voice. Governor Cass, aware of this discontent, made plans to do something about it. The first change came in 1819, when the Michigan Territory was granted the right to elect a delegate to Congress. The first man sent to represent the territory was William Woodbridge, a close friend of Cass. In 1825, Father Gabriel Richard was elected representative and became the first Roman Catholic priest ever to sit in the halls of Congress.

Detroit's first mayor: John R. Williams, for whom John R. Street is named. Top, Michigan's territorial and state capitol, erected in 1823, and pictured here in the 1850s. It later was used as the city's union school, above right.

In 1824, the rule of the Governor and Judges came to an end, replaced by an elected legislative council. Detroit reorganized its city government that same year, and the people elected a mayor, a clerk, and a board of five aldermen. The first man to be elected mayor was businessman John R. Williams. Several years later, Detroiters honored their first mayor by naming two streets after him. The first, Williams Street, has long since disappeared, but the second, John R. Street, is still one of our city's major thoroughfares.

For the new legislative council to have a place to meet, a capitol was built. Under the Woodward Plan of 1807, such a building was supposed to have been erected in Grand Circus Park, but it was still too far out in the country in 1824. Another site was selected, the small triangular plot of ground fronting on State Street and the head of Griswold, today known as Capitol Park. Finally completed in 1828 at a cost of $21,000, this beautiful building could easily have passed as a New England church.

The building served as the capitol until 1847, when Lansing — because of its location near the center of the state — became the capital city. After Detroit ceased to be the center of government, the Old Capitol, as the building eventually came to be known, was used for a variety of purposes. In 1893, while serving as the city's high school, it was destroyed by fire.

When Lewis Cass resigned as governor in 1831 to go to Washington as Secretary of War, he was succeeded by George B. Porter. Porter, not known for his diligence, was frequently absent from Michigan. As a result, Stevens T. Mason, the young territorial secretary, was called upon to serve as acting governor.

Those who were able did what they could for those who contracted cholera, but in truth, there was little that could be done.

It was while Mason was serving as acting governor in 1832 that the state militia had to be called out. The troops were sent to Chicago to help quell the Indian uprising in northern Illinois known as Black Hawk's War. The war itself never touched Detroit directly, but one incident connected with the war did, and with disasterous results.

On its way to Chicago from Buffalo with more than 300 soldiers, the steamer *Henry Clay* stopped at Detroit on July 4, 1832. After docking, local health officials were called aboard to identify the illness that had struck down several of the soldiers. Their findings could not have been worse — the disease was the dreaded cholera. The vessel was ordered to cast off at once. The disease spread so quickly among the troops though that the *Henry Clay* was forced to stop at Port Huron. There, about 150 of the soldiers deserted the ship, and headed back to Detroit on foot. Many were able to reach the city, but many others died along the way.

The disease spread rapidly among the townspeople of Detroit who, living close to the waterfront, drew their water and passed their water indiscriminately along the riverbank. On July 6, Detroit recorded its first death. Cows, pigs, goats and other domestic animals spread the epidemic. Many citizens fled the city in fear for their lives, but when they tried to enter nearby towns, they found the roads barricaded and were turned back by armed guards.

Those who were able did what they could for those who contracted the disease, but in truth, there was little that could be done. Father Richard made a daily circuit of the town in a cart to collect the dead for burial. He also nursed the sick until, with the epidemic already on the wane, he contracted cholera and died on September 13, 1832. He was one of the 96 to die of the disease that summer.

Cholera struck again in 1834, but this time with added horrors. During a three-week period in August, 122 people, seven percent of the city's population, died of the disease. The custom of ringing the church bells to announce a death was abandoned, for the ceaseless tolling only added to the panic of the residents. With

Father Martin Kundig turned the Most Holy Trinity Roman Catholic Church into a hospital during the 1834 cholera epidemic, and used parishioners as nurses. The church was located at the northwest corner of Bates Street and Cadillac Square.

Stevens T. Mason was sworn in as Territorial Secretary in 1831 by Gov. Lewis Cass. Three years later, he would take over as governor when Gov. Porter died from cholera.

bells, horses' hooves, and hawkers' cries stilled, the city was eerily peaceful. The streets were choked from the smoke of pitch, which people burned in the belief it warded off the disease. The Capitol and Most Holy Trinity Church were turned into hospitals. Father Martin Kundig tore out the pews and set up litters, and the men and women of the parish served as nurses. Altogether, Detroit suffered four cholera outbreaks. The third was in 1849, and the fourth and last epidemic occurred in 1854.

It was during the city's second outbreak of cholera, in July 1834, that Governor Porter died. As a result, Stevens T. Mason became acting governor on a full-time basis. He did such a creditable job that, in 1835, when Michigan declared herself a state, he was elected the first governor, though he was only 24 years old. The citizens of the territory also adopted a constitution, although because of a boundary dispute with Ohio, it was not until January 26, 1837, that Michigan was officially admitted to the Union as the 26th state.

The two decades following statehood were a time of continued growth for Detroit and Michigan. After 1830, fur was no longer a major factor in Detroit's economic life. In that year, the records listed 232 diverse businesses established within the city.* By the mid-1840s the city had lost most of its characteristics of a riverfront trading post. It had become a town of businessmen and shopkeepers, of busy commercial houses and of quiet tree-lined residential avenues.

The commercial center of the city remained concentrated near the river front, the

---

*Included were 5 bakers, 12 blacksmiths, 60 carpenters and joiners, 3 coopers, 1 coach and chaisemaker, 10 gunsmiths, 24 grocery and dry-goods merchants, 16 grocery and provision stores and alehouses, 6 hatters, 5 harness makers, 8 innkeepers, 23 masons, 3 painters, 3 printers, 12 shoemakers, 7 watchmakers, and 5 wheelwrights.

Detroit in 1837: Above, a view of the city from the Canadian shore shows a busy river crowded with lake steamers. Right, a humorous rendition of a Democratic rally on the grounds of the capitol at the first state election in 1837.

principal streets being Atwater, Woodbridge and Jefferson. Above Jefferson was the residential district extending north to about Adams, with Third the western boundary and St. Antoine the eastern. Gradually, some of the more prosperous citizens moved out East Jefferson. A few of the old houses dating from the 1830s and 1840s may still be seen there. Others moved up Woodward, and as business encroached north of Jefferson, the residential area pushed north of Grand Circus Park. In 1836, Detroit's population was 6,927. By 1840, it had reached 9,124. Then it took a significant jump to 21,019 in 1850, and by 1860, just before the Civil War, Detroit boasted a respectable population of 45,619.

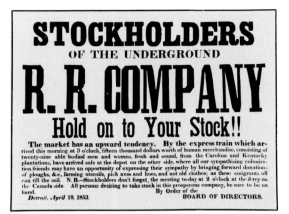

Escape for some, battle for others: Left, an 1853 handbill reports the successful arrival in Canada of 29 escaping slaves and of the next meeting of the Detroit "stockholders." Below, the Michigan 24th Regiment of the famous Iron Brigade on the first day of the Battle of Gettysburg, July 1, 1863. The Iron Brigade's trademark was the black hat and feather.

Because of its location across the river from Canada and its accessibility from the border states, Detroit became an important last station on the Underground Railroad.

Civil war

During the 1840s and 1850s, a zealous wave for reformation swept across the United States. It began in western New York state in the 1820s and one of its most important goals was the abolition of slavery. Because many of Detroit's settlers in the 1820s and 1830s were from western New York, it is understandable why a strong anti-slavery and pro-abolition sentiment developed in the city.

Slavery had existed in Detroit since its earliest days, and persisted well into the 19th century. As late as 1830, slaves were still owned by those who had lived in the city during the British period; a provision in the Jay Treaty of 1794 allowed settlers to keep "all their property of every kind." Since slaves were considered property, those residents who owned slaves were allowed to keep them. Records show that 175 slaves were in Detroit when the Americans arrived in 1796. About half were Indians, the rest were blacks who had been brought from raids into Kentucky during the Revolutionary War. There were also a number of free blacks living in the town at this time. One William Lee worked on the Macomb farm and a free woman known as Black Betty worked as a cook for several of the town's well-to-do families.

After 1796, no new slaves were brought to Detroit and the anti-slavery movement took hold and grew. Finally, in 1835, when the new state constitution was signed, the institution of slavery was at last abolished in Michigan.

Just prior to this, however, Detroit was jolted by a serious racial incident.

In 1831, a slave named Thornton Blackburn and his wife Ruth escaped from Kentucky and made their way to Detroit. In the summer of 1833, they were traced by slave hunters and claimed by their owner. The Blackburns were arrested and held in the city jail pending their return to the South. A large crowd, made up mostly of blacks, stormed the jail on Gratiot between Farmer and Library Streets demanding the Blackburns' release. A woman obtained permission to visit Mrs. Blackburn and once inside, changed clothes with her, thus enabling Mrs. Blackburn to escape to Canada. A couple of days later, while her husband was being escorted to a boat to start his journey back south, the crowd rushed the sheriff and severely beat him, in the melee that followed, Blackburn was spirited away. It appeared that Blackburn and his rescuers had made good their escape in a cart by way of the post road, but when a posse overtook them some miles from town, they found the cart empty. Blackburn had joined his wife in Canada.

During the year following the Blackburn Riot, Erotius Parmalee Hastings organized the first anti-slavery society in Detroit. Two years later, in 1836, a group of Quakers, Congregationalists, Methodists and Presbyterians met in the Presbyterian Church in Ann Arbor and established the Michigan Anti-Slavery Society.

Because of its location across the river from Canada and its accessibility from the border states, Detroit became an important last station on the Underground Railroad. Thousands of slaves escaping from the South were passed along the "Railroad" through Ohio, Indiana and Illinois into Michigan and on to Detroit. The slaves were hidden during the day by sympathetic townspeople and farmers in barns, attics, haystacks, cellars and church steeples and transported at night from one station to the next. In Michigan these stations were located about every fifteen miles. Seven main routes were in operation by 1840, with the Detroit River as Route No. 1.

Once in Detroit, many fugitives were hidden in the livery barn of Seymour Finney's Temperance House. The hotel was at the corner of Woodward and Gratiot, which today is the site of the park area known as the Kern Block. The stable was a block away at the northeast corner of State and Griswold, across the street from the

The Underground Railroad: The livery barn of Seymor Finney's Temperance House, above, at Griswold and State Streets, was one of the important stations on the Underground Railroad. Right, another important station was the Second Baptist Church, at Monroe and Beaubien. The church was founded in 1836 by 13 ex-slaves. Its first pastor was the Rev. William C. Monroe, who taught the first classes for black children in Detroit in the church's basement. The first celebration of the Emancipation Proclamation was held here on January 6, 1863.

Top, Detroit in 1855. Above, Woodward Avenue in 1856, looking south from Cadillac Square to the river; in the foreground, old City Hall, today the site of the Soldiers and Sailors Monument.

old Capitol. A bronze plaque on the wall of the Detroit Bank & Trust Company branch offices now marks the location.

Another important station was the Second Baptist Church. On any night of the week, the church could expect the arrival of passengers on the railroad. The pastor would receive a note from one of his members which might read: "Pastor, tomorrow night at our 8:00 meeting, let's read Exodus 10:8." In Underground language, that meant "Conductor No. 2 will be arriving at 8:00 p.m. with ten slaves, eight men and two women."

At each of these stations, the stationmaster would hide, feed and instruct the passengers during the day, then take them to waiting barges and canoes during the night, and send them across the river to Canadian sanctuary. As a result, a sizable and energetic black community developed in Windsor, and from there Henry Bibb's *Voice of the Fugitive* eloquently advanced the anti-slavery cause. Passengers also traveled through Detroit to Amherstburg, Colchester, New Canaan, Gosfield, Chatham, Shewsbury, Dresden and London. Today, large numbers of blacks in southwestern Ontario trace their ancestry to passengers on the Underground Railroad.

The Civil War was to bring to an end a need for the Underground Railroad although the movement remained active by helping freed slaves relocate in the North. On April 7, 1870 Detroiters celebrated the radification of the 15th Amendment which guaranteed all citizens the right to vote regardless "of race, color, or previous condition of servitude." George DeBaptiste, a local leader in the railway movement, displayed a sign on his store which read:

"Notice to Stockholders of the Underground Railroad: This office is closed. Hereafter all stockholders will receive dividends according to their merits."

On March 12, 1859, Detroit was to experience an incident of quite a different sort. On that date the noted black orator and abolitionist Frederick Douglass was in

March 12, 1859: A most interesting meeting of the minds took place on that day in Detroit, when abolitionist Frederick Douglass, left, met the fiery John Brown, right, at the home of William Webb, below right, on East Congress. William Lambert, below left, owner of a clothes cleaning shop at Bates and Larned, and one of the leading abolitionists in Detroit, listened with others as Brown outlined his plan of armed uprisings throughout the South. Others there that night were Rev. William C. Monroe, George DeBaptiste, and Henry Bibb. America would later hear of John Brown at Harper's Ferry.

Detroit to give a lecture. On the same day the fiery, fanatical abolitionist John Brown arrived in town with 14 escaping slaves from Missouri. After the passengers had been safely delivered to conductors for transfer to Windsor, Brown went to the home of William Webb, a local black leader with whom Douglass was staying. There, by candlelight, in the quiet, two-story frame house on Congress Street, Brown outlined his plan for the organization of simultaneous armed slave uprisings all across the South. George DeBaptiste, one of the men attending the meeting, suggested that the rebellion include the wholesale elimination of planters. Douglass, however, was far too discerning to commit himself to such a course. Brown did receive promises of help, though, from some of the others present; he then moved on to Chatham, Ontario, to recruit a band of followers. His next and most historic stop was Harper's Ferry, in 1859. The Webb house, where the Detroit meeting took place, was on the north side of Congress near St. Antoine. The site today is marked by a state historical plaque.

Citizens' meeting: The date was April 18, 1861, and citizens hold a meeting in front of the new post office on the northwest corner of Griswold and Larned. In the distance, at the head of Griswold, the old state capitol.

On April 12, 1861, a Detroit telegraph operator received the news that Fort Sumter had been fired upon. Five days later, President Lincoln announced a state of war. The next day, a citizens' mass meeting was held in front of the newly built post office and customs house, at the northwest corner of Griswold and Larned Streets, and a wave of patriotic fervor swept the city.

The first to answer Lincoln's call for volunteers was the First Michigan Infantry, composed of militia companies drawn from Detroit and several other Michigan towns. Orders for the formation of the First Michigan were issued April 24 and, on May 2, the regiment was mustered into service. The troops were trained at Fort Wayne, located south of Detroit on the river. Construction of the fort was begun in 1841 because of the fear of invasion during Canada's Patriot's Rebellion. Completed in 1851, Fort Wayne never fired a shot in anger, though it was garrisoned almost continuously until World War II.

Receiving the colors: The First Michigan Infantry, in an impressive ceremony, above, receives its colors in Campus Martius, May 11, 1861. Right, a view of Detroit and river from Fort Wayne in that same year. Far right, the First Michigan Infantry was a three-month regiment; upon its return to Detroit, the troops were welcomed at the Detroit and Milwaukee Railroad Station by the elderly Lewis Cass.

RALLY ROUND
THE FLAG, BOYS!
100 MEN WANTED!!
For the 23d Mich. Infantry.

Enlist before April 1st, secure the Government Bounty of $300 00,
AND "KEEP OUT OF THE DRAFT!"

Government Bounty, $300; State Bounty, $100; Town Bounty, $100.
Apply to WM. SICKELS, St. Johns, or
O. L. SPAULDING,
Lieut. Col., 23d Mich. Infantry, Corunna.
March   , 1864.

On May 11, an impressive ceremony was held in Campus Martius in which the ladies of the city presented the First Michigan with its colors. Two days later, the regiment left for Washington to become the first troops from the area west of the Alleghenies to reach the nation's capital. Their arrival reassured President Lincoln that the western states would remain loyal. He is said to have exclaimed, "Thank God for Michigan." In all, Detroit would send about 6,000 soldiers to the battlefields during the four years of the Civil War. Michigan would send nearly 90,000.

Another distinguished regiment was the Twenty-fourth Infantry, composed almost entirely of Detroit and Wayne County volunteers. It trained at the old fair grounds, then at Woodward and Canfield Avenues, and arrived at the front in time to take part in the battle of Antietam. Later it was incorporated into the famous Iron Brigade. It opened the battle of Gettysburg on July 1, 1863, and was almost completely destroyed while holding up the Confederate advance until the mass of the Army of the Potomac could get into position. Its casualty rate was the highest of any Union regiment in the battle.

As it became obvious that the war was going to be a long and painful struggle, the call went out for more volunteers. As a device to encourage local enlistments, Detroit officials decided in July 1862 to pay a bounty of $50 for each single man, and $100 for each married man who volunteered. In all more than $200,000 in bounties was paid by the city during the war.

In addition to these funds, a number of organizations also made contributions of money and materials to the various societies which provided special services to the city's soldiers and sailors. These included the Michigan Soldiers' Relief Organization, which gave aid to the sick and wounded, the Ladies Aid Society, which packed and shipped supplies for the men at the front, and the Michigan Christian Commission, which ministered to the soldiers' spiritual needs.

In addition to its young men, Detroit supplied munitions and food for the Union army throughout the war. The city, in fact, was a principal distribution point for supplies from Michigan towns and farms.

Detroit's Civil War record was tarnished in March 1863, by a race riot. The city's

More than $200,000 was paid in bounty by Detroit to induce men to join the Michigan regiments fighting in the Civil War.

unskilled Irish and German immigrants were incensed over the newly passed national conscription law, because the affluent could escape the draft by paying a $300 fee. The white immigrants associated it with the kind of discrimination that had caused them to leave their homelands. Most of these immigrants had relatively little interest in the war to preserve the Union. They were more concerned about the competition of black laborers for unskilled and service jobs. As a result, race relations in the city were severely strained.

The actual incident which touched off the riot occurred when William Faulkner, a black, was arrested, tried and convicted of raping two nine-year-old girls, one black, the other white. An angry mob attempted to lynch Faulkner as he was being taken to jail from the courthouse on the morning of Friday, March 6. Held back by federal troops, the crowd turned and started down to Beaubien Street where most of the city's blacks lived. Armed with guns, clubs, axes and a rope, the mob swept through the area. A large part of the district was burned and damaged from fire; looting and vandalism was extensive. A large number of blacks were beaten and two men were killed. Others were forced to flee their homes, and some escaped across the river to Canada.

Among the blacks who sought temporary refuge in Canada were Robert and Frances Pelham. Pelham, a good mathematician, bricklayer, mason and contractor, had left the South during the hysteria that followed John Brown's raid on Harper's Ferry. In 1862, the family arrived in Detroit and rented a house on Congress Street. During the next hundred years, the Pelhams were to become one of Detroit's leading families.

The riot continued throughout the day. Order was not restored until nightfall, when troops from Fort Wayne and Ypsilanti arrived. Ironically, William Faulkner was later proven innocent when the two girls confessed that they had perjured themselves.

Lt. Ulysses S. Grant, above, lived with his wife for a time in Detroit, on Fort Street between Russell and Rivard, right. He slipped on the ice one day in front of the grocery store of Zachariah Chandler; the later prominent Republican would, below, become Secretary of the Interior in Grant's cabinet.

It is also interesting to note that the First Michigan Colored Infantry was mustered into service and left Detroit just a few months after the riot. The regiment, which had been raised through the efforts of Detroit's black leaders, was comprised of men from Canada as well as Detroit. In all, about 1,400 blacks enlisted, and of these, some 1,000 had been born in slave states. In the spring of 1864, the regiment became the 102nd United States Colored Infantry. This unit saw service in South Carolina and Florida and took part in several engagements. Mustered out in Charleston on September 30, 1865, the soldiers returned to Detroit shortly thereafter.

As the Civil War continued for four long years, Detroiters took pride in the fact that the Union's most famous general once lived in the city. From 1848 to 1851, Lieutenant and Mrs. Ulysses S. Grant made their home in Detroit while Grant was commanding officer of the Detroit Barracks. The Grants lived in a small frame house typical of the workingman's home of the day. It was on the north side of Fort between Russell and Rivard. During the 1930s the house was donated to the State of Michigan by the Michigan Mutual Liability Company and moved to the Michigan State Fair Grounds. Each year during the Fair, it is furnished in the style of the period by the Detroit Historical Museum and is opened to the public.

Twice while living in Detroit, Lt. Grant was in the public notice: he once slipped and fell on the icy sidewalk in front of Zachariah Chandler's grocery store. He unsuccessfully sued the merchant, who later became a leader in the Republican Party and his Secretary of the Interior when Grant was elected President. On the other occasion, Grant was fined for riding his horse too fast through the city's streets.

The Civil War ended on Palm Sunday, April 9, 1865, when Lee's armies surrendered at Appomattox. The Union was preserved. The wreckage was surveyed, and the task of rebuilding begun. The United States faced the future uncertainly, little knowing that it stood on the threshold of an industrial expansion which, in little more than half a century, would make it the richest and strongest nation in the world. Detroit was to play a vital role in this industrial growth.

Mourners for Lincoln: The announcement of President Lincoln's assasination, right, was issued by Mayor K. C. Barker on April 15, 1865. Above, on April 25, a Lincoln memorial service was held in Cadillac Square. This view looks west across Woodward Avenue. In the central background is the dome of the old state capitol.

CITY OF DETROIT

Mayor's Office,

APRIL 15, 1865.

To the Citizens of Detroit:

To-day we have received the astounding intelligence that our Chief Magistrate has been daringly assassinated at a public theatre in our Capital. The Nation, lately so joyous over victories and the assurance of peace, is to-day shrouded in gloom. The feeling is universal that no greater loss could befall our country. Sorrow sits upon every countenance. Under such circumstances, and while bending beneath the weight of this great calamity, it seems proper that I should invite all citizens to suspend their ordinary avocations, and to give testimony to their sense of the country's affliction.

I therefore request that all public and private places of business be closed and remain closed during the day.

I request that all the bells of the city be tolled one hour, from 12 to 1 o'clock, this day.

I also respectfully invite the citizens of Detroit to meet at the

CITY HALL, AT 3 O'CLOCK

To take such action as shall be appropriate to the solemn occasion.

K. C. BARKER, Mayor.

The beginnings of major growth: the
Michigan Central Railroad roundhouse
and freight yard about 1868.

2

3. The age of industry

Sault Ste. Marie canal was opened to shipping in 1855. Charles T. Harvey (on horseback), the man principally responsible for the planning and building of the canal, surveyed the construction site in the summer of 1854.

Copper, iron and lumber

The growth of manufacturing that followed the Civil War had its beginnings in Detroit and Michigan in the early 1840s. Initial sources of this expansion came from copper, iron and lumber.

The existence of copper in Michigan's Upper Peninsula had been known from the earliest days. The French had learned of it from the Indians, and the exploration of the upper Great Lakes was due in part to the desire to locate these copper deposits. It was not until 1841, however, that extraction and refining of copper ore began on a commercial basis. A need for metals used in the manufacture of steam-ship and logging engines caused copper and brass to become important factors in Detroit's economy in the 1850s.

In 1844, about the time the copper industry was beginning to grow, substantial deposits of iron ore were discovered in Michigan's Upper Peninsula. In 1855, the new canal at Sault Ste. Marie was completed and it was not long before great shipments of iron ore were on their way down the lakes. With iron ore and limestone — the necessary materials for the production of pig iron and steel — now readily available, Detroit was gradually becoming a center for heavy industry. A number of foundries and machine and boiler works were built in which boilers and engines for the new mining industries, ships, and sawmills were produced.

A number of sawmills were always in Detroit, but the city never became a major lumbering center as did Saginaw, Bay City, Muskegon and several other Michigan cities. Nevertheless, large amounts of Detroit capital went into lumbering, and several Detroiters amassed great fortunes from the industry in the latter part of the 19th century. Included were such men as Russell A. Alger, John S. Newberry, William H. Murphy, Eber B. Ward and David Whitney, Jr.

Detroit's first heavy industry was the manufacturing of railroad cars, wheels and other railway equipment. At this time, there were no rail connections beyond Michigan's borders, so most of what was needed in the way of rolling stock and equipment had to be produced locally. The Pontiac and Detroit Railroad (whose first

A new house for government: The new city hall, above, as it was then called, was completed in 1871, in what is now Kennedy Square. In the foreground is the Soldiers and Sailors Monument which was dedicated in April, 1872. The old city hall, built in 1835, right, was across the street from the new building, and on July 18, 1871, below, the mayor and city council, attired for the occasion, marched across Woodward Avenue from the old city hall to formally occupy the new one.

*The public gathers: looking toward the
northwest corner of Michigan and
Woodward in 1870.*

cars were drawn by horses) had begun operations in the spring of 1838 when the
line reached Birmingham. By 1852, Detroit was connected by rail west to Chicago,
and by 1854, to the east through Canada.

The first major production of rail equipment began here in 1853 when a physician,
Dr. George B. Russel, organized a firm which became the Detroit Car &
Manufacturing Company. Operations began in a small shop on Gratiot. As the
business grew, the firm moved to larger quarters at the foot of Beaubien Street.
Before long, other companies entered the field. These included the Michigan Car
Company in 1865, and the Peninsular Car Works, founded in 1885.

In 1868, Detroiter William Davis perfected his refrigerator car and persuaded local
meat packer George H. Hammond to provide the needed capital to set up his
business. The first shipment by refrigerator car was made from Detroit to Boston in
1869.

67

Woodward Avenue ca. 1870: Above, the west side of Woodward from Clifford northward; the clump of trees marks the location of Grand Circus Park. Right, the east side of Woodward Avenue between Gratiot and Grand River; a century later it was the site of the J. L. Hudson Company's downtown store.

Stove capital: Detroit was the nation's leading stove manufacturer in the late 1800s, and the statement from the Michigan Stove Company, above, which manufactured "all kinds of Cooking Parlor and Heating Stoves," were performed with a flourish. Right, as the symbol of Detroit's importance to the industry, this giant stove was constructed for the Chicago Columbian Exposition in 1893. Located for years on the grounds of the Detroit-Michigan Stove Company at Jefferson and the Belle Isle Bridge, it may now be viewed at the Michigan State Fairgrounds.

The Real McCoy: Elijah McCoy, inventor of the automatic railroad lubricating cup.

Two years later, a man by the name of George Pullman bought a plant near Monroe and St. Aubin Streets, and for the next several years Detroit was the center for the manufacture of the Pullman sleeping car. In 1879 the company's headquarters was moved to Chicago, but cars continued to be built in Detroit until 1893.

In addition to railroad cars, a substantial number of other new railroading ideas and mechanical improvements came out of local shops. One of these was the railroad track cleaner and snow plow, the invention of August Day.

Another major contribution was made by a black mechanical engineer named Elijah McCoy. McCoy's invention, the automatic lubricating cup, allowed railroad engines to be lubricated automatically while the train was moving, thus preventing the problem of overheating. Prior to this, it was necessary to stop trains every so often to lubricate them — a process that took considerable time. In all, McCoy is credited with more than 80 inventions and some 57 patents. Because of the quality of Elijah McCoy's workmanship, railroad men would insist on his design when buying a lubricator. From then on people referred to the genuine article as "the real McCoy."

In 1975, the site of McCoy's home on Lincoln Avenue near Hobart Street was designated an historic area by the Michigan Historical Commission and commemorated by the erection of an historical marker.

Another industry that had an early start in Detroit was the manufacturing of stoves, which began locally in the 1830s. At that time, most stoves were made either at Albany or Troy, New York. Because it took so long to get a replacement part from the east, the Hydraulic Iron Works in Detroit began making parts for the local market and was successful enough to branch out into the production of complete stoves. In 1861, Jeremiah Dwyer, who had worked in an Albany stove works and as an apprentice with Hydraulic, opened his own stove company in Detroit. He did well, and three years later, two Detroit industrialists put up the necessary capital for expansion. First called the Detroit Stove Works, Dwyer's operations grew and in 1871 the firm became the Michigan Stove Company. During the 1870s and 1880s, other firms such as the Peninsular Stove Company began operations. As a result, for more than 50 years, the manufacturing of stoves and kitchen ranges was Detroit's leading industry.

The drug and pharmaceutical industry, another business venture of great importance to Detroit, grew from the activities of a number of local druggists who began to manufacture their own medicines. The industry was to include not only the

Chemical concoctions: top left, on the southwest corner of Woodward and Clifford was the store of James Vernor; it was in that store in 1876 where his famous ginger ale was first made. Bottom left, this first Parke Davis plant was located on the corner of Cass and Henry Street. Right, another concoction, beer, was being produced in the 1880s in the Stroh Brewery.

James McMillan, top, one of Detroit's leading businessmen of the 19th century, made his fortune in the railroad business. Bottom, John J. Bagley earned his wealth in the tobacco business; he went on to become a director in several banks, a power in the Republican Party and governor of Michigan in 1872.

manufacture of over-the-counter "patent medicines," but a large wholesale pharmaceutical business as well.

The industry got its start in Detroit in 1845 when Jacob Farrand began to manufacture pills in his grocery and drugstore on Woodward near Jefferson. Before long his business grew, and Farrand, Williams & Company became one of the leading wholesale drug firms in the Midwest.

In 1865, Frederick Stearns opened a drugstore on Jefferson near Brush Street and soon he too was manufacturing pharmaceuticals. As his business grew, Stearns moved to a number of locations, finally building a large factory and laboratory on East Jefferson at Bellevue.

Detroit's largest pharmaceutical concern, Parke, Davis & Company, dates to 1866. Its founder, Dr. Samuel Duffield, a member of a distinguished local family, began making pharmaceuticals in a drugstore at Cass and Henry. It was not long before the entire building was turned into a factory, and Duffield was joined by partner Hervey C. Parke and George S. Davis. A short time later, Duffield left the business, and the firm became Parke, Davis & Company. In 1873, the firm moved to a new plant on the river near the foot of Joseph Campau. The company's greatly expanded operations are still located on this site.

Not all druggists went into the business of manufacturing pills. For example, Theodore Eaton, who had begun a wholesale drug business in 1855, eventually went into the production of chemicals and dyestuffs. Another druggist, James Vernor, liked to mix soft drinks in his store where he produced a very fine ginger ale. It was not long before the soft drink business outgrew the drugstore, and for more than a century Vernor's Ginger Ale has been enjoyed by millions.

Along with railroad equipment, stoves and drugs, several other important industries were established in Detroit about the time of the Civil War. These included paints and varnish, soap, shoes, seeds, tobacco and steel. The great company names were the Berry Brothers, Detroit White Lead and Color Works, Queen Ann Soap, D. M. Ferry Seed, American Eagle Tobacco Company, Pingree-Smith Shoe Factory and the Eureka Iron and Steel Works, where the first commercial Bessemer steel was produced in 1864. The men who made these and other companies prosper and grow included John J. Bagley, Daniel Scotten, Henry R. Baldwin, Richard H. Fyfe, Hazen S. Pingree, Dexter M. Ferry, James McMillan and Eber B. Ward.

In addition, there was Gernhard Stroh, grandson of a German innkeeper who also brewed his own beer. Young Stroh immigrated to Detroit and founded the Lion

Marketing Detroit's wares: samples of 19th century posters, cards and broadsides; clockwise, from top, the almost perfect seeds of D. M. Ferry & Co.; new and reliable turnip seeds by Ferry; "All the Novelties in Boots and Shoes" at C. R. Mably's Department Store; an ad for Harmony Chewing Tobacco from one of the country's then largest tobacco companies, Scotten, Lovett & Cos.; and frogs in men's clothing, a poster for "J. L. Hudson, Clothier, Etc."

In the 1880s and '90s, the corner of Michigan and Woodward was the site of Fred Sanders' confectionary store, above. It was in 1875 that Sanders served the first ice cream soda. Below, Mabley & Company on Woodward Avenue was Detroit's leading department store in the 1880s.

Brewery, later to become the Stroh Brewery Company. About this time, R. L. Polk and Company was incorporated and issued its first directory. Roehm and Wright established a jewelry firm and when Roehm decided to leave the business, John Kay became Wright's partner, and they moved into a new store at Woodward and Campus Martius. Fred Sanders opened his confectionery store on Woodward Avenue and served the country's first ice cream soda. Ira and Clayton Grinnell opened their music store and several years later began manufacturing pianos.

For their shopping needs, Detroiters of this period could choose from a number of excellent department stores such as Mabley's (the city's first big department store), the Newcomb-Endicott Company, the Ernst Kern Company, People's Outfitting, and Partridges, which in 1908 became the Crowley-Milner Company.

Without a doubt, the leading merchant was Joseph Lowthian Hudson. In 1877, Hudson moved to Detroit as manager of Mabley's clothing department. Four years later he opened his own store, establishing the J. L. Hudson Company in the Opera House on Campus Martius.

In 1891, Hudson moved into a new building at the corner of Farmer and Gratiot. Over the years, the building was expanded and enlarged until 1946 when it filled the entire block bounded by Woodward, Farmer, Gratiot and Grand River. Carrying everything from grand pianos to spools of thread, $500 designer dresses to jasmine tea, original oil paintings to electric trains, Hudson's grew into the third largest department store in the United States.

In its heyday, Hudson's downtown store was "the" shopping place for Detroiters. Its 25 stories made it the tallest department store in the world. Its nearly two million square feet made it second only to Macy's New York store in space under one roof. Hudson's had the largest sales force, the biggest switchboard — second only to the Pentagon — and the world's largest American flag. It covered six stories of the building when it was hung on the Woodward side each Flag Day.

In 1897, just down Woodward from Hudson's, the notions business of Kresge and Wilson was established. A short time later, when Sebastian S. Kresge bought out his

In 1881, J. L. Hudson opened his clothing store on the first floor of the Opera House on Campus Martius, above. Next door was the jewelry firm of Roehm & Wright, later known as Wright Kay and Company. Hudson's later became one of the largest department stores in the nation, boasting the largest sales force, the biggest private switchboard and the largest American flag, above. Left, the Kresge & Wilson "Big 5 and 10c Store" on Woodward Avenue. Opened in 1897, it was the forerunner of the great S. S. Kresge chain.

partner, the business was moved across Woodward to the corner of Grand River where a wide variety of merchandise was offered in the attractive price range of five to ten cents — "nothing over ten cents." This store, still in operation, became number one in the billion dollar nation-wide Kresge chain.

Detroit's banking system did not develop until well into the 19th century. The first, the Bank of Detroit, opened in 1806, but its capital of $10,000 disappeared with the cashier. The next attempt at a bank did not come until 1818, when the Bank of Michigan was lawfully chartered. It served the community well, and in 1842 when its charter expired, it closed its doors, but with no losses to the depositors.

Since then, a large number of banking institutions have been established in Detroit. One of the most sound was the Detroit Savings Fund Institute. This bank began operations in 1849 at the northeast corner of Griswold and Woodbridge, on property that is now part of the civic center. After a few years, it changed its name to the Detroit Savings Bank and thrives today, Michigan's oldest banking institution, as the Detroit Bank & Trust. The bank's present main office is at the southeast corner of

Banking's beginnings: the Detroit Savings Bank building at Griswold and Larned in 1881, above, was erected in 1878 and known as the Bank Chambers; it was the home of the Detroit Savings Bank (today the Detroit Bank & Trust) until 1906. Inset left, the bank staff on the steps of the Bank Chambers in 1881. Inset right, 19th century Michigan state bank notes: Bank of Pontiac; Detroit Bank (Detroit's first and founded in 1806, this note bears the signature of bank president Augustus B. Woodward); the State Bank of Michigan.

Fort and Washington Boulevard, on the site of old Fort Lernoult.

In general, however, the city's current large banking structure dates from the Depression. Several new banks were organized to replace others closed in the 1930s by government proclamation, that story will be told later.

The growth of industrialization, and to a degree of all commerce in the area, was facilitated by the availability of electricity, provided initially by a variety of companies which eventually consolidated in 1903 into the Detroit Edison Company. In fact, Detroit was the home of the country's first power plant actually built for that purpose. This was Station A, a two-story brick building built in 1886 on the corner of Washington Boulevard and State Street.*

---

*While Station A has long since been replaced by giant power plants producing hundreds of times the amount of electricity far more efficiently, much of the machinery that produced electricity in Station A is now housed in a replica of the original building in Greenfield Village. To this day it is operated by retired Detroit Edison employees and viewed by thousands of visitors to Greenfield Village each year.

Above, St. Albertus Church on the southwest corner of East Canfield and St. Aubin about 1880. Inset above, typical of the working class homes in Corktown, these houses date from the latter part of 19th century.

The pre-Civil War industrial development and that which followed required a substantial labor force. While many who found jobs in the shops, factories and stores were native-born Americans, there was a great increase in immigration. The Germans and Irish were the first to immigrate en masse to Detroit. Many Germans fled the political unrest of their homeland in the early 1830s. Most were educated, many came with some capital, and they settled on the city's near east side around Gratiot, where they established small shops and businesses, as well as religious, social and cultural institutions. Many were skilled tradesmen and found a ready market for their crafts.

The Irish came shortly after. Forced to flee their native island because of the potato famine and political troubles, large numbers began to arrive in Detroit in the 1840s. In all, it is estimated that more than a million people fled Ireland between 1845 to 1850. Unlike the Germans, the Irish arrived in Detroit lacking professional skills, and of necessity became laborers, working on public projects such as road and rail construction and in factories. Many of the young women became domestics and the men who traditionally had a way with horses manned the livery stables. The Irish settled on the lower west side around Most Holy Trinity Church at Porter and Sixth Streets. They called the area Corktown because many had immigrated from County Cork. By 1850, one of every seven Detroiters was Irish.

The largest ethnic group to adopt Detroit as its new home was the Poles. A few Poles had arrived at a relatively early date, but the heavy influx began in the

Streets and politics: Top a Detroit street repair crew about 1900.

Robert A. Pelham, Jr., was the leading black politician in Detroit from 1882 to the end of the century. In 1896 he was active in the Republican National Convention and held various government positions on the state and national level.

mid-1870s. Unlike the Germans and Irish, the Poles were actively recruited through immigration offices or bureaus which the state of Michigan maintained from 1869 to 1885. Agents of the commission also met the immigrant ships at eastern seaports and channeled the new arrivals to the city. They were greatly needed at the time as common labor in the railroad shops and stove works, although some among the first arrivals were employed in the fields of D. M. Ferry seed farms. The first Poles to arrive in Detroit settled close to the German community, but as their numbers grew, they formed their own community around St. Albertus Church on St. Aubin Street, which was founded in 1872. Later, about 1910, other citizens of Polish descent began to settle in Hamtramck. That suburb, with as many as 56,000 residents, was for years more a Polish than an American city, and today it retains its Polish character.

After the Germans, the Irish and the Poles, immigrants from all over the world began descending upon Detroit. Most settled in areas with others of the same nationality for support, for companionship and to retain their ethnic heritage. This was necessary in a society that recognized them as little more than a tool for getting the job done, instead of appreciating the richness of culture and tradition they brought to their new land.

In 1860, Detroit's population stood at 45,619. By 1870, it had grown to 79,577, and by 1880, to 116,000. A large percentage of this growth came from the new immigrants, and indeed, they came from everywhere. In 1880, the census records showed the following breakdown of countries represented in its foreign born citizenry:

British America 10,754; Germany 17,292; Ireland 6,775; England 4,200; Scotland 1,783; Poland 1,771; France 721; Bohemia 557; Switzerland 421; Holland 275; Italy 127; Russia 77; Wales 71; Hungary 64; Sweden 55; Norway 27; Austria 15; China 11; India 9; Spain 8; Mexico 6; Malta 3; Cuba 3; Africa 2; Gibraltar 2; Greece 1.

Black entrepreneurship: Upper left, the "Plaindealer Boys," founders of Detroit's first successful black owned newspaper; from left, Robert A. Pelham, Jr., Walter H. Stowers, William H. Anderson; seated, Benjamin B. Pelham and Bryon G. Redmond. Upper right, one of several black-owned barber shops at the turn of the century. Lower left, a drugstore on Rivard owned by two brothers, both prominent black doctors, Albert H. and William E. Johnson. Lower right, typical homes owned by Detroit's black leadership in the 1890s, on tree-lined Canfield Avenue.

Another segment of Detroit's population that was experiencing considerable change at this time, particularly in the field of business, was the city's black community. Following the Civil War most of Detroit's black businessmen continued to turn their services and skills into small businesses serving white clientele. These included barber shops, clothes-cleaning stores, construction firms, tailor shops, delivery services, carpentry shops and grocery stores.

In the early 1880s, however, an important change found black businessmen turning from serving the white population to serving the black community. As the city's black population grew and settled along the lower east side, the number of black businesses grew and diversified.* During the next two decades, black businessmen were to be found as owners of moving companies, coal yards, lumber yards, drugstores, groceries, funeral homes, restaurants, news dealerships, hotels and saloons — all largely serving the black community. The period was also to witness the rise of the city's first black financial and realty agencies.

One of the major forces in this change was the city's first successful black owned newspaper, the *Plaindealer.* Organized in 1883 by Robert A. Pelham, Jr., Walter H. Stowers, William H. Anderson, Benjamin B. Pelham and Byron G. Redmand, the *Plaindealer* was an important landmark in the history of black Detroit. During its 11 years of publication, the paper was a champion of racial unity, promoter of black business, and a leading force in local politics.

*In 1880, Detroit's black community numbered 2,921, nearly 2½ percent of the city's total population.

Detroit street sweepers, above, in Cadillac Square about 1900. Right, Detroit's first streetcars, drawn by horses, began operation in 1863 on Jefferson Avenue. The first electric streetcar ran out Woodward in 1893; this is a view of the end of the line at Woodward and Baltimore in 1882; the horse drawn streetcar is heading back to town.

In 1879, the city purchased Belle Isle, a lush island in the midst of the river; it had been used by farmers as a rooting place for hogs.

By 1890, Detroit had lost most of its small town characteristics and had become a city, big and bustling. The population had grown to 206,000; the boundaries had been pushed out north to Grand Boulevard, east to Baldwin Avenue (near Mt. Elliott), and west to Livernois, and the new residential sections were developed in what only a short time before had been open countryside. Hugh elm, maple and chestnut trees shaded the streets. Homes, most of them frame and painted either white or dark green, gave the newer residential areas an air of comfort and well-being.

In 1879, the city purchased Belle Isle, a lush island in the midst of the river. It had been used by farmers as a rooting place for hogs until the realization that it would make an idlyllic setting for a city park. Landscape architect Frederick Law Olmsted (who designed New York's Central Park) transformed the island into a beautiful park that has since become a retreat for Detroiters.

Recognizing the many positive aspects of their city, the Board of Commerce coined a new municipal slogan, "Detroit, where life is worth living."

79

People on the streets: Hurdy-gurdy men, upper left, were familiar scenes on the streets of Detroit at the turn of the century. Far left, a policeman keeps watch as strollers walk along Woodward Avenue in 1890 (looking north from Gratiot). Left, City Hall (now Kennedy Square) at the turn of the century. Above, the epitome of elegance in the 1890s, a couple with horse and fashionable curved-body cutter. Right, the city's Central Market in Cadillac Square, completed in 1880, had meat stalls on its first floor, while, ironically, the Board of Health, along with the Superior Court and other governmental agencies occupied the second and third floors.

Life in the late 1800s: Above left, draymen stop to water their horses at a watering trough on Jefferson Avenue. Far left, boys cluster around an ice cream vendor in 1880. Left, a tricycle and a parking problem on Woodward Avenue in the 1880s; the trees in the distance are in Grand Circus Park. Above, the east side of Woodward between Atwater Street and the river in 1890. Above right, Woodward looking south from Parsons in the 1880s; the three churches are the Woodward Avenue Baptist at Winder Street, St. John's Episcopal at Vernor Highway, and the Central Methodist at Adams on Grand Circus Park. Center right, homes of the well-do-do who built on Woodward as the city grew; this is the west side between Davenport and Parsons about 1890. Below right, a typical view of Detroit's busy waterfront in the 1880s.

The pleasures of their times: Rowing has always been a popular sport in Detroit; left, a group gets ready to "shove off" from Belle Isle, while a group of children, above, take it feet first. Right, three fashionable young maidens pick wild flowers on Belle Isle.

The new era commences: The quiet tree lined streets, such as Second Avenue, left, before the intrusion of the motor car. The first horseless carriage to appear on Detroit's city streets was built by Charles B. King, below, at the tiller with his young assistant Oliver Barthel. Right, Henry Ford and his "quadricycle." Below right, Woodward Avenue becomes mechanized; this view looks south towards the river around 1910. The Pontchartrain Hotel opened in 1907.

The horseless carriage

Although Detroit was indeed a big city by 1890, it was the motor car that was to transform its destiny to that of one of the world's major urban centers.

On the cold snowy evening of March 6, 1896, Charles Brady King drove the first horseless carriage on the streets of Detroit. It was a machine of his own design that had been assembled in John Lauer's machine shop on the east side of St. Antoine Street, just south of Jefferson Avenue.

King drove his car west on Jefferson to Woodward, where he turned north and chugged up to Cadillac Square. There the motor died and the machine was towed back to Lauer's shop. Significant as this short trip was, it stirred only casual public interest. On the following day, the *Free Press* carried only a brief account, buried on its back page: "The first horseless carriage seen in this city was out on the streets last night. The apparatus seems to work all right, and it went at the rate of five or six miles an hour at an even rate of speed." The longest account of King's feat was a quarter column on an inside page of the *Journal*. The *Tribune* gave it only three lines.

Charles King was not the only local mechanic working on a horseless carriage. A young man named Henry Ford was also building a machine. Ford was the night shift engineer at the Edison Illuminating Company (the present-day Detroit Edison

The good old days: in such environments as the early day auto plant, below, Detroit began manufacturing automobiles. Left, the Olds Motor Works on East Jefferson at the Belle Isle Bridge, 1899. Above, the curved-dash Oldsmobile.

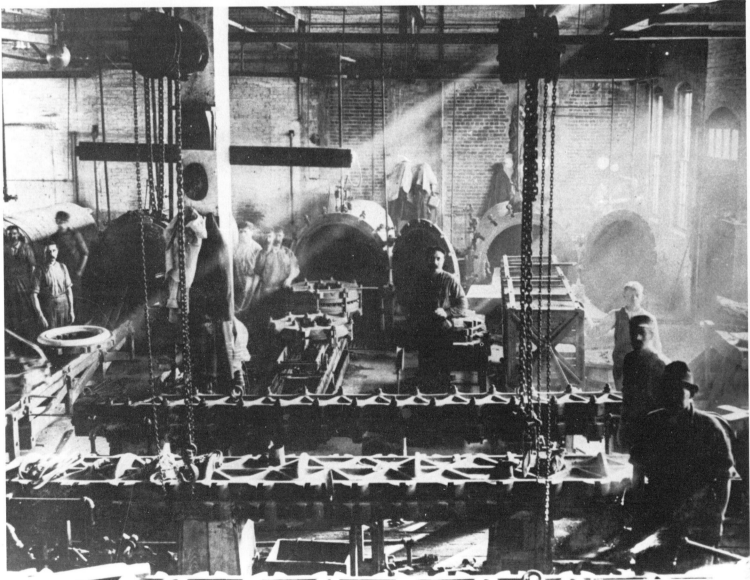

Company). In his spare time, he worked in a small brick shed at the rear of his Bagley Avenue home. Ford completed work on his machine on June 4, but he discovered too late that to get it onto the street, he had to knock out part of the shed's wall. This done, Ford cranked up his quadricycle, as he called it, and no one was more surprised than he when it started.

At the time, neither Ford nor King had any idea they were launching a great industry, and neither one was the first to begin the production of automobiles in Detroit.

The first to open an automobile plant in Detroit was Ranson E. Olds. Working in his hometown of Lansing, Olds had built what he called the Oldsmobile, but to produce his car in quantity, he needed capital. He came to Detroit and met Samuel L. Smith who had made a fortune in lumber and copper. Smith agreed to back Olds, and as a result, the Olds Motor Works was founded. Production began in a small factory on East Jefferson near the Belle Isle Bridge, where the Uniroyal plant now stands. The first Oldsmobiles were good machines, but they cost $2,382, which only the wealthy could afford. However, they ran well on paved streets and the company sold all it could make, which was not very many.

Then, on March 9, 1901, a fire completely destroyed the Olds plant, including all the plans and machinery for producing the Oldsmobile. Only a small experimental model car with a curved dash was saved. Olds decided not to rebuild in Detroit and moved back to Lansing, where he began production of his smaller car. As a result, Olds was able to drastically cut his price to $625. Within a year, the company was turning out the first popular low-priced car and making about 25 percent of all the autos built in the United States.

Above, the Ford Motor Company's first factory at Mack and Beaufait in 1905. Below, the legendary Barney Oldfield at the tiller of Ford's "999" racer two years earlier.

During this time, Henry Ford continued to make improvements on his machine. Charles King, on the other hand, decided to follow other interests. Ford's major thrust, though, was not in producing cars but in racing them. He induced driver Barney Oldfield to race his cars, and in 1901, Oldfield set a record of 60 miles an hour on the Grosse Pointe track. Ford personally drove a race on the ice of Lake St. Clair in 1904, setting a new world speed record of 93 miles per hour.

Finally Ford decided to begin producing cars in quantity, and after several unsuccessful starts, he was able to obtain financial backing for a new company. On June 16, 1903 the Ford Motor Company was incorporated, beginning operations in a factory on Mack Avenue at Bellvue. Among those who furnished the money

James Couzens started out as Henry Ford's accountant; he went on to become one of Detroit's wealthiest and most influential citizens.

The early assembly of automobiles was crude and often dangerous. Unguarded moving belts, above left, which drove lathes, drills and other machines, led to many serious injuries. The Model T became America's favorite because the assembly line operation made it plentiful and affordable; below left, a Model T engine is installed; below, the final stage at Ford's Highland Park Plant, with bodies being joined to chassis. Right, the durability of the finished product was one its most important selling points; the year: 1911.

(actually only $28,000 in working capital was paid in) were Alexander Y. Malcomson, a coal dealer; John S. Gray, a banker; and Horace H. Rackham, an attorney. The Dodge brothers, John and Horace, contracted with Ford to make parts in their machine shop on Beaubien at Fort. They were given shares in the company as payment.

Malcomson's bookkeeper, James S. Couzens, put up $2,500 and joined the Ford Motor Company as its business manager. In 1919, Ford bought him out for $29,308,857, a substantial part of which Couzens returned to the community in philanthropy.

Ford's plan was to build a car that would provide basic transportation for farmers and small town residents as well as for city dwellers. He envisioned a mass-produced, low-priced automobile, so simple in construction that any handy-man could repair it. The idea paid off from the start, and in 1906, Ford moved to a larger plant on Piquette Avenue at Beaubien. It was in this plant in 1908 that Ford began production of probably the most famous automobile of all time — the Model T. The car was so popular that the company was soon unable to meet the demand. Within just two years, Ford was six months behind in deliveries. So the decision was made to move again, this time far out Woodward Avenue to the City of Highland Park. The new factory was designed by noted architect Albert Kahn, ground was broken early in 1909, and by year-end the Highland Park plant was in partial operation.

With production well underway at the new plant, Ford introduced a revolutionary procedure. In 1913, the first automatic assembly line was put in operation. Ford had already perfected the standardization of parts at the plant, and now these parts were made to flow in a continuous stream to the moving line. The required part reached the line just as it was needed by the worker, who now performed only a single task. At the end of the line, the body of the car slid down an incline just as the completed chassis arrived. The two were bolted together, and the finished auto was driven away under its own power. With this system, production was more economical and efficient, and had an almost unlimited quantity potential.

While the assembly line was an important milepost, Ford's next innovation staggered the competition. On January 12, 1914, Ford announced that henceforth each production worker in his plant would be paid $5.00 for an eight-hour shift. To workers for whom $2.75 or less for a ten-hour day was standard pay for unskilled or semi-skilled labor, this sounded like a new gold strike. Men from all over Michigan left the lumber camps and farms and headed for Detroit. Job seekers came from other states as well, and even from Europe. Thousands lined up at the Highland Park plant gates. So dense was the throng of job applicants that it was necessary on one occasion to use fire hoses to disperse them.

In 1904, the first Buick model was test-run from Flint to Detroit, above, by Chief Engineer Walter Marr, the driver, and David Buick's son, Tom. Others were beyond the testing stage, left, as couples took their motor cars out for a drive on Belle Isle. Below, the old Pontchartrain Hotel was the starting point for the 1909 Glidden Tour which ran from Detroit to Denver, a distance of 2,636 miles; the Interstate system was not even a dream.

William C. Curant, top, was a wagon manufacturer who bought out Buick and started a company in 1908 he called General Motors. Above right, an early view of the Packard plant illustrates the method of building cars prior to the moving assembly line. Frames were assembled on sawhorses and the components were brought to the frames. Above, in 1900, the White Company built its first truck, a steamer, and introduced "horseless" delivery service.

In 1903, the same year Ford founded his company, another Detroit industrialist entered the automotive field: Henry M. Leland and his associates put their first car on the market under the name of Cadillac. Not long afterward, the name of Leland's firm was changed to the Cadillac Motor Car Company. Leland's first plant was located at Cass and Amsterdam.

Olds, Ford and Leland were not alone, though. There was engineer David D. Buick, who had met with considerable success in the plumbing supply business. He became interested in automobiles and in 1903 built a car which he named for himself. Unfortunately he depleted his resources in doing so, and was forced to sell out. His company was purchased by wagon-maker William C. Durant and moved to Flint.

With Buick as his base, Durant formed the General Motors Company on September 16, 1908. In the next two years he bought in quick succession Cadillac, Oldsmobile, Oakland (manufactured in Pontiac and forerunner of the Pontiac car), and several other smaller auto producers. Financial difficulties, however, forced Durant out of General Motors in 1910, so he joined forces with Swiss-born mechanic and racing driver Louis Chevrolet and launched the Chevrolet Motor Car Company in Detroit in 1911. In 1915, Durant was able to regain control of General Motors and he brought with him the Chevrolet. With the Chevrolet, which he moved to Flint, Durant had the inexpensive auto that could compete with Ford's "Tin Lizzie." Other firms, particularly companies making parts and accessories, were also added to the corporation. With its headquarters in Detroit and its production sites widely scattered, Durant had General Motors well on its way to becoming the giant of all American industrial enterprises.

Along with Cadillac, Buick and Ford, the year 1903 was to witness the beginnings of another car in Detroit. It was the Packard, which had originally been produced in the town of Warren, Ohio. While on a trip to New York, two wealthy Detroiters, Henry B. Joy and Truman H. Newberry, saw a new Packard parked on the street. While they were inspecting the car, a fire engine went by. The owner dashed out of a nearby building, started the motor with one spin of the crank, and went off in pursuit. Joy and Newberry were impressed, and shortly thereafter, they purchased the Packard Company, moved it to Detroit, and began production in a plant designed by Albert Kahn on East Grand Boulevard near Mt. Elliott.

The year following the move of Packard to Detroit, Jonathan Maxwell obtained financial backing to build his new car, which he called, not surprisingly, the Maxwell. A former Olds' factory manager, Maxwell soon had his automobile in production at a factory at East Jefferson near Connors. During the depression that followed the First World War, however, the company fell on hard times. To help get the firm back on its feet, one-time railroad master mechanic Walter P. Chrysler was called in. Chrysler, who had previously worked for Buick as plant superintendent, reorganized the company, and in 1925 the last of the Big Three was born.

Walter P. Chrysler, from a 1929 John Coppin sketch.

First of the line: Above left, the first Chevrolet, in 1912; admiring the car are Louis Chevrolet (at left without hat) and William C. Durant (far right with derby). The firm turned out 2,999 cars the first year. Left center, Horace Dodge (left rear) and John Dodge (right rear) take delivery of the first Dodge, November 14, 1914, in front of the John Dodge estate, 75 East Boston Boulevard. Below left, Roy Chapin at the wheel of one his first Hudson automobiles. Below, two Detroiters take a spin in their new Brush automobile.

*The Central Oil Company built in 1910
what may have been the first drive-in
gas station with an island. Above, in
1915, the company's second such facility,
at the corner of Woodward and High
(now Vernor Highway). Below, two
pictures of Broadway and Gratiot; top,
in 1906, men on bicycles and brewers
wagons were commonplace, but by
1920, bottom, the motor car, trucks,
traffic towers and pavement markers had
made their mark.*

During the years prior to World War I, a number of other cars were
produced in Detroit: Hupp and Paige; Krit and Saxon; Liberty and
Richenbacker. In 1909, the Hudson Motor Car Company was organized
by Roy D. Chapin. Chapin, a former Olds employee, obtained his
financial backing from department store owner J. L. Hudson. But the life of these
early automobile companies was a precarious one. Of the 202 different makes of
automobiles being produced in 1910, only four remain today: Buick, Cadillac, Ford
and Oldsmobile. Chevrolet and others would follow.

In 1914, the Dodge brothers left Ford and organized their own company,
producing their automobile in a new plant in Hamtramck. The Dodge Brothers
Company grew with a line of well-built, moderately-priced cars and durable trucks.
In 1920, however, with the tragic deaths of both brothers, the company began to
falter. The company's situation continued to deteriorate until April 30, 1925, when a
New York banking interest headed by Dillon Read & Company bought the Dodge
properties for $146 million. At the time, this was the greatest cash transaction in the
history of American industry. Three years later, with his eye on the success of
General Motors, Walter Chrysler obtained control of the company and it became the
Dodge Division of the Chrysler Corporation.

Within a relatively short time, Detroit had become the heart of the automobile
industry. There are several reasons why. First, for several years, the city had been the
center of the marine gasoline engine industry. Second, Detroit was also the center of
the malleable iron manufacturing industry. It had plants which could turn out springs,
copper and brass parts and fittings, and paints and varnishes. Third, the lumber era
was coming to an end in Michigan and a supply of unemployed labor was at hand.
Finally there was money back here, and lots of it. During the second half of the 19th
century, fortunes had been made in lumber, mining and shipping. Wealthy Detroiters
had capital that they could afford to risk in ventures that gave promise of being
economically sound. Thus it was that Detroit, more than any other city, possessed
the necessary elements at just the right time: capital, labor, material.

Now that Detroit was producing better cars, local motorists began to demand
better roads. In general, rural roads most of the year were muddy and difficult, and
people were no longer satisfied being restricted to city driving. In response, the
Wayne County Road Commission laid the world's first stretch of concrete highway in
1909 on Woodward Avenue between Six and Seven Mile Roads. In 1911, County

Early motorists had their problems, and road construction was truly in its infancy. Roads generally were poor, tires were always going flat and drivers had little protection from the weather. From left across top: mired in the mud; pavement breaking ceremonies at Grand River Avenue and West Chicago Boulevard on April 23, 1908; horse power participating in road construction in 1916; a road crew repairing Grand River Avenue, August 22, 1912. Far right, a first step toward the improvement of roads was taken in 1909 with the laying of the first mile of concrete highway in he United States on Woodward Avenue between Six and Seven Mile Roads.

Not only have automobiles changed over the years, but fire fighting apparatus has made its own significant strides: Above, the men (and the neighborhood boys) of Engine Co. No. 12 proudly show off their new Silsby steam pumper in December 1886. Drawn by two horses, the engine had shoe type brakes on the rear wheels and could pump 500 gallons of water per minute. Left center, the city's first motorized pumper, a Webb Model K, went into service in June 1910. The engine had a 700 gpm rotary pump, detachable pneumatic tires, and it carried a thousand feet of hose. Sixty-five years later, in July 1975, this cab-forward Han engine, below left, began service at Engine Co. No. 5 at Cass and Alexanderine.

Heavy traffic firsts: the first traffic light appeared on Detroit streets in 1915, right; it was a kerosene railroad switch lantern borrowed from the Michigan Central. Set atop a stand, the lamp had two green and two red slides, and was turned by the police officer to direct and stop traffic. Below, in 1907, few automobiles were on the streets and policemen still rode bicycles. Two officers issue what some claim to be the first traffic ticket in the city, at Woodward and Adams. Note the right hand drive.

Woodward Avenue about 1910.

Road Commissioner Edward N. Hines had the world's first white center line painted on the River Road near Trenton. To control all the traffic on the new roads, young Detroit police patrolman William L. Potts invented the electric red-amber-green traffic light. The first unit was installed on a high tower at the corner of Woodward and Michigan Avenues in October 1920.

By 1916, the automobile was big business in Detroit, and the city was on its way to becoming the Motor Capital. Yet Detroit was not a one-industry town. Between 1915 and 1916, industrial production rose from $600 million to $900 million, and while automotive products accounted for the largest portion of this figure, the manufacture of stoves, furnaces, paints, pharmaceuticals, marine equipment and tobacco continued to be important. For example, in 1916, more than a million cigars a day were being produced in the city.

Attracted by Detroit's supply of skilled labor, other industries were established. In 1904, the Arithmometer Company of St. Louis moved to Detroit, opened a plant at Second and Amsterdam and began the production of adding machines. The next year, it was incorporated as the Burroughs Adding Machine Company, later becoming the Burroughs Corporation. The salt mining and chemical industries also helped to produce many of the city's new jobs.

The Detroit Board of Commerce was organized in June 1903 to coordinate and stimulate this business activity. During its first year of operation, Board of Commerce membership numbered 142 firms and its projects included the organization of a Convention Bureau, now the Metropolitan Detroit Convention and Visitors Bureau, and the Adscript Club, now the Adcraft Club. Over the years, the concept and functions of the Board of Commerce have multiplied, and today it is the Greater Detroit Chamber of Commerce.

World war and the 1920s

On April 6, 1917, the United States officially joined the war against Germany which had been raging in Europe since 1914. Detroiters had taken an active interest in the war long before 1917, however. Because Canada had been involved since 1914, many Detroiters crossed the river and entered the Canadian army and air force.

In 1915, Henry Ford had tried to settle the whole European conflict himself by chartering a "Peace Ship" and transporting a group of "peace delegates," technical staff, newspaper reporters, and students across the ocean for the purpose of "gettin nthe boys out of the trenches by Christmas." Ford accompanied the party to Norway, but he promptly returned when he sensed the futility of the effort. The expedition, needless to say, came to nothing. In fact, no informed person ever gave it a chance to succeed.

Following the declaration of war, the Michigan National Guard was called into service to form the 32nd Division. The troops from Detroit, the 31st Infantry, became part of the 63rd Brigade. They were joined by a medical detachment, a headquarters unit, the 119th Field Artillery, a machine gun company, and part of a cavalry squadron. Two base hospitals were also organized; No. 17 was made up of doctors and nurses from Harper Hospital, and No. 36 represented the Detroit College of Medicine. In addition to these Detroiters, thousands of others volunteered and went into the regular army, navy, and marine corps.

Woodward Avenue, left, on the eve of the First World War. Inset left, Henry Ford's "Peace Ship," Oscar II, leaves the pier at Hoboken, New Jersey, on the morning of December 4, 1915; his idealism would not reach reality. Below, the "Victory Arch" in front of the Opera House on Campus Martius in 1916.

Guardsmen and volunteers, however, did not provide the total manpower needed. On June 5, 1917, all Detroit men between the ages of 21 and 30 went to voting booths, schools, and other public places to register for the draft, two later registrations were necessary before the war ended. Altogether, Detroit sent 65,000 men and women to serve in the armed forces during World War I. Of those, 1,360 would not survive the conflict.

One Detroit regiment, the 339th Infantry, was sent to Archangel in northern Russia in 1918 to fight the Bolsheviks and to serve as what was hoped would be a rallying force for non-Communist Russians. Poorly armed and equipped, the regiment, along with several other military units, served through the extremely severe winter of 1918 and 1919. Finally brought home in July 1919, they were given the name, Polar Bears.

World War I production: Above left, Detroit's automobile industry played a major role in the allied victory; here two-ton White trucks in a convoy somewhere in France; above right, at the Ford Highland Park plant, Red Cross workers were trained using Ford ambulances; the date: July 17, 1918. Also at the Highland Park plant, below right, Ford tested the new Whippet tanks. Below left, another type of machine introduced by Henry Ford (in center of photo) during the war was his famous Fordson tractor; it was credited with saving the British from starvation during the German blockade, and later helped mechanize farming around the world.

In 1918, coal shortages were so severe that during a cold spell, all non-essential businesses were required to shut down for five days.

At home during the war, Detroiters actively supported the "Liberty Loan" bond drives. Through these drives, bonds were sold directly to the public by "4-minute speakers" who gave high-powered sales talks in theaters, hotels and restaurants. Ministers made pleas from their pulpits for the purchase of bonds, and mass meetings were held in the downtown area. In addition, many Detroiters earnestly supported the Red Cross, Knights of Columbus, Jewish Welfare Board, YMCA and Salvation Army and the services they provided to men and women in the armed forces.

The war caused serious shortages of food and fuel in Detroit. Breadless and meatless days were proclaimed, nonessential businesses were encouraged to close on Mondays to save coal, and early in January 1918, the fuel shortage became so acute during a prolonged spell of bitterly cold weather that all businesses except hotels, restaurants, and drug stores were required to shut down for five days.

The severe winter of 1917 saw an epidemic of influenza. It returned again in 1918 and almost every Detroiter was stricken to some degree by the Spanish flu, as it was called. Hundreds died, and for weeks many were seen wearing gauze masks in the false hope that the face coverings would give some protection from the flu.

Submarine chasers: Not only did Ford diversify his automobile production during the war, the company constructed Eagle boats at its Rouge plant. Top, construction of an Eagle on July 3, 1918. Above left, Ford Eagle Boat No. 13; above right, mass production techniques enabled workers to build Eagle Boat No. 59 in just 10 days; here work is completed as the boat is moved out of the assembly building.

Along with its citizens, Detroit's automobile industry also went to war in 1917. And, for the first time in history, the industry became a principal factor in the production of war materials. In fact, it was the industry's production capacity that helped to bring about the Allied victory.

The automobile industry turned out a variety of military equipment, including guns, ammunition and helmets, all produced in large quantities. Detroit also supplied thousands of trucks, ambulances and staff cars. Not only did these motorized vehicles help defeat the German army, they also brought an end to the use of cavalry and horse artillery.

In addition, Detroit produced the famous Liberty aircraft engine. It was built by Ford, Packard, Cadillac and the newly organized Lincoln Motor Company. Ford also produced Eagle boats, small but fast submarine chasers, at the new Rouge Plant, using a revolutionary new moving assembly line technique similar to the one the company had already pioneered. At the Highland Park Plant, Ford was building a newly designed armored tread-operated vehicle called the Whippet tank. To test it, Ford built some artificial hills on the grounds just north of the plant on Woodward Avenue, and because of minimum security, the public could easily watch the Whippet being tested.

Armistice November 11, 1918: when announced, top, Detroiters flocked into downtown to celebrate. During this time, Detroit's municipal government was modernized, due largely to the efforts of Hazen S. Pingree, above left, Detroit's mayor several years earlier; above right, Pingree and his daughter Hazel (on horseback) oversee formal start of paving of Grand Boulevard just east of Woodward, August 10, 1891.

In the late summer of 1918, the German armies began to collapse and on November 11, the armistice was signed. When word reached the city, Detroiters poured into downtown to celebrate.

It was during the era of the First World War that Detroit's municipal government was modernized. It began in 1890 when Hazen S. Pingree was elected mayor. Pingree, or Ping, as his fellow citizens fondly called him, served six years and gave Detroit one of its most productive administrations. He cleaned up the graft-ridden city departments and laid the foundations for the relatively clean nonpartisan form of municipal government that was later to be adopted.

Civil response: Above right, looking south along Woodward Avenue from in front of the city hall in 1912; this was the year the Detroit Citizens' League was organized. Above, one of the most important moments in the civil rights movement was the trial of Dr. Ossian Sweet and 10 members of his family and friends; from left, Sweet's brother Henry (a defendant) and defense attorneys Julian Perry, Tom Chawkes and Clarence Darrow.

In 1925, Detroit was to experience the beginnings of a reform movement of a very different nature — improved housing for its black citizens.

During the first two decades of the 20th century, Detroit's population grew at an unprecedented rate. In 1900, the city's population was 285,704. By 1910, it had reached 465,766, and mushroomed to 993,678 in 1920. Detroit was becoming too big and too complex to operate with an inefficient municipal government. In 1912, the Detroit Citizens League was organized. One of those responsible for its formation was Henry M. Leland, thus marking one of the first instances when the automobile industry demonstrated its concern about civic improvement. One of the League's first projects was the publication of *The Civic Searchlight,* a journal which has become the standard for the independent voter. As a result of pressure by the Citizens League and church groups, the Board of Education was reorganized in 1916, and public education was largely removed from the area of partisan politics.

On June 25, 1918, Detroit voters approved, by a large margin, a new city charter which embodied several unusual features. The large 42 member council (two elected from each ward) was replaced by a nine member council chosen at large. The power of the mayor was spelled in detail and enlarged. All of the officials, including judges, were to be chosen on a non-partisan basis. James Couzens, Henry Ford's former associate, became the first non-partisan mayor under the new charter, and in 1920, the reform movement was further advanced by the reorganization of the municipal courts.

In 1925, Detroit was to experience the beginnings of a reform movement of a very different nature — improved housing for its black citizens. At this time blacks were by and large restricted to purchasing homes in several well defined areas. These included: the East Side District, bounded by the river, Mt. Elliott, Mack and Brush; the Warren-Tireman District; the Holbrook-Clay District; and the North Detroit or Carpenter Avenue Area. In the fall of 1925, Dr. Ossian Sweet, a black gynecologist who had graduated from Howard University and who later studied under Madame Curie in France, purchased an $18,000, two-story brick house at Garland and Charlevoix, a comfortable middle-class neighborhood in which there had been some racial mixing. But the Sweet family was not welcomed. In fact, they received threats from their new neighbors even before they moved in. On September 8, the Sweet's moving van pulled up under police escort, but that night a crowd gathered, and during the next two days it became menacing. Several friends and relatives joined the Sweets to help them defend their home. Ten policemen were assigned to keep the crowd away, but despite their presence, rocks were thrown at the windows. At one point, the crowd surged toward the home, and panic swept over those inside the house. Suddenly there was a blast of gunfire from an upstairs window, and a white man sitting on his porch across the street was struck and instantly killed.

The selling of Lincoln: In 1922, Ford Motor Company purchased the Lincoln Motor Company, owned by the Leland family. Signing the sale documents, top, are, seated, sons Edsel B. Ford and Wilfred Leland; standing, fathers Henry Ford and Henry M. Leland. Above, on land purchased in 1916, Henry Ford built his great Rouge plant, one of the world's largest industrial complexes.

Dr. Sweet and ten of his companions, including his wife, were arrested and tried for murder. The case not only united the middle-class black community but brought to Sweet's defense famous lawyer Clarence Darrow — a defense financed largely by the National Association for the Advancement of Colored People. The judge to whom the case was assigned was Frank Murphy.

The trial was lengthy and its sensational aspects, together with the presence of Darrow, attracted front-page attention across the country. The first trial resulted in a hung jury, but the retrial jury deliberated only briefly before bringing in a verdict of acquittal.

The trial prompted Mayor John Smith to appoint an interracial committee, the first in the city's history, to find jobs and housing for blacks. This was really the first major breakthrough in both of these areas for the city's black citizens.

Shortly after the end of the war, Detroit experienced a short recession but, by 1923, the worst was over and the economy was again on the upswing. Unfortunately, the good times became somewhat too good. Serious inflation began, and people began complaining about the high cost of living. Wild speculation in the stock market and in real estate, and considerable overspending caused no particular widespread concern. Inflation continued, speculation continued, spending continued, and Detroit, along with the nation and much of the world, was heading toward the crash of 1929.

It was during Detroit's post-war years that the automobile industry reached maturity. During the 1920s, the domestic production of cars and trucks rose steadily until 1929, when the five million unit mark was passed for the first time. Not until 1948 would that figure again be attained.

In 1927, Detroit experienced one of its most famous fires; on April 23, fire destroyed the block-long Briggs Manufacturing plant at Russell and Harper. More than 1,200 were at work when the fire broke out; it burned for two days, killing 21 and causing more than $2 million in damage, Detroit's greatest loss to that date. During the '20s, Ford made more major moves: above Henry Ford with his company's 10 millionth car — a 1924 Model T, alongside the 1896 quadricycle; above left, in the fall of 1927, Ford began production of his new car — the Model A; this is one of the first, a 1928 coup; and during the 1920s, Detroit was a major center for the aircraft industry; below left, the Stout Air Pullman's "Maiden Detroit," forerunner of the famous Ford Tri-Motor.

Woodward Avenue in the 1920s, top, looking north from Cadillac Square. Above, during the 1920s, downtown Detroit experienced a major boom which included the construction of the Penobscot Building (1928), for nearly 50 years the city's tallest building.

Several factors contributed to this growth. Millions of soldiers learned to rely on the automobile during the war, it being one of the first things they wanted when they returned. The industry now producing cars that were safer, faster and more comfortable, spent millions of dollars researching such innovations as clear, unbreakable safety glass, and more dependable brakes. The invention and perfection of the self-starter — thereby eliminating the crank — made the automobile available to those without strong right arms. By 1920, it was standard equipment on virtually all cars. Also during the 1920s, the closed car, originally regarded as a luxury model, became the standard. In 1925, for the first time, the sale of closed cars passed the sales of the open models.

Despite production increases, however, fewer automobile companies were able to survive. Difficulty in obtaining financing necessary to adjust to new marketing conditions and to technological changes brought numerous companies to their knees. By the late 1920s, Ford, General Motors and Chrysler had become the "Big Three", although Hudson, Packard, Hupp and Graham-Paige were still in production.

This period did see the end of one best-selling car, however — Henry Ford's Model T. For nearly 20 years, the Model T had remained substantially unchanged. But the American public was looking for something new, and they found it in the Chevrolet. Chevrolet, which had been outsold 15 to one in 1921, was selling more than half as many cars as Ford in early 1927. And so the decision was made. On May 30, 1927, the last of 15,007,003 Model T's rolled off the assembly line. In 1928, the Model A made its appearance and Ford was back in competition, but the company never again had the field to itself as it did during the heyday of the Model T.

Gradually the automobile industry began to decentralize. The companies found it more economical and efficient to assemble cars in plants close to the consumers. Before long, Detroit proper was producing relatively few complete automobiles. But the major offices remained in the city and Detroit continued to be the industry's nerve center.

NEW CENTER DEVELOPMENT CORP
ALBERT KAHN INC. ARCHITECT
H. G. CHRISTMAN-BURKE CO
CONTRACTOR
No. 11 DATE 1-6-28

Above left, General Motors' impressive world headquarters on West Grand Boulevard; construction began in 1919. In the fall of 1927, the Fisher Building was begun, above. Left, the S.S. South American on the Detroit River; in the background a Bob-Lo boat and the Ambassador bridge. Below left, the Bob-Lo steamer Ste. Claire (built in 1911) docking at the foot of Woodward Avenue. Below, a flyer dated September 4, 1914.

Landlubber sailors: Above right, Detroiters disembark from the Bob-Lo boat pier, at left, at the foot of Woodward Avenue in 1928. Another favorite pasttime was a cruise aboard a fine lake steamer; below right, an ad for the South American dated July 28, 1918.

Almost immediately after the end of the First World War, Detroit's skyline underwent a major facelifting. Included in the huge building program of the 1920s were skyscrapers that attracted the attention of architects throughout the country. The Penobscot Building (1928), the tallest in the city for nearly 50 years, was the highlight of downtown along with the new Buhl (1925) and Guardian (1929) buildings. The Book brothers took the lead in transforming Washington Boulevard into a replica of New York's Fifth Avenue. The Book-Cadillac Hotel at Michigan and Washington was the showplace of the new development.

In 1919, General Motors began construction of its new headquarters, at the time the largest office building in the world. This marked the beginning of the New Center Area at Second and West Grand Boulevard. In 1928, the beautiful Fisher Building was completed across the street from the General Motors Building.

The Detroit River was also the scene of great building activity. In 1928, the Detroit-Windsor Tunnel was completed, providing motorists with an alternative to the antiquated and inadequate ferry service. The following year, the Ambassador Bridge was open to traffic.

By early 1929, industry in Detroit was at a new peak, providing employment for nearly 330,000 workers. Although the automobile industry unquestionably ranked first, pharmaceuticals, tobacco, copper, steel, printing, meat packing and leisure goods industries all contributed to Detroit's phenomenal economic boom. Then on October 24, 1929, the New York Stock Exchange collapsed. The market continued its plunge until November 13, and ushered in the greatest economic depression the United States had ever experienced.

Bootlegging was for a time one of Detroit's principal industries, and the booze came in a variety of forms of transportation. Left, a lugger with a cargo of bootleg whiskey on June 15, 1929. Below, customs agents unload contraband liquor from the back of a hearse. Below right, police ride up the Detroit River in a captured rum-runner's speedboat.

4. The turbulent years

The Great Depression

The causes of the Great Depression which followed the stock market crash did not, of course, begin in Detroit. They were world-wide. The origins can be found in the aftermath of the war with its ensuing inflation, and the European financial and political collapses. The fall of the stock market in itself was a devastating blow. Thousands lost their money in the market. Everything tightened up and people stopped buying. The era of good times, easy credit, and unprecedented prosperity was over.

At the time of the Depression and during the years immediately preceding it, Detroit had two major industries — the manufacture of automobiles and the distribution of bootleg Canadian liquor.

The latter began in 1916, in that reform-minded period of the First World War. That year, Michigan amended its constitution to prohibit the manufacture and sale of intoxicating liquor. On the night before the ban became law on May 1, 1918, many Detroiters gathered in their favorite saloons in an effort to consume a good portion of the remaining supply.

For the next year and a half, most of Detroit's bootleg booze came from Ohio. Then on Jaunary 16, 1920, with the signing of the 18th Amendment to the U.S. Constitution, prohibition became national, Canada became the chief source of supply, and bootlegging began across the Detroit River. Within a short time, Canada became the source not only for Detroit but also for Chicago and much of the American Midwest. Syndicates, such as the one led by Al Capone, moved in and the smuggling of beer and whiskey from the Windsor area became a well-organized business.

No one really knows the value of the liquor carried across the Windsor-Detroit border in the 1920s and 1930s, but it was in the hundreds of millions of dollars. It was said that 85 percent of all the liquor smuggled into the United States from Canada crossed at Detroit. At times, the business amounted to 500,000 cases a month.

There was, in fact, no place along the St. Clair and Detroit Rivers where smuggling was not carried on. Each night, fast, high-powered boats made runs to the

Rum running in the act: Right, a blind pig on Grand River Avenue just down the street from the Wesley Methodist Church, April 19, 1930. Center, rum running at the foot of Riopelle Street, April 15, 1929; this photograph was taken by a Detroit News photographer hidden in a warehouse loft. Below, bootleggers await a signal to cross the river and land liquor at 17th Street, April 27, 1929.

When customs agents were on patrol, rumrunners were warned by a system of signals tooted by the locomotive engineers in the railroad yards along the river front.

U.S. customs agents unload a cargo of captured beer, September 27, 1931.

Canadian shore and back, all in a matter of minutes. After the Ambassador Bridge and the Detroit-Windsor Tunnel were opened, booze came across by the truckload. Individuals brought in single bottles hidden under their coats or in the upholstery of their cars. Women, safe from search by authorities, tucked bottles inside their girdles and waddled blithely through customs. This contraband was known as girdle or panty whiskey.

Every sort of ingenious device was used to get liquor across the border and to distribute it. A bank vault in St. Clair Shores, used as a storage place, held more whiskey than currency. In at least two instances, windlasses were rigged on the American shore and sled-like contraptions were hauled over the river bed. When customs agents were known to be out on patrol, rumrunners were warned by a system of signals tooted by the locomotive engineers in the railroad yards along the riverfront.

With beer and liquor no longer legally available from their friendly neighborhood tavern, Detroiters turned to the speakeasy — or as they were more commonly called — blind pigs. This term, used to describe an illegal establishment where alcoholic beverages are sold, dates to the 1870s. In those days, in an effort to evade the law, a store or saloon owner would advertise that he owned a pig that was blind and for a 10-cent admission charge he would allow a customer to view this pig. There was, of course, no sightless farm animal to be seen and upon payment of his dime, the customer was handed instead a glass of whiskey. During prohibition it was estimated that at one time there were as many as 25,000 blind pigs in Detroit.

In downtown Detroit, many different storefronts were used to disguise these illegal drinking spots. For example, one was located in a well-equipped radio store where several salesmen were ready to wait on customers. If one were a preferred customer, however, he was ushered into the stockroom and through an unmarked door, which opened into a completely furnished barroom. There was a similar set up in a luggage shop, another in a laundry. There is also the record of a blind pig in a funeral home where the liquor was stored in caskets.

Advanced stages of illegal activity: top right and left, members of the Purple gang, which along with the Licavoli gang ran rampant during prohibition. Above, Blossom Heath on Jefferson Avenue in suburban St. Clair Shores. Center right, downtown Detroit in 1930 looking upriver towards Belle Isle. Below right, Woodward Avenue in 1934 looking north from Jefferson Avenue.

The exploits of the Purple gang and the Licavoli gang during the Depression left a bloody mark on the city. Murder was commonplace.

Gangland killing: On July 22, 1930, popular radio commentator Jerry Buckley was gunned down in the lobby of the La Salle Hotel; the killers weren't caught, but police theorized they were members of the Licavoli gang. Top, close to 30,000 admirers of Buckley filed past his coffin as his body lay in state before his funeral.

While many blind pigs did nothing more unlawful than sell a little illegal booze, others expanded their operations into another business. Gamblers took advantage of police nonintervention and several casinos were opened in and around Detroit. The Aniwa Club, for example, on Van Dyke just off East Jefferson, was patronized by the well-to-do from Grosse Pointe. There were others, such as Blossom Heath, Chesterfield Inn, the Club Royale, Doc Brady's and Lefty Clark's.

In order for all of this to work, considerable corruption existed among officials, much of which was uncovered by the post-prohibition grand jury investigation conducted in 1940 by Circuit Judge (later U.S. Senator) Homer Ferguson. As a result, the mayor of Detroit and scores of other officials were indicted and eventually jailed.

As was noted, the illicit liquor traffic was, within a short time, under the complete control of the big city gangs. In Detroit, two principal gangs ran rampant during the prohibition period — the Purple gang, and the Licavoli gang.

The exploits of these two groups of organized hoodlums left a bloody mark on the city. Murder became so commonplace as to make newspaper headlines one day, only to be forgotten the next when some new act of violence occurred.

The worst outbreak of gang murder in Detroit happened in 1930. During the first two weeks of July, ten men were gunned down by gangsters, and the month became known as Bloody July. Then on the morning of July 22, occurred one of the most sensational murders in Detroit's history. It was the shooting of prominent and popular radio commentator Jerry Buckley in the lobby of the La Salle Hotel at Woodward and Adelaide Street. Once a gangland hangout, the La Salle is now a respectable retirement home for the elderly known as Carmel Hall. Buckley's murder was never solved; no one was ever really certain of the motive and no one ever went to jail. The police, however, believed they knew the identity of one of the triggermen — a member of the Licavoli gang.

The death of Buckley, official corruption, and the boldness of the gangsters led to a public disillusionment with prohibition, and a strong movement began to grow for its repeal. Finally, in 1932, Michigan repealed its state prohibition statutes. On December 5, 1933, the 21st Amendment was ratified, and prohibition was finally over.

The Depression, however, did not end. Detroit had been one of the first cities to feel the Depression, due to its industrial make up and heavy dependence on the automobile industry. In 1929, more than 5,337,000 vehicles had been produced. In 1930, production was down to 3,363,000 and in 1931, it fell to 1,332,000. As a result, extensive layoffs left thousands of Detroiters out of work.

On the eve of the Depression, Charles Bowles was elected mayor, a victory that came as a surprise. Bowles had been attacked with unsubstantiated charges that he had Ku Klux Klan endorsement and that he was going to create a "political machine" that would destroy the city's non-partisan government.

Unfortunately, Bowles was unable to carry out this campaign pledge of economy

The Ford Hunger March: On March 7, 1932, 3,000 demonstrators attempted to march to Dearborn to present Henry Ford with demands for union recognition, fuller employment and better working conditions; they didn't make it. Top, marchers cross over the Rouge River on Fort Street. Above, the march halts as Dearborn police are sighted at the Detroit/Dearborn city limits. Here, at Miller Road, one of the leaders on a truck urges the marchers on; the march resumed shortly after and resulted in four being killed and a number injured. Right, two marchers help a wounded comrade to safety.

Top, Mayor Charles Bowles was elected mayor on the eve of the Depression and ousted seven months later. Frank Murphy, above, began a long public career when he replaced Bowles. Below, Father Charles Coughlin gained a large radio following, only to be silenced by his superiors.

because of the Depression-caused welfare burden. The majority of his recommendations aroused intense opposition, and as a result, on June 22, 1930, less than seven months after his inauguration, Mayor Bowles was ousted by Detroit voters in a special recall election.

Bowles' successor, Frank Murphy, a judge of recorder's court, became mayor at a time when the Depression was creating almost unsolvable problems for the city.

A liberal and a humanitarian, it became Murphy's task to alleviate the widespread distress. It was obvious that to avert starvation and homelessness, public assistance in the form of a substantial welfare program was essential. The mayor adopted a middle-of-the-road policy in the heated controversies between welfare advocates and the proponents of rigid economy. He ordered the public welfare officials to meet the steadily rising relief needs of the unemployed, and at the same time, he maintained the financial integrity of the municipal government.

Frank Murphy's program for Detroit attracted national attention, and in 1933, President Roosevelt appointed him governor general of the Philippines. In 1936, Murphy successfully sought the office of governor of Michigan, and subsequently served as U.S. attorney general and as a justice of the U.S. Supreme Court.

During the Depression, Detroit families, like millions of other Americans, gathered around their radios every Sunday to listen to the inspiring and hypnotic voice of Father Charles Coughlin. A Roman Catholic priest and pastor of the Shrine of the Little Flower in suburban Royal Oak, Father Coughlin's first programs were of a religious nature. A persuasive and eloquent speaker, he soon began to talk about the social, economic and political problems of the day. He quickly gained a tremendous influence by his attacks on international bankers at whose doorstep he placed all the world's problems. Before long, he was the number one radio personality of the day.

Along with his radio programs, Father Coughlin began to publish a magazine called *Social Justice,* for which he claimed 600,000 subscribers. But then, apparently carried away by his own eloquence and sense of power, Father Coughlin's speeches began to deteriorate into bitter and abusive verbal attacks of anti-Semitism and isolationism. He was finally silenced by his superiors in the church and his magazine was barred from the mail early in 1942 because of its opposition to the U.S. war effort.

Another voice focusing on the problems of the day was that of Reverend Gerald L. K. Smith, a Protestant evangelist who had been allied with Senator Huey Long of Louisiana. Father Coughlin and Reverend Smith represented the extreme right. On the opposite side was the U.S. Communist Party, more active in Detroit than in many cities, working to make converts among the unemployed and welfare recipients.

The most dangerously explosive event of the Depression occurred on March 7, 1932. A Communist-inspired demonstration, it has become known as the Ford Hunger March.

The march began peaceably enough. The demonstrators, about 3,000 strong, assembled in downtown Detroit, intending to go to Dearborn and present Henry Ford with a list of demands which included union recognition, fuller employment and better working conditions.

As the marchers attempted to enter Dearborn, however, they were stopped by a squad of Dearborn policemen. The marchers were met by a barrage of tear gas, a melee followed and shots were fired. Four marchers were killed and a hundred were injured. The marchers finally dispersed when Detroit police arrived on the scene, having never reached the Ford plant.

The next few days saw a series of Communist demonstrations, and an estimated 15,000 walked in the four-mile funeral procession for the dead marchers. At graveside, 30,000 gathered to hear the band play "The International" and the funeral march of the 1905 Russian Revolutionaries. Observers said later that the affair had all the ingredients for the start of a Communist revolution. That it did not come off may be attributed to the fact that most of Detroit's workers had more innate confidence in the U.S. Constitution than in the red banner. But as one writer said in retrospect, "It was the best chance the Communists ever had in the United States."

Another dramatic incident of the Depression occured on February 14, 1933, when Detroit and Michigan banks were closed by decree of Governor William A. Comstock. In 1933, Detroit's banking system was dominated by two large holding companies, the Guardian Detroit Group, established in 1929, and the Detroit Bankers Company, founded in 1930. Each of these organizations was based upon a major Detroit bank, along with trust companies and other financial institutions acquired by purchase or merger. The two central banks were the Guardian National and the First National. By early 1933,

EIGHT-DAY HOLIDAY FOR ALL BANKS IN MICHIGAN

CITY EDITION

DETROIT TIMES

Only Detroit Newspaper Carrying International News   EVENING   Universal Service and Complete Sport Dispatches

EXTRA

33D YEAR, NO. 137   DETROIT, MICHIGAN, TUESDAY, FEBRUARY 14, 1933   24 PAGES   THREE CENTS

Proclamation Closing Banks to Protect State

Whereas, in view of the acute financial emergency now existing in the city of Detroit and throughout the state of Michigan, I deem it necessary in the public interest and for the preservation of the public peace, health and safety, and for the equal safeguarding without preference of the rights of all depositors in the banks and trust companies of this state and at the request of the Michigan Bankers' Association and the Detroit Clearing House and after consultation with the banking authorities, both national and state, with representatives of the United States Treasury Department, the Banking Department of the State of Michigan, the Federal Reserve Bank, the Reconstruction Finance Corporation, and with the United States Secretary of Commerce, I hereby proclaim the days from Tuesday, February 14th, 1933, to Tuesday, February 21st, 1933, both dates inclusive, to be public holidays during which time all banks, trust companies and other financial institutions conducting a banking or trust business within the state of Michigan shall not be opened for the transaction of banking or trust business, the same to be recognized, classed and treated and have the same effect in respect to such banks, trust companies and other financial institutions as other legal holidays under the laws of this state, provided that it shall not affect the making or execution of agreements or instruments in writing or interfere with judicial proceedings. Dated this 14th day of February, 1933, 1:32 a. m.

WILLIAM A. COMSTOCK, Governor of the State of Michigan.

ERNIE SCHAAF SUCCUMBS TO BRAIN OPERATION AFTER KNOCKOUT

NEW YORK, Feb. 14.—Ernie Schaaf, Boston boxer knocked unconscious in his bout with Primo Carnera Friday night, died at Polyclinic Hospital at 4:20 o'clock this morning.

Mortgage Holiday Asked in Nebraska

LINCOLN, Neb., Feb. 14.—Gov. Charles W. Bryan today issued an "emergency" proclamation in which he asked farm and home mortgage holders to suspend all foreclosures until Congress, the state Legislature and a board of conciliation can act.

Banking Holiday Here Ties Up 720 Million

Funds on deposit in Detroit banks, according to statements of December 31, 1932, were:

First National Bank, Detroit	$423,557,897
Guardian National Bank of Commerce	161,992,934
Detroit Savings Bank	54,911,949
Commonwealth Commercial State Bank	13,966,633
United Savings Bank	11,633,934
Industrial Morris Plan Bank	3,600,612
Detroit Trust Company	38,140,944
Union Guardian Trust Company	31,438,601
Equitable Trust Company	1,960,763
	$722,091,787

War Supply Bill Hiked $24,000,000

WASHINGTON, Feb. 14.—The War Department supply bill, carrying a total of $373,000,000 in appropriations for the next fiscal year, $24,000,000 more than the House bill, was approved by the Senate. An amendment by Senator Couzens, appropriating $25,000,000 for the care of homeless youths was included.

Prisoner Is Slain By Fellow Convict

HUNTSVILLE, Tex., Feb. 14.—Clyde Thompson, who admittedly killed two boys in Eastland County in 1928 "just to see them kick," and whose death sentence was commuted to life imprisonment, today was listed by state prison officials as the slayer of a third man, this time a fellow convict.

Utility Chief Took Life, Coroner Says

CHARLOTTE, N. C., Feb. 14.—Death of Roy L. Peterman, vice-president of the Southern Public Utilities Co., was pronounced a suicide by a coroner's jury. Peterman was found shot to death in his home Saturday night.

Lay $230,000 Theft To High School Boy

OMAHA, Neb., Feb. 14.—Roy Winger, 19-year-old high school student, was to be returned to Idaho today to answer charges of stealing $230,000 worth of state bonds.

STATEMENTS BY OFFICIALS

GOVERNOR COMSTOCK

"At 3 p. m. Monday, February 13, I was requested by telephone to reach Detroit from Lansing at the earliest possible moment to take part in an important conference relative to the general banking situation. This conference was precipitated by an unforeseen and acute situation which had suddenly arisen in the affairs of one of our leading financial institutions, the Union Guardian Trust Company.

"It was the consensus of opinion after long conference by those present that the difficulties might be ironed out provided time could be had for negotiations. As matters stood it would have been necessary to close the doors of the institution involved on the morning of February 14th, which would likely bring in its train disaster to many others of our banking institutions in Michigan.

Crisis Caused by Threatened Withdrawals and Frozen Assets

"The crisis was caused by the inability to realize immediately upon the assets of the institution to meet threatened withdrawals. For the protection of smaller depositors in our institutions and to prevent the withdrawal of large sums from the state of Michigan it was deemed wise to declare a banking holiday for a period sufficiently long to allow the situation to be cleared up.

"The conference was participated in by representatives of all clearing house banks of Detroit, representatives of the Michigan Bankers Association, Secretary of Commerce of the United States Roy D. Chapin, Undersecretary of the United States Treasury Arthur A. Ballantine, the deputy governor of the Federal Reserve Bank for the seventh district, the chief national bank examiner for the seventh district, representative of the Reconstruction Finance Corporation and the Michigan Banking Commission.

"I am convinced that the action taken is in the best interest of the people of this state and especially the smaller depositors in our banking institutions."

Gives Federal Agencies Time To Work Out Stabilizing Plans

ROY D. CHAPIN
Secretary of Commerce

"After discussion of the Detroit banking situation with the various authorities in Washington, the undersecretary of the Treasury, Arthur A. Ballantine, and I came to Detroit Saturday to co-operate with the bankers here. Certain conditions had developed in which Detroit bankers deemed assistance of federal agencies necessary. The requirements as well as the time involved to arrange all the details, which were changing rapidly, made it seem wise to the bankers and to us that a public holiday be requested of Governor Comstock. He has seen fit to declare this and during its period an opportunity is provided to work out plans which we hope will stabilize the entire Michigan situation."

Under Secretary of Treasury Pledges Fullest Aid of U. S.

ARTHUR A. BALLANTINE
Undersecretary of the Treasury

"From close contact during some days with phases of the banking situation existing in this state I believe that Governor Comstock acted very wisely in making his declaration of public holidays. All agencies of the federal government touching the banking field have been giving closest attention and fullest support to these state problems. The time available proved to be too short for final solutions, but further time and effort should be productive of constructive results. The governor's action gives opportunity for this."

All Detroit Banks and Trust Companies to Close for Holiday

"In accordance with the proclamation of Governor Comstock, declaring a bank holiday during the period from Feb. 14, 1933, to Feb. 23, 1933, and believing it to be in the best interests of the financial and business institutions of the state of Michigan, all Detroit banks and trust companies will not be open for business until termination of the holiday proclaimed by the governor."

This statement was made by Detroit banks and trust companies, and also by the Michigan Bankers Association for banks and trust companies throughout the state.

Appeal From Detroit Bankers For Eight-Day Breathing Spell

"To his excellency, the governor of the state of Michigan:

"In view of the acute financial emergency now existing in the city of Detroit and throughout the state of Michigan, we

(Continued on Next Page, Col. 3)

UNION GUARDIAN TRUST CO. DIFFICULTY CAUSES ORDER; BRINGING U. S. AID

Governor William A. Comstock at 3 o'clock this morning issued a proclamation closing all banks, trust companies and all other financial institutions in Michigan for an eight-day period from February 14 to February 21 inclusive.

This action, ties up for at least a week, $650,523,979 in deposits in Detroit banks alone. In addition, $71,567,808 of trust deposits are impounded.

About 500 banks and trust companies are affected by the bank holiday.

Governor Comstock, in a signed statement, announced the bank holiday in Michigan was due to difficulties in which the Union Guardian Trust Company found itself.

"It was the consensus of opinion," the governor asserted, "that the difficulties might be ironed out, provided time could be had for negotiations."

The governor's statement said the Union Guardian Trust Company would have had to close its doors today, and it was in fear this step would cause disaster to other banking

(Continued on Next Page, Col. 1)

120

Shock of reality: On the morning of February 14, 1933, left, Detroiters awoke to these newspaper headlines: without warning they found all their banks closed, top left. On March 24, an apprehensive crowd filled the main floor of the old First National Bank on Cadillac Square; it is now the National Bank of Detroit. In April, 1933, with its treasury empty, the city issued $8 million of scrip to pay its employees.

City Treasurer Albert E. Cobo devised a Depression era plan enabling property owners to extend delinquent tax payments over a seven year period.

unknown to the public, the two banking groups were in serious trouble, their condition a reflection of the speculative days of the 1920s and the economic setbacks of the early 1930s. The banks held mortgages on which jobless borrowers could not keep up their payments. They had also granted large loans and now found that the collateral they had accepted, most of it stocks and bonds, had shrunk to a fraction of its original value.

Detroit also had four independent banks, smaller, more conservatively managed, and in relatively good shape. It was feared that if the two large banks collapsed, sound banks in Detroit and outstate might also be pulled down. So attempts were made to obtain a large government loan to bolster the Guardian. When this failed, Comstock had no choice but to close all the state's banks.

On the morning of February 14, Detroiters were in a state of shock and disbelief. People who transacted their business by check found they had no funds. Merchants could not pay their bills and employers could not meet their payrolls. Business operations throughout the city and state were suddenly at a standstill. The only money that was available was that which people had in their pockets or in cash registers, or in safety deposit boxes. The large corporations, with banking connections outside the state, had currency shipped in to them, but even this source disappeared on March 6, when President Roosevelt declared a national bank holiday.

By March 21, all the solvent banks had reopened, although under tight restrictions. The two large Detroit banks, however, with their more than 800,000 depositors, were not allowed to reopen and were put through the process of liquidation. The large depositors waived their claims so that the smaller ones could be paid off, and the remaining good assets were sold to two new banks, the Manufacturers National and the National Bank of Detroit. Fortunately, by 1934, sufficient recovery had been made so that Detroit's banking community was once again on a sound footing.

Just as the causes of the Depression were at work before the people became aware of them, so was the process of recovery. Following his inauguration in 1933, President Roosevelt presented Congress with a program of relief measures, among them the establishment of the Civilian Conservation Corps (CCC), the Civil Works Administration, the Works Progress Administration (WPA), and the Public Works Administration (PWA).

Other relief included a federal agency created to enable distressed homeowners to refinance their mortgages, thus avoiding foreclosure of their homes. Detroit City Treasurer Albert E. Cobo also produced a beneficial plan which enabled property owners to extend payments of delinquent taxes over a seven-year period. This freed them from the fear of losing their homes through tax foreclosure sales. Known as the Seven Year Plan, this arrangement won Cobo such public favor that in 1949, he was elected mayor and became one of the city's most progressive chief executives.

Thus, gradually, a better financial base was built and purchasing power was restored. People's confidence returned and with it came signs of prosperity. Just as Detroit was one of the first cities to feel the Depression, so it was one of the first to find the recovery road. A car-hungry nation began again to buy automobiles and in 1936, the auto industry produced nearly 4,500,000 cars and trucks.

It was during the trying times of the Depression years that Detroit proclaimed itself

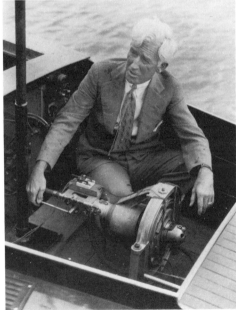

Breadlines, a common sight during the 1930s, above, did not keep Detroiters away from their favorite sports. Left, Joe "Ducky" Medwick of St. Louis, at bat, and Mickey Cochrane, Detroit catcher, during the 1934 World Series. Below left, Augie Galan of the Cubs is forced out at 2nd by Billy Rogell as Billy Herman hits into a double play during the second game of the 1935 World Series.
Far left, Gar Wood, powerboat designer and driver.

The Brown Bomber: above, Joe Louis with his mother on the front porch of their Detroit home; right, Louis being readied for a fight by his trainer, Jack Blackburn. Below, Detroiter Eddie Tolan, who won two gold medals at the 1932 Olympics. Bottom, Detroit Red Wings Peter Kelly, Modere Bruneteau, Earl Robertson and Walter Kilrea celebrate winning the Stanley Cup over the New York Rangers, April 15, 1937.

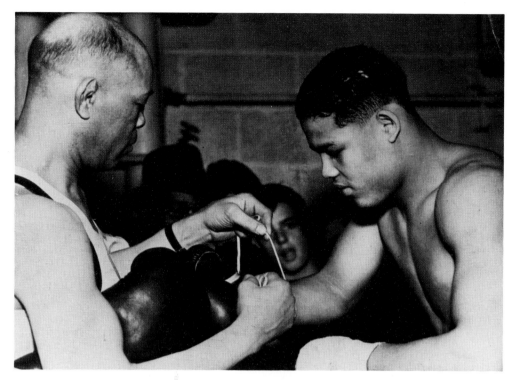

the "City of Champions." It all began with Gar Wood when he successfully defended the Harmsworth Trophy — the most coveted international prize for unlimited powerboat racing — in a race on the Detroit River in 1931. Then Eddie Tolan, a young black man from Cass Technical High School and the University of Michigan, won two gold medals in the 1932 Olympics, capturing the 100 and 200 meter races. The Detroit Tigers won the American League pennant in 1934 and then again in 1935, when they won the World Series. The Detroit Lions won the National Football League championship in 1935. The Red Wings won hockey's Stanley Cup that same year, then again in 1937.

The claim "City of Champions" was topped off in 1937 when Joe Louis Barrow, known as Joe Louis — the Brown Bomber — defeated Jim Braddock to win the world's heavyweight boxing championship.

Born on an Alabama sharecropper's farm, Louis moved with his family to Detroit in 1926 when he was 12. Rising out of Brewster's East Side Gym, he became the pride of Detroit and heavyweight champion of the world. Louis reigned as champion for 11 years and eight months and defended his title 25 times, records unequalled by any heavyweight boxer before or since.

In all, Louis won more than $4.6 million but he spent it and gave it away as fast as he earned it. Following his retirement as undefeated on March 1, 1949, Louis was so heavily in debt for back taxes that he tried to make a comeback. But age had caught up with the Brown Bomber. He lost his two title challenges and retired permanently in 1952.

Though not a native Detroiter, Joe Louis was raised in the city, and once his professional career was established, he retained close ties with Detroit — he lived in the city part of each year; he bought a farm not far from it; he contributed to Detroit charities; he worked with the young people of the Motor City; and a great many Detroiters have remained his close friends.

But Joe Louis was more than a citizen of Detroit. His major impact was on America as a whole. As a symbol during the turbulent 1930s and 1940s, the Brown Bomber's public image was often ambiguous, reflecting the uncertainties of his age. But beneath the ambiguity was a clear message. Louis was a beacon of hope for his race as well as a champion admired and respected by white Americans.

Joe Louis will never be forgotten. In tribute to this great Detroiter, the City Council on June 22, 1978, voted to name the new riverfront sports arena for Joe Louis. They could not have made a more fitting choice.

Five months later, another group made up of such celebrities as Frank Sinatra, Muhammad Ali, Cary Grant and Joe DiMaggio, staged a testimonial dinner for the Brown Bomber in Las Vegas. Said old timer Eddie Futch, a lightweight on the amateur boxing team on which Louis was the light-heavyweight: "He was the champion, is the champion and always will be the champion."

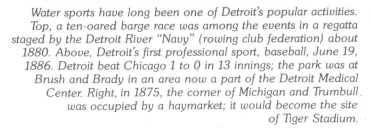

Water sports have long been one of Detroit's popular activities. Top, a ten-oared barge race was among the events in a regatta staged by the Detroit River "Navy" (rowing club federation) about 1880. Above, Detroit's first professional sport, baseball, June 19, 1886. Detroit beat Chicago 1 to 0 in 13 innings; the park was at Brush and Brady in an area now a part of the Detroit Medical Center. Right, in 1875, the corner of Michigan and Trumbull was occupied by a haymarket; it would become the site of Tiger Stadium.

Top, Tiger Stadium in 1968. Above, Tiger owner Walter O. "Spike" Briggs and son at the ball park, May 13, 1936. Below, Tiger owner Frank Navin at the batting cage, September 20, 1930. Above right, Detroit Tiger Hall-of-famer Harry Heilman, left and the greatest of them all — Ty Cobb.

Sports, of course, were nothing new to Detroit. Along with horseracing and sledding on the frozen river, boating was one of the earliest forms of organized sport enjoyed by the people of Detroit. In 1839, for example, the Detroit Boat Club was founded and its members actively participated in rowing and sailing. It is today the oldest rowing club in the U.S.

Detroit's first major professional sport was baseball. A team called the Detroits was formed in 1881, and, obtaining a franchise previously held by Cincinnati, became a member of the National League. The Detroits, based at Recreation Park at Brush and Brady Streets, beat St. Louis for the world's championship in 1887.

With professional baseball drawing ever larger crowds, a bigger and more accessible field was needed and the club owners acquired a new lot at Michigan and Trumbull in 1896. A grandstand was erected on the site and was named Bennett Field after the club's star catcher, Charley Bennett; and the team was renamed the Tigers when the players appeared in black and orange striped stockings. In 1901, Detroit joined the American League and has played in it ever since.

Ownership of the Tigers was acquired by Frank Navin in 1903, and nine years later the field's name was changed to Navin Field. Later, when millionaire auto body manufacturer Walter O. Briggs bought the ball club, it became Briggs Stadium. When ownership passed to his successors, the name was again changed to its present Tiger Stadium.

The Tigers won several league penants in the early part of the century, but their golden era began in 1905 when a flashy young Georgian, Tyrus Raymond Cobb, joined the team and began a 24-year career that made him a legend. Throughout the succeeding years, others came to play at the corner of Michigan and Trumbull;

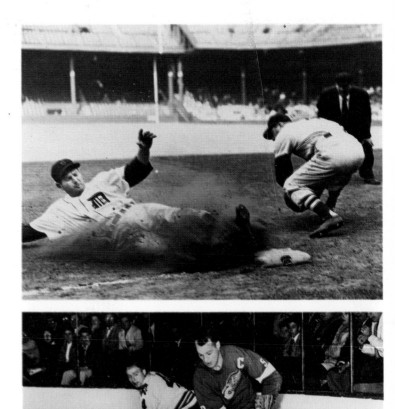

The stars of their times: top left, Mickey Cochrane, left, and Charlie Gehringer compare a new and old ball, May 20, 1938. Top right, George Kell slides safely into third on a triple to left center, May 25, 1950. Above left, Al Kaline, for more than 20 years the Tigers' premier right fielder, sends one into the seats at the 365 foot marker, July 31, 1966. Above right, Gordie Howe, No. 9, in action. Left, pitcher Harold "Hal" Newshouser. Right, the greatest quarterback in Detroit Lion history — Bobby Lane, August 7, 1955.

Victory is sweet: in 1968, Detroit defeated St. Louis in a dramatic come-from-behind victory to win the World Series and the town went wild, top left and right. Above left, Detroit Lions' great middle line-backer No. 56, Joe Schmidt, with teammates Jim Martin (47), Charlie Ane (50), and Lou Creekmur (76), on November 30, 1957. Upper right, The Detroit Express in action. Below, all-star Bob Lanier of the Detroit Pistons.

players such as Harry Heilmann and Mickey Cochrane, Hank Greenberg and Charlie Gehringer, Hal Newhouser and George Kell, Al Kaline and Norman Cash, and in 1961 a young black man from Detroit's Northwestern High School, Willie Horton.

The growing auto town took to the club in its early years and supported it through good times and bad. Detroiters made local celebrities out of anyone who donned the Tiger stripes, and went wild in times of triumph such as 1940 and 1945, then again in 1968 when a world series victory over the St. Louis Cardinals united a city torn by racial strife.

Although there had been some professional football in Detroit as early as World War I, the city joined the big leagues in 1934 when a franchise was purchased from Portsmouth, Ohio, and the Lions entered the local arena. Over the years, the Lions have produced some of Detroit's greatest sports moments with the glory years of Bobby Layne and Joe Schmidt during the 1950s. In 1975, the team moved from Tiger Stadium to the newly constructed Silverdome in suburban Pontiac.

In 1926, the Detroit Hockey Club was organized and purchased the Cougars of Victoria, British Columbia. The team was renamed the Falcons in 1930, and a short time later became the Red Wings. Their home rink, Olympia, was built in 1927. One of the most powerful hockey teams of all time, the Red Wings have given Detroit fans some unforgettable moments and probably the greatest player the game has ever known — number 9, Gordie Howe.

Professional basketball came to the city in 1957 when the Pistons were brought to Detroit from Fort Wayne, Indiana. Soccer has grown in popularity in recent years and in 1977 the Detroit Express joined the North American Soccer League.

The union men

The union movement in Detroit began in the 1850s, but the first important labor leader was Richard F. Trevellick, top, who in 1864 led the organization of the Detroit Trades Assembly. Above, one of the leading forces in formation of the Michigan Federation of Labor in 1888, Joseph Labadie. Left, by the 1930s, the assembly line technique had been developed to the point where cars could be assembled as fast as men could work.

It was out of the Depression and its turbulent years that a strong labor movement grew in Detroit. But the history of the labor movement in the city begins many years earlier.

Although a Mechanics Society (an early type of labor union) was organized as early as 1818 in Detroit, the city's first real labor organization was formed by the printers in the 1830s. The group's structure at first was rather informal but in 1848, the printers established the Detroit Typographic Union. Still in existence today, it is Detroit's oldest trade union.

The union movement itself began to grow in Detroit during the decade of the 1850s, when a small handful of local unions first became affiliated with national organizations. The period during the Civil War saw further growth of unionism because of the wartime atmosphere of full employment, high wages, and still higher prices.

In 1860, the iron molders founded a highly successful union. During the next four years, the machinists, blacksmiths, carpenters and plasterers also organized. In May 1863, the Brotherhood of Locomotive Engineers, the first permanent railroad union in the country, was founded in Detroit as the Brotherhood of the Footboard. By the end of the war, the labor movement was large enough to form a separate division in the city's 1865 Fourth of July parade.

The first important local labor leader was Richard F. Trevellick, who was instrumental in establishing the Detroit Trades Assembly in 1864. The assembly was a coalition of most of the trade unions in the city and soon boasted a membership of 5,000, about 10 percent of Detroit's population. However, the Depression of 1873 set the movement back and marked the end of the Detroit Trades Assembly.

Although the assembly lasted only a few years, it was for a time a powerful force in Detroit. It served as spokesman for organized labor in economic matters and functioned effectively in city politics. Politicians actively sought assembly support at election time, and occasionally, workingmen themselves ran for city office, often successfully.

In 1879, the Knights of Labor, which had been founded 10 years earlier in Philadelphia, sent representatives to Detroit and by the middle 1880s had enrolled a large local membership. Yet many trade union people were frankly suspicious of the Knights (the organization had originally been a secret fraternal society). In 1881 the Detroit Council of Trades and Labor Unions was formed, later the Council became the Detroit Federation of Labor, composed of representatives from each of the leading trade unions in the city. It took an active interest in problems affecting workers, and on various occasions even endorsed candidates for political office. In 1888, it assumed a major role in the formation of the Michigan Federation of Labor. One of the moving forces behind the Council was Joseph Labadie, a printer of unusual literary talents and an outspoken advocate of reform. Along with Trevellick, Labadie was one of the outstanding champions of the labor cause in Detroit and Michigan.

By 1892, the Detroit Council of Trades counted 37 local unions as members, many of which still thrive. Others, however, have been lost in the parade of progress, and their names and functions today have a quaint sound, such as the Horse-Collar Makers Union, the Cigar Packers Union, the Broommakers and the Stove Mounters. Another which flourished at the time was the Florence Nightingale Union most of whose female membership was employed in local shoe factories.

Between 1900 and 1910, the labor movement in Detroit seemed to lack the vitality of the era that had seen the formation of the Detroit Council of Trades. In fact in the opinion of many labor leaders, Detroit at this time was a "poor union town."

The unusual growth of the city between 1910 and 1920 resulted in a large increase in membership of many craft unions. During the boom time of the 1920s, the highly specialized craft unions continued to grow.

Throughout all this period, however, one group in Detroit remained largely unorganized — these were the factory workers, particularly the workers in the automobile plants. As early as 1903, the Detroit Council of Trades made some effort to organize automotive workers but met with little success. Other efforts were made in 1910 and 1916, but they too lacked results.

The unions had achieved little headway in the auto plants for several reasons. First of all, the auto industry was a high-wage industry. In 1910, for example, an auto

Mass Meeting

Sunday, June 30, 1935

4 P. M.

at State Fair Grounds Coliseum

Sponsored by the

**AUTOMOBILE INDUSTRIAL
WORKERS ASSOCIATION**

for the purpose of acquainting all Automobile
Workers with the necessities and advantages
of Organized Labor

SPEAKERS

REV. FATHER CHARLES E. COUGHLIN
"National Union for Social Justice"

Congressman, WILLIAM P. CONNERY
of the Wagner-Connery Labor Bill

Representative, WILLIAM LEMKE
Frazier-Lemke Farm Bill

RICHARD FRANKENSTEEN
Secretary of Dodge Bros. Collective Bargaining
Representative Board

It is Your Duty to be Present

25

The union notice: common sights in the 1930s were such posters for labor organizational meetings, above; this one was called a year and a half before the UAW-CIO staged the auto industry's first major sit down strike in December 1936, against General Motors at Flint, above right and center. Below right, union officials lead Cadillac strikers out of their plant on January 17, 1937; from left, Julius Hochman, Richard Frankensteen, Leo Krzycki, Homer Martin, and Walter Reuther.

The National Industrial Recovery Act, part of the new deal, gave workers the right to organize and required employers to bargain collectively with them.

The Battle of the Overpass: the UAW had contracts with GM and Chrysler but Ford was adamantly opposed to union recognition. However, a blunder by Henry Ford's special assistant, Harry Bennett, caused the public tide to go in favor of the union when, on May 26, 1937, UAW people, distributing leaflets at Ford's Dearborn plant gates, were met head on by some of Bennett's men. Press photographers recorded the rest: Above left, Robert Kantor, Walter Reuther, Richard Frankensteen and J. J. Kennedy watch approaching Ford Service Department men just prior to the battle. Above, Richard Frankensteen with his coat pulled over his head. Left, Reuther and Frankensteen after their beating.

worker in Michigan averaged $2.78 a day, while the statewide rate for men in general factory work was $2.19. Then in 1914, Henry Ford announced his $5-a-day wage scale. In addition, the craft union leaders of organizations such as the American Federation of Labor were just not interested in organizing auto workers. Most importantly, though, auto workers were essentially unskilled, and it was said that a new hire could be taught his job on the assembly line in two or three days. The industrial worker was not only easily replaceable, he was undoubtedly the most expendable tool in the auto plant. The workers themselves could see that with a large untapped pool of easily recruited and cheap southern labor — both black and white — they were in no position to openly demonstrate an interest in organizing. This situation continued through the boom times of the 1920s.

All this changed in 1932 with the election of Franklin Roosevelt and the passage of the National Industrial Recovery Act. This piece of New Deal legislation not only gave workers the right to organize, but even encouraged them to do so. It also required employers to bargain collectively with them.

As a result, a considerable amount of automotive union organization occurred in 1933, 1934 and 1935. Then in August 1935, the American Federation of Labor accepted the organization of a consolidated auto union and that marked the beginning of the United Automobile Workers. In 1936, when the Committee for Industrial Organization (under the leadership of John L. Lewis and renamed the Congress of Industrial Organizations in 1938) split with the AFL, it was joined by the UAW.

The UAW-CIO met with little success until December 1936, when General Motors employees in Flint staged the auto industry's first major sit-down strike. The strike continued until February 1937 when General Motors finally agreed to recognize the

It took four years of union persistence following the Battle of the Overpass to win recognition of UAW by Ford Motor Company. Far left, a union protest leaflet for a meeting held shortly after the confrontation. Left, a solemn Harry Bennett signs the first Ford contract on June 20, 1941; union officials express a somewhat different feeling. Lower left, Walter Reuther, veteran of the Battle of the Overpass, celebrates his election to the UAW's top office in 1946. Right, the skyline of Detroit in 1939.

Walter Reuther became president of the UAW-CIO in 1946 and until his death in 1970 played a strategic role in the affairs of the United States.

UAW as sole bargaining agent. This was the first major breakthrough. It was soon followed by an equally successful Chrysler sit-down.

While the UAW now had contracts with General Motors and Chrysler, it still had its toughest customer to deal with. That was Henry Ford. Ford had announced that despite hell, high water or the law, he would never recognize the union. To enforce his policies, Ford called upon his special assistant, Harry Bennett, who directed the company's private army of Service Department men.

That the union was finally successful can largely be attributed to a blunder by Bennett. On May 26, 1937, a group of UAW people went to the Ford Gates in Dearborn to distribute union leaflets. Among them were Walter Reuther and Richard Frankensteen. They were met at the Miller Road overpass to the Rouge Plant by members of Bennett's Service Department, who gave the unionists an unmerciful beating. Two were severely injured; the others, bloody and with their clothes half torn off, were turned back, but not before press photographers recorded the entire disgraceful affair. The incident became known as the Battle of the Overpass and from that moment, the union, helped greatly by public opinion, gained the upper hand. After a long and bitter struggle, Ford finally capitulated, and in May 1941, the UAW won out as the sole bargaining agent. Since then, the UAW has remained the unchallenged voice of labor in the automotive industry.

Throughout World War II, the union observed the wartime no-strike pledge, but in 1946, the UAW staged a bitter strike against General Motors which lasted 113 days. The strike proved the soundness of the new union strategy of striking only one of the Big Three at a time, thereby placing its target at a competitive disadvantage.

In 1946, Walter Reuther was elected president of the UAW-CIO and brought to the union a strong administration. It was not accomplished easily, however, and internal union friction sometimes took a violent turn. In 1948, Reuther was critically wounded by a would-be assassin. The assailants were never apprehended, but they were believed to have been Communists whom Reuther had purged from the union.

For the next 22 years, Walter Reuther continued to head the UAW, and as its president played a major role in the economic, political, and social affairs of the United States. On May 9, 1970, while traveling to northern Michigan, Reuther's light plane crashed and he was killed. Reuther was ably followed as president of the UAW by Leonard Woodcock, and after his retirement in 1977, by Douglas Fraser.

The Great Depression that witnessed the growth of the labor movement in Detroit was to last for more than 10 long years. By the end of the 1930s, a measure of prosperity had returned to Detroit, but full recvovery was not to come from social legislation and financial pump-priming. Full recovery was to come with the onslaught of the blitzkrieg and the marching feet of invading armies.

Union problems took a back seat to the menace of World War II, as Ford began production of the famous B-24 Liberator bombers at the company's Willow Run plant, below. Left, military service and rationing put many automobiles into storage for the duration of the war.

Arsenal of democracy

The domestic problems of the Great Depression had tended to obscure the international scene for most Detroiters. Many had come to accept the theory that American participation in World War I had been a great mistake, and that the nation had been dragged into the war by British propaganda, by the munition makers, and by the banks who wanted to secure the loans they had made to the Allies.

When the Nazis invaded Poland on September 1, 1939, many Detroiters felt that the United States should stay out of this new war and that military aid, given to the Allies, was all that was needed to defeat the Axis powers. Others, however, were calling for direct American involvement.

Then on the morning of December 7, 1941, all speculation ended. With the Japanese attack on Pearl Harbor, the United States had no other alternative. The nation was once again at war.

As early as the fall of 1940, however, Detroit had begun to feel the impact of the war. On October 15, the Michigan National Guard was called into federal service after a summer of maneuvers. Once again, the 32nd Division was mobilized and other Michigan units were to follow, including the 210th Anti-Aircraft Artillery regiment, and the 182nd and 177th Field Artillery regiments. While the guard and reserve units were being called up, more than half a million Detroit men registered on October 16, 1940, for possible duty under the Selective Service Act.

Altogether, 613,542 men and women from Michigan served in the armed forces during the Second World War, with Detroit furnishing about one-third of that number.

There was mobilization on the home front as well. The day after the attack on Pearl Harbor, army guards from Selfridge Field were posted at the entrance to the Detroit-Windsor Tunnel and the Ambassador Bridge to prevent sabotage, which was considered a very real danger. As a precaution against air raids, a civil defense organization was created. The organization was responsible for providing a technical training program to more than 100,000 Detroit men and women as air raid wardens, medical service volunteers, special police and auxiliary firefighters.

Thousands of military men and women, many of them aviators, were trained in the Detroit area at Selfridge Field and Grosse Ile Naval Base. Large military airports were also maintained at Romulus and Willow Run. The Dearborn Naval School, in cooperation with the Ford Motor Company, gave instruction to hundreds of mechanics.

In addition, many Detroiters did their part by purchasing war bonds on a payroll deduction plan. Others participated in the activities of the Red Cross, the USO and other service and relief organizations.

Many who stayed home cultivated victory gardens. Boys and girls collected scrap metal and milkweed pods, the floss from which was used to fill life jackets. And families gathered around the radio each evening to hear the latest war news.

The declaration of war brought price controls and rationing to Detroit — geared to assure enough material for the U.S. armed forces and its hard-pressed allies, rationing of gasoline and tires was ordered, thus severely limiting automobile travel. Later in 1942, shortages of commodities resulted in the rationing of meat, canned goods, shoes, clothes, and unhappily for many, liquor and cigarettes.

Behind the actual fighting front, the chief contribution to the war effort was made by American industry; in this, the role of Detroit's automobile industry was one of the most important. During the war, the United States was called the "Arsenal of Democracy", and this designation came to be applied particularly to Detroit.

In August 1941, the production of automobiles and trucks for the civilian market began to be curtailed. On February 9, 1942, the last automobile was produced, the last truck on May 31. Production was not resumed until late 1945 and early 1946. All the industry's efforts were now concentrated on the production of war material.

To build the needed war materials, new plants were constructed by the government and turned over to the auto companies to operate. Chrysler ran the great tank arsenal in Warren, Hudson Motor Car Company took over the Navy gun arsenal in Center Line, and General Motors operated a tank arsenal near Flint. The Ford Motor Company assumed the responsibility for building B-24 Liberator

The war effort: military trucks by the thousands rolled off Detroit assembly lines, top left. Top right, the automobile companies produced 57% of all tanks delivered to U.S. and Allied armed forces during the World War II; the ones shown are Patton tanks. Above left, while most able bodied men were involved with the more vicious elements of war, the industrial backup was handled by "Rosie the Riveter," as those women who joined the work force were called. Significantly, the war was also to result in black women entering the work force in areas where they had not before been welcome.

bombers at the Willow Run plant, which was constructed at a cost of more than $100 million.

The extent of the auto industry's involvement in the production of war material was evident in both variety and volume. The Chrysler tank arsenal turned out more than 25,000 tanks, the rate of output sometimes reaching 1,000 tanks a month. In addition, Chrysler plants turned out Bofors anti-aircraft guns, light ammunition, pontoons, aircraft engines and aircraft fuselage sections and parts.

At Willow Run, the first B-24 bomber came off the lines on September 10, 1942. A total of 8,685 of the huge aircraft were built there, more aircraft than were produced at any other U.S. plant. Other Ford plants were producing aircraft engines, amphibians, tank destroyers and gun directors.

General Motors manufactured more than 2,300 separate items, ranging from tiny ball bearings to 30-ton tanks. The corporation also produced airplanes, airplane engines and parts, guns, shells, and marine diesel engines.

The plants of the other automotive companies were equally productive. Packard built thousands of Rolls-Royce aircraft engines and marine engines for PT boats; Studebaker produced Wright Cyclone aircraft engines; Nash turned out two-stage, supercharged, 2,000-horsepower Pratt and Whitney airplane engines; and Hudson built engine parts and suspension units for M-5 tanks. In addition, the companies turned out military vehicles of all types in a seemingly unending stream. At the Ford Rouge plant, a new kind of light vehicle was developed and tested; it was named the Jeep. Ford built them and so did the Willys plant in Toledo. Both Ford and Willys were also producing jet buzz bombs near the end of the war.

Proud and patriotic: workers pose at the Reo plant during the war; they were building military trucks, one of which is in the center of the picture draped with two American flags.

Blacks, crowded into segregated areas where they were forced to live under indescribable conditions, were victimized by unscrupulous landlords.

One of the most difficult problems facing the automobile industry was to secure enough labor. With so many men and women in the armed services, the pool of skilled and unskilled workers was drained. To help meet this need, women were hired to fill jobs previously held only by men; it was the era of Rosie the Riveter and it was soon apparent that women could indeed do this work and do it well. And so, a new social pattern was set, an outward symbol of which was the wearing of slacks by women. Previously unacceptable, slacks were a necessity in a factory. Thus the war and Detroit's automobile industry, in a real sense, promoted the women's cause; when the war was over, many women did not return to their homes but remained in the labor force.

The need for additional workers though could not be filled with local women alone. Thus thousands of blacks from the South and whites from West Virginia, Kentucky and Tennessee were recruited to work in Detroit factories. As a result, Detroit faced a rapid deterioration of race relations.

Although Detroit's racial troubles had many roots, the one single development that can best explain what happened in the early 1940s is the problem of housing for blacks. By 1941, the housing situation had become intolerable. Blacks, crowded into segregated areas where they were forced to live under indescribable conditions, were victimized by unscrupulous landlords. Their resentment ran high, and whites in bordering neighborhoods feared them as a menace to their own somewhat precarious way of life.

It was not until the 1930s that Detroit's first public housing was built. However, none of the first projects were in black neighborhoods, nor were they intended for black occupancy. Officials were aware of the need for low-cost black housing and planned a project on the lower east side; but, for some reason, federal authorities changed the site location to an all-white, predominantly Polish neighborhood on the northeast side. It was named the Sojourner Truth Project, after the one-time slave woman who had been active in the emancipation movement. Detroit officials and

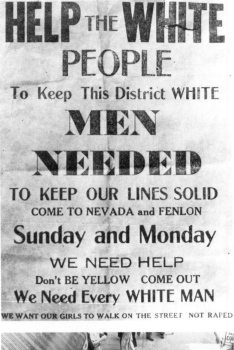

The first major attempt to provide public housing for blacks turned into a vacillating battle of local and federal governments and eventually, in June 1943, a black and white battle in the streets. Top left, the Sojourner Truth housing incident produced hate literature such as this. Above, a young black is attacked by a group of whites. Although members of the Detroit Urban League traveled to Washington, D. C. to protest the government's actions in handling the housing project, top right, it did not prevent the riot. Center right, a crowd watches an automobile burn on Woodward Avenue; such actions resulted in patrolling by military troops for 10 days, below right.

Aftermath: Wrecked cars and court appearances. Many of the rioters, both white and black, were young men and boys.

black leaders objected to the change, pointing out that to move blacks into that location would certainly lead to trouble.

The result was called shameful vacillation and weakness on the part of federal officials. When white residents of the area protested, the National Housing Administration announced that the project would be occupied by whites. A month later, however, that decision was reversed and black occupancy was ordered. When blacks did begin to move in on February 28, 1942, a white mob gathered, wielding knives, bricks and clubs. The mob was quieted with assurance that the policy had again been changed and that no blacks would be admitted. However, officials reversed their position again and the project went back to the blacks, who, protected by a cordon of 1,750 troops and police finally moved in. If it was a victory over discrimination, it was also an example of how inept government could be in handling a difficult racial situation. Neither the white people in the area nor the black community would soon forget Sojourner Truth.

A year later, in early summer of 1943, people sought relief from the heat in the city's parks. Because there were so few places for them to go, many blacks flocked to Belle Isle. It was on the island that the trouble started on the night of Sunday, June 20. No one knows what incident touched it off, but after sundown there were a series of fights, which were carried across the Belle Isle Bridge to the mainland. Then a fight between blacks and 200 sailors broke out at the nearby Brodhead Naval Armory. Before long, the mob had grown to an estimated 5,000 and the police riot squad was called.

Word of what was happening spread swiftly through the black districts. Wild rumors were circulated, and blacks surged into the streets of the lower east side. Whites, unaware of what was happening, went to work as usual on Monday, some driving through riot-torn streets. Some were attacked and beaten, and at least one was killed.

As news of what was going on spread across the city, white mobs gathered and started to counterattack. General fighting broke out, the worst between Vernor and Forest along Woodward and John R. Streetcars were stopped and blacks were taken off and beaten; automobiles carrying blacks were tipped over and set on fire. Later in the day, the white mob of shouting men and boys, many of them in their early teens, moved downtown and gathered around City Hall. Blacks on their way home from work were caught in Cadillac Square as they transferred from one streetcar to another. One black was beaten to death on the Fort Street steps of the Federal Building.

Realizing that the police could no longer control the situation, Governor Harry F. Kelly proclaimed martial law and called for federal troop intervention. About 9:30 p.m. on Monday, June 21, the first contingent of 2,500 arrived in the city. By nightfall, order was restored, but for the next 10 days, Detroit was an armed camp. The troops remained until June 30, encamped on the lawn of the Public Library and at other strategic locations. No further major incidents occurred.

Altogether, 34 persons, 23 of them blacks, were killed during the riot. Hundreds were injured, 1,800 arrests were made, and property damage ran into the millions of dollars.

Within a few short days, Detroit was back to its wartime pattern of life. Unfortunately, some bitter feelings lingered and little was accomplished in attacking the many problems that had brought on that dreadful week of rioting.

Peace and celebrations: It was August 1945, the Japanese had just surrendered, and citizens of Detroit partied, top and right. A month before Japan capitulated and two months after Germany's surrender, Ford produced its first postwar civilian automobile, a 1946 Super Delux two-door sedan; it was presented to President Harry S. Truman, above, by Henry Ford II.

Before Suburbia: three views of Woodward Avenue in the 1940s.

Detroiters held their first United Foundation Torch Drive in 1949, a drive which today supports nearly 200 agencies; below, a recent "Miss Torch Drive" and four young Detroiters before the United Foundation Torch.

On June 6, 1944, the great Allied armada landed on the beaches of Normandy. Gradually, the enemy was pushed back and on May 8, 1945, Nazi Germany surrendered. The war effort did not slacken, however, and on August 6, the United States crushed any last Japanese war hopes when the first atomic bomb was exploded over Hiroshima.

With the dreadful destruction caused by the A-Bomb, the Japanese realized that their cause was lost. On August 14, the shattered and defeated Japanese Empire surrendered.

When the news reached the city, a half million cheering, shouting Detroiters flocked into the downtown area for a great victory celebration, expressing their joy that at long last the war was finally over.

The years immediately following World War II were a time of prosperity for Detroit. True, there was a post-war period of adjustment as the sudden demobilization brought with it equally sudden problems. There were shortages, inflation, strikes, and a surge of growth that brought Detroit to its peak of population of 1,849,568 in 1950. But the auto industry was booming and the first steps of urban renewal were being taken.

In 1949, Detroiters held their first United Foundation Torch Drive. Today, this massive fund-raising effort supports nearly 200 agencies in the metropolitan area. The Fund drive, which has never failed to make its goal, has been so successful that the idea has been widely adopted by communities throughout the United States.

On July 24, 1951, the city celebrated the 250th anniversary of its founding by Cadillac. A grand parade was held on Woodward Avenue and that evening, thousands of Detroiters gathered in Grand Circus Park to join in the lighting of a giant birthday cake. There was a feeling of optimism in the air. The future indeed looked bright.

A decade before Henry Ford's death in 1947, Edsel Ford was president of the company and posed for this picture with his family at their Gaulker Pointe home in Grosse Pointe; from left, Edsel, Eleanor Clay, Henry II, Benson, Josephine, and William Clay. Edsel Ford died in 1943, and two years later Henry II ascended to the top position. Below, the Kaiser-Frazer Corporation assembly line at its Willow Run plant; its automobile production ceased in 1955.

5. Detroit today

A city on the move

As Detroit entered the decades of the 1950s and 1960s, it was to undergo a number of important changes, some of the most important of which were to occur within the automobile industry.

On the night of April 7, 1947, Henry Ford died at his home at the age of 83, and an automotive era came to an end. In 1919, Ford's only son, Edsel, had become president, but when he died in 1943, the elder Ford resumed control. In actuality, the corporation was now run by Harry Bennett, head of the company's Service Department; as a result of some of his decisions, operations began to suffer. In 1945, Mrs. Edsel Ford and other members of the family gained control of the company and young Henry Ford II, Edsel's son, became president. Bennett was forced out and major changes were made at the corporation's executive level. The Ford Motor Company once again had a sound management structure and a promising future.

Another important change occurred in 1954 when Nash, a Wisconsin-based company, became American Motors and absorbed the Hudson Motor Car Company. Shortly thereafter, the Nash and Hudson lines were discontinued, and American Motors turned to the production of the smaller Rambler automobile. The year 1954 also saw the Packard Motor Company taken over by the Indiana-based Studebaker Corporation. In 1956, the Detroit Packard plant was closed and the last Packard was built in 1958. Then, in 1963, Studebaker ended all auto production in the United States and built cars only in Canada. But the move was short lived, and three years later the final Studebaker was built. The company closed its doors for the last time.

A new line of automobile was introduced to the American public in 1946 when Kaiser-Frazer began production in the old bomber plant at Willow Run. In 1953, the company merged with the Willys Corporation of Toledo, then ceased passenger car production in 1955 while continuing to manufacture trucks and jeeps. In 1970, the company merged with American Motors, which dropped the production of trucks while expanding the production of the jeep line. By this date, the manufacturing of passenger cars in the United States was down to the Big Three and the much smaller American Motors.

Several production milestones were marked in the decades of the 1950s and 1960s for the auto industry. In 1955, production passed the nine million mark at 9,169,292 with nearly eight million passenger cars and more than 1.2 million motor trucks and buses manufactured. Ten years later, another all-time one-year production record was set when 11,057,366 motor vehicles were produced. Then, in 1967, General Motors turned out its 100 millionth unit, a Chevrolet, and a few days later Ford passed the 70 million mark. The following year, the U.S. automotive industry manufactured its 250 millionth vehicle.

During the 1970s, the automobile industry faced a new and different challenge. Much of the industry's research and development efforts were devoted to meeting government regulations in safety and emission-control areas. There was also a rising tide of consumerism, and the industry faced critics in Congress. With the rising costs of gasoline and stronger competition from imports, U.S. manufacturers also began production of the sub-compact, and began to reduce the size and weight of larger cars to meet new federal fuel-consumption levels.

However, these restrictions did not curtail sales. In 1972, a new record of 11,270,745 units was reached, only to be broken the following year with a total of 12,637,335 vehicles. A good portion of this growth came from the sale of recreational vehicles — travel trailers, truck campers, camping trailers, and motor

Detroit's freeways began accommodating the automobile in 1950, and in the next 25 years 265 miles of freeways were either built or were under construction. Top, the Fisher/Lodge Freeway interchange under construction, June 9, 1969. Above, the same year, the Ford Freeway (I-94) looking east; the Lodge interchange is at the bottom of the photo, and the Chrysler Freeway interchange is at the top.

homes. In 1972 these sales reached 747,500 and passed the 750,000 mark the next year. Ten years earlier, in 1962, only 80,300 recreational vehicles had been sold.

Along with the changes in the automobile industry, Detroit was to see a major change in the type of roads upon which these cars and trucks were to travel — the city's freeways, or expressways, as they were first called. It began in 1950 when the first portion of the north-south John C. Lodge was opened.* The Lodge was soon followed by the east-west Edsel Ford. With the passage of the Federal Highway Act of 1956, when the Interstate System was initiated, the city's freeway network was expanded. During the 20 years that followed, the Detroit expressway system grew to include the Chrysler, the Fisher, the Jeffries, and the Reuther. By 1974, almost 200 miles of freeways in the Detroit metropolitan area were complete with approximately 65 miles under construction or scheduled for construction. This gave Detroit one of the most extensive freeway networks in the country.

These giant roadways created problems as they solved others. While they allowed the rapid movement of vast numbers of cars and trucks across the city, they dislocated the thousands of people who lived in their path. By 1970 alone, an estimated 20,400 homes in the Detroit metropolitan area were demolished for freeway construction. In addition, the freeways divided or destroyed many of the city's neighborhoods. This was particularly true in Detroit's inner-city, because most of the freeways converge upon the downtown area. For example, a predominantly Mexican-American neighborhood west of the central business district became practically inaccessible.

---

*Although a 1½ mile stretch of expressway had been built along Davison Avenue in Highland Park during the early 1940s, Detroit's freeway system dates from the construction of the John C. Lodge.

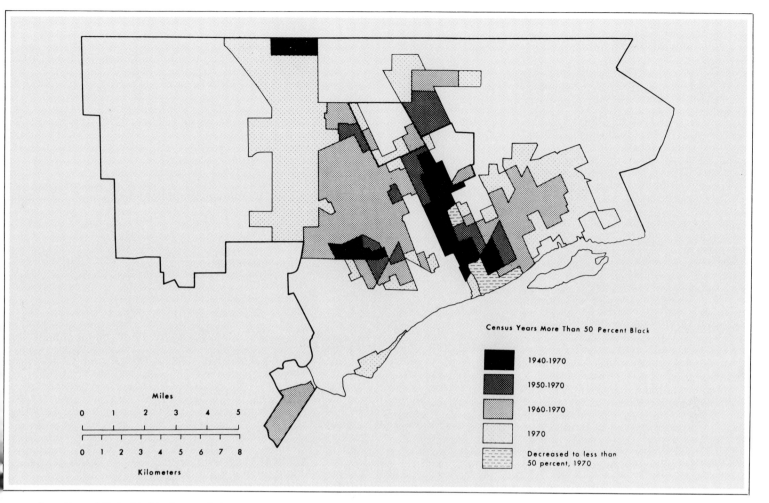

Location of Detroit's black population from 1940 to 1970.

As the freeways provided easy access to the plentiful land to the east, west, and north, Detroit's population began to seep outward. The city's lack of natural boundaries or nearby cities promoted this movement and Detroiters discarded inner city property as if it were a three-year-old car. White ethnic groups tended to move out along the nearest radial. Blacks also gained mobility and access to more desirable neighborhoods.

In 1950, the city's population was at an all-time high of 1,849,568. The population of the suburban area was 1,166,629. By 1960, the city's population had fallen to 1,670,144 while the suburban population had almost doubled to 2,092,216. In 1970, these figures stood at 1,511,482 and 2,688,449 respectively. By 1975, 1,335,185 resided in Detroit, while more than 3,195,000 lived in the suburbs.

The move to the suburbs has been almost exclusively a move by Detroit's white population, resulting in a dramatic shift in the city's racial composition. Over the past two decades, from 7,000 to 9,000 Detroit households have changed from white to black each year. In 1950, more than 300,000 blacks were living in Detroit, about 16 percent of the city's population; in 1975, the number was estimated to be in the neighborhood of 750,000, more than 56 percent of the total population.

In the past, integrated neighborhoods were few. Normally, whites accepted a few black families in their neighborhoods, but when a critical proportion was reached, an exodus of white homeowners followed. In many instances this was prompted and encouraged by such tactics as blockbusting, harrassment of homeowners, and steering of black families in and white families out of target neighborhoods. This transition often brought on instability and turmoil, leaving a legacy of neighborhood depreciation and blight. In recent years, however, this situation has changed as efforts have been made by local community groups to combat the more adverse effects of the transition process. These groups have recognized the need for neighborhood stabilization and the realization that this stabilization can only come about through a high degree of ethnic integration. Fortunately for Detroit, the efforts of many of these groups have met with considerable success.

The change in the make-up of Detroit's population has resulted in a change in leadership of the city government.

Major changes came to Detroit's skyline and to its political structure in the 1950s and '60s: The first major building to inaugurate the replacing of dilapidated downtown sections was the Veterans' Memorial Building, right, dedicated on June 14, 1950. Eleven years later, Jerome P. Cavanaugh, above, took his campaign to the people, propelling the previously little known attorney into the mayor's office.

Cavanaugh's first job was to tackle the city's growing fiscal problems; he called upon Alfred Pelham to become city controller.

I n the mayoral election of 1961, a young unknown lawyer, Jerome P. Cavanaugh, challenged the incumbent Louis Miriani. Miriani represented the establishment, while Cavanaugh took his campaign to the people, particularly to the black neighborhoods. When the votes were counted, Cavanaugh was the new mayor who, for the next eight years was to bring to city government a progressive administration.

Cavanaugh's first job was to tackle the city's growing fiscal problems. To assist him with this task he called upon Alfred Pelham to become city controller, the most important position next to that of mayor. It marked the first time a black had been named to a major post in city government. One of Detroit's most distinguished citizens, Pelham had long served as county budget director and more recently as associate professor of political science at Wayne State University. Few had as good a grasp of the intricacies of urban government and its finances than did Pelham.

To balance the city's budget, Cavanaugh succeeded in having a municipal income tax enacted — one percent on residents and one-half percent on nonresidents working in the city. For the first time since the Depression, Detroit was on such sound financial footing that its bonds were accorded a prime rating.

In 1965, Cavanaugh was reelected, but in the summer of 1969, he announced that he would run for the U.S. Senate. That fall Wayne County Sheriff Roman S. Gribbs defeated county auditor Richard H. Austin, a black, by the smallest margin in the city's history. In 1973, Gribbs choose not to seek another term, and that November, State Senator Coleman A. Young was elected the first black mayor of Detroit, defeating former city police commissioner John F. Nichols. Then in 1977, Young won reelection by defeating black city councilman Ernest C. Browne, Jr. This was the first time two blacks had run in a mayoral election in a major U.S. city.

During his first term of office, Young took active steps to implement affirmative action programs for minorities and women in the police and fire departments, and to establish police mini-stations throughout the city. Through diligent efforts at the national level, he obtained commitments from the federal government for more than $800 million in federal monies for the city. He was instrumental in getting the Detroit

The second major building in the effort to rejuvenate downtown was the Henry and Edsel Ford Auditorium in 1956, top. Above, Cavanaugh announces the appointment of Al Pelham as his city controller, November 15, 1961.

Tigers to remain at Tiger Stadium (the Detroit Lions had left the city for the new Silverdome in suburban Pontiac) and in preparing plans for the construction of a new sports arena on the waterfront where the Red Wings would play their home games.

When he began his second term, Mayor Young stated that his chief objectives were to reduce crime (it dropped 20 percent in 1977 over 1976), lower unemployment, reduce polarization between the races, and continue to rebuild the city with a "coalition of labor, business, the private sector and the people."

Major changes came also to Detroit's downtown skyline in the 1950s and 1960s. For many years, the area between Jefferson Avenue and the river had consisted of rundown, delapidated warehouses, lofts and dock structures. Unsightly buildings, they cut off public view of the water. In the belief that the river was one of the city's principal assets, plans were made to tear down these old buildings and develop a civic center where Detroiters could enjoy the view of their waterfront. In the early 1950s, the civic center was begun as the area between First and Randolph Streets south of Jefferson Avenue was cleared. The first building, the Veterans' Memorial, dedicated June 14, 1950, stands at the foot of Shelby Street, about where Cadillac landed in the summer of 1701.

Next came the Henry and Edsel Ford Auditorium. Constructed at the foot of Woodward Avenue, the building was opened in 1956 as the new home of the Detroit Symphony Orchestra. The auditorium was the gift by the Ford Motor Company and the Ford and Mercury dealers of America, as a memorial to the two Fords.

The initial phase of the civic center development was completed in 1960 with the opening of the giant Cobo Hall and Arena. Built at the western end of the center, they have become one of the nation's leading accommodations for conventions and exhibits.

The unique feature of the civic center is, without a doubt, old Mariners Church. Built in 1849 on the west side of Woodward Avenue between Jefferson and Woodbridge, it stood directly in the path of the civic center. Over the years the church had deteriorated into a run-down building used primarily for commercial

One of the new buildings in Detroit's new civic center was the City-County Building; on September 23, 1955, Mayor Cobo and city officials marched down Woodward Avenue from the now "old" city hall, above, to occupy their new governmental home. Right, Mariners Church in the 1870s; in the mid-1950s, the old Episcopal church, in the path of the civic center construction, was saved by literally moving it 880 feet.

Woodward Avenue looking south from Elizabeth Street, 1950.

purposes. The question now became, should it be torn down or could it be saved. Preservation won, the church was saved, then moved from its original location to the eastern end of the civic center. A long and slow process, the move was begun on December 17, 1954 and completed on April 12, 1955 — four months to move 880 feet. Once in place, this venerable Episcopal church was beautifully restored. Today it stands as one of Detroit's outstanding historic sites.

As the civic center began to take shape, other new buildings began to rise in the downtown area. These included the City-County Building, the Pontchartrain Hotel, the National Bank of Detroit Building, and the Howard Johnson Motor Lodge. These were followed by the headquarters of Detroit Bank & Trust Company, Michigan Consolidated Gas Company, the First Federal Savings and Loan Association, and the Blue Cross Blue Shield of Michigan Building. These were the first buildings to be erected in downtown Detroit since the Depression. Along with this new construction, several older but structurally sound offices and stores were remodeled and refurbished inside and out.

The revitalization of Detroit was not limited to the downtown area. With the aid of federal funds, the city began a massive urban renewal program. With some exceptions, the areas selected for urban renewal were located within Grand Boulevard and comprised the worst of Detroit's housing; virtually all of it was residential. The areas also comprised some of the most vital and colorful of Detroit's ethnic and working class communities: Black Bottom, Paradise Valley, Bagley, Corktown, and Chinatown — all important parts of Detroit's heritage. In all, the urban renewal program in this area has accounted for more than 1500 acres of land which at one time contained more than 17,000 housing units and nearly 2,000

---

*Construction continued during the late 1960s and into the 1970s. This included the Frank Murphy Hall of Justice, Manufacturers National Bank Building, the Edison Plaza, and the McNamara Federal Building.

The old houses went to make room for the new Detroit: below, houses face the demolition crew near Cadillac and Bewick Streets, near Eastern Market and in the University City District in the early 1970s. Right, Detroit's civic center in the 1960s.

businesses. More importantly though, an estimated 7,660 families and 6,730 single individuals had to be relocated.

In some areas, the urban renewal process has proven to be highly successful. On the lower east side, for example, several highrise luxury apartments have been built, and Lafayette and Elmwood Parks, residential areas of tree-lined, spacious apartments and condominiums, have lured people back to the central city. Several areas were renewed for industrial use, while others, notably in the University City and Medical Center areas, were designed for institutional use.

As in most American cities, the urban renewal process in Detroit has been long, complicated and bureaucratic. Thus, much of this land has stood vacant for long periods. As a result, vacant land has been a pervasive and accepted part of the Detroit inner-city landscape for more than two decades. This land has taken on various hues and physical characteristics, from bare earth and weeds, to green rural-like tranquility, to western sagebrush, and to a recent Detroit speciality, white wooden fences, which gave vacant blocks in the heart of the city the appearance of Kentucky horse farms.

Unfortunately, throughout much of the program there was little real attempt to understand the plight of the residents involved. Projects were discussed and planned with little local participation. Residents felt themselves to be at the mercy of a frightening combination of federal officials, city government, and the institutions that would benefit from development.

In recent years, however, an important change has taken place. Local resident organizations gained greater control of what was happening in their neighborhoods. This was brought about by federal revenue-sharing stipulations, model neighborhood examples, the growing power of citizen councils, and a changing attitude on the part of city officials as to what constitutes "development."

This concept of citizen involvement and control has also spread beyond the urban renewal areas. Throughout the city, residents have joined together in associations and block clubs to work for improvements. Included are such neighborhoods as Boston/Edison, Green Acres, Jefferson/Chalmers, Palmer Woods, Sherwood Forest, Rosedale Park, Grandmont, Berry Subdivision, Chandler Park Drive/Cadieux, Harmony Village, West Canfield, and, in one of the most historically interesting neighborhoods, Indian Village.

Located out East Jefferson Avenue about three and one half miles from downtown, the area known as Indian Village was purchased by Abraham Cook from two French farmers, Gabriel St. Aubin and Francois Rivard, during the first decades of the nineteenth century. The vicinity, known as the Cook Farms, was a race track

One of Detroit's most significant historic areas of architectural heritage is Indian Village about 3½ miles from downtown and built in the late 1800s and early 1900s. Above are representative homes of the area.

from 1836 to 1839. In 1894, Cook's heirs subdivided the property and named it Indian Village. The first home was built in 1895 and Indian Village developed into a distinctive single family residential community of more than 300 homes representing a diversity of popular styles of the late 1800s to early 1900s. Due to the unique combination of social and architectural history, Indian Village is one of the most significant neighborhoods in present-day Detroit. Beautifully restored and maintained, it was listed in the National Register of Historic Places in 1972.

Unfortunately, some neighborhoods have not fared as well, because of one of the most detrimental aspects of the urban renewal process — the destruction of whole neighborhoods. Two of the best known of these communities were Black Bottom and Paradise Valley.

During the decade of the 1920s, Detroit's black population increased dramatically from 41,000 to 120,000, largely as a result of the expansion of the automobile industry. These new residents found plenty of jobs, but housing was a different matter. There were only a few neighborhoods into which blacks could move, and one of these was on the near east side close to downtown between Woodward and Chene. The area was largely inhabited by Italians, Greeks, Jews, and Poles. Within a short time, though, it became the predominantly black residential section commonly known as Black Bottom.

Within Black Bottom, in an area roughly bounded by Brush, Gratiot, Hastings, and Vernor, was the area's business district. It contained shops, music stores, grocery

The days of Paradise Valley: the black business district of Black Bottom, it was black owned, but during the 1930s and early '40s, clubs such as the Horse Shoe Bar and Club Three 666 were congenial melting pots. Right, the staff of the 606 Horse Shoe Bar. Below, a menu cover for Club Three 666.

stores, bowling alleys, hotels, restaurants, policy offices and 17 nightclubs — all black owned. It was known as Paradise Valley.

Although Paradise Valley was black owned, its nightclubs during the 1930s and early 1940s were true melting pots. Blacks and whites drank, danced, and were entertained side by side without undue tension or incident. The atmosphere, in fact, was cordial and happy.

Crimes of violence in Paradise Valley were practically non-existent. Black policemen assigned to patrol the Valley partied with the night crowd. But they set absolute rules forbidding criminal disorder.

Paradise Valley attracted all of the best black entertainers in the country. Many aspiring young singers, dancers and musicians got their first big break at the Club Plantation, the 606, the B & C Club, and Club 666. They all played the Valley — Earl Hines, the Inkspots, Ethel Waters, Pearl Bailey, Billie Holliday, Dinah Washington, Ella Fitzgerald, Bojangles and many more.

Even those established entertainers who worked at the Greystone Ballroom or the

It was in the Valley's nightclubs that many black entertainers got their start: the Inkspots, Pearl Bailey, Billie Holiday, Dinah Washington, Ella Fitzgerald, Bojangles and many more played the Valley, including organist Teddy Harris, above. Above right, the 606 Horse Shoe on Adams in the early 1950s. Of the one-time 17 nightclubs, only the Horse Shoe remains; right center, then-owner William T. Johnson sits with a table of patrons in the place where "you would rather be than anywhere else in the world." Below right, Johnson, congratulates white-hatted Satchel Paige after he pitched a no-hitter. Black ball players found the Valley a haven when they were denied access to the city's white hotels and restaurants.

Local politicians were frequent visitors to Paradise Valley, including Mayor Cobo. From left, Dr. Samuel Milton, Forester B. Washington, Cobo and Horse Shoe proprietor William T. Johnson.

In the basement of the Biltmore was "The Hole", the place to go for soul food in Paradise Valley.

Michigan Theater, such as Duke Ellington, Lena Horne, and Cab Calloway, frequented the Valley's nightclubs after their acts. Here they relaxed and entertained at jam sessions, playing into the early hours of the morning. In those days, the downtown hotels would not accept black guests, and so they stayed at the hotels in the Valley — the Dewey, the Biltmore and the Norwood.

Along with the nightclubs were a number of other well-known establishments in Paradise Valley. Long's Drug Store was the information center. The best restaurant was Pekins. Broscher's Restaurant was known for its biscuits. In the basement of the Biltmore was "The Hole," the place to go for soul food.

Another very popular spot was the Paradise Bowl, owned in part by Joe Louis with a restaurant stocked from his Utica farm. This was a favorite stop for the "flyboys," black airmen stationed at Selfridge Field who bussed into the city to come to the Valley.

Also located within its boundaries were the offices of the *Michigan Chronicle, The Detroit Tribune,* St. Antoine YMCA, Lucy Thurman YWCA, and St. Mathew's Episcopal Church. Nearby were the offices of the Detroit Urban League.

Another important aspect of the valley's economy was gambling, particularly the policy operation (a southern black gambling game that originated in St. Louis) and later the numbers racket. For many years they flourished here, but they also marked the beginning of the end for Paradise Valley. In 1939, a woman committed suicide and left a note implicating many police and city officials in these illegal activities. A grand jury investigation followed in 1942.

Then in 1943 came Detroit's race riot; many whites were now afraid to visit the Valley. Investigations following the riot also revealed the substandard, crowded conditions under which blacks were forced to live. This eventually brought about opportunities for blacks to move out of the area. Many club owners also left for more suburban locations.

Black Bottom and Paradise Valley continued to survive into the 1950s but the final blow came with urban renewal and the building of the expressways. The Chrysler Freeway obliterated Hastings Street. Stroh's Brewery took St. Antoine Street. Hudson's Warehouse took Brush and Beaubien. Finally, Black Bottom was transformed into Lafayette Park. Detroit was committed to the progress of expressways and urban renewal. But it was progress with a price. Today Black Bottom and Paradise Valley are only memories.

Detroit's "Walk to Freedom" was led on June 23, 1963 by Dr. Martin Luther King, Jr., left. Below, troops stand an uneasy guard during the July 1967 riot.

The unrest of the '60s

After the riot of 1943, Detroit experienced a period of racial calm and considerable progress in the area of race relations. Detroit was fortunate in having a strong black middle class with such men as John Dancy of the Urban League who worked closely with enlightened and responsible white organizations. Dancy's role in improving conditions for Detroit's black citizens had been a long and active one. He began his work in Detroit as executive director of the Detroit Urban League in 1918, a position he held until his retirement in 1960. He was ably succeeded by Francis A. Kornegay who had joined the League in 1944 as head of the Vocational Services department. Since 1956, he had served as the League's assistant executive director.

It was also during the late 1940s that another barrier against open housing was brought down. A black man, Orsel McGhee, bought a house in an all-white neighborhood on Detroit's west side in the area of Grand River Avenue and Grand Boulevard. But once he had purchased the home, McGhee was told that a clause in the deed stated that it could not be owned by anyone other than a Caucasian. Whites in the neighborhood sued to have the clause enforced and the local court found it to be valid. The case was appealed however, and on May 3, 1948, in a unanimous decision, the U.S. Supreme Court ruled that the clause was in violation of the 14th Amendment. It was a landmark decision, for this was a ruling which was to have a significant effect not only for Detroit, but for the nation as well.

Although advances in education, housing and job opportunities had indeed occurred, many black Americans were growing impatient with how slowly these changes were coming about. As a result, in the late 1950s and early 1960s, moderate organizations such as the NAACP and the Urban League — which had been in the civil rights movement for decades — were suddenly considered contemptible and obsolete.

John Dancy, for more than 40 years the executive director of the Detroit Urban League and one of Detroit's most influential citizens.

Where it all began: in the early morning hours of July 23, 1967, police raided the blind pig on the second floor of this building on Twelfth Street, above; that incident touched off Detroit's disastrous riot. Left, a looted pawn shop, where savings were even greater than usual. Above right, groceries and homes came under destructive attack during the riot.

In Detroit, the feeling of most civic leaders was that a riot such as that which had occurred in Watts could not possibly happen.

Now activist groups such as SCLC (Southern Christian Leadership Conference), and militant organizations such as SNCC (Student Non-violent Coordinating Committee), CORE (Congress of Racial Equality), the Republic of New Africa, and the Black Panthers, advocated confrontation instead of negotiation and litigation.

In 1955, a new era in the civil rights movement was ushered in when a young black minister, Dr. Martin Luther King, Jr., led a successful boycott of the Montgomery, Alabama, bus system. Slowly but surely the black struggle for equal rights spread.

In the spring of 1963, the Detroit Council for Human Rights began plans for a march to commemorate the 20th anniversary of the Detroit riot. Asserting that "the same basic, underlying causes for the disturbance are still present," the council's chairman, Reverend Clarence Franklin, scheduled the "Walk to Freedom" for Sunday, June 23, 1963.

On that hot, summer Sunday afternoon, 125,000 members of Detroit's black community marched a mile down Woodward Avenue to the riverfront. Not since the days of the Depression had the city seen a demonstration like it. At Cobo Hall and Arena, 26,000 flocked inside, all the two buildings could hold, and there, in his resonant voice, Dr. King revealed "a dream." In that dream, white men and black had been "walking together, hand in hand, free at last, free at last."

During the early 1960s similar marches were held in many of the nation's largest urban centers. But it seemed that little progress was being made, and in the summers of 1965 and 1966, many militant blacks turned from marching and non-involvement to rioting. In the Watts district of Los Angeles, blacks rioted in the summer of 1965; 34 died and property losses ran to $40 million.

I n Detroit, the feeling of most civic leaders was that a riot such as that which had occurred in Watts could not possibly happen, and it seemed a reasonable enough expectation. Fully 40 percent of the black family heads owned their own homes. No city had waged a more massive and comprehensive war on poverty. Under Mayor Cavanaugh, the city had obtained more than $42 million in federal funds for its poverty programs. "We learned our lesson in 1943," said the city fathers. They were to find, however, that there was more to learn.

In the early morning hours of Sunday, July 23, 1967, Detroit police led a raid at a blind pig on Twelfth Street near Clairmount. As those arrested were being taken from the building, a crowd of about 200 blacks gathered and began taunting the police. A bottle was thrown, a brick was tossed, a fire was started, a store was looted. The crowd turned into a mob.

Patrol cars immediately began arriving on the scene, but police made no effort to beat back the mob, a decision that was to be bitterly denounced by black and white moderates alike. When this policy became evident, the looters ran rampant.

As the riot spread, U.S. Representative John Conyers, Jr., one of the city's two black congressmen, and the Reverend Nicholas Hood, the city's only black councilman, arrived at the scene hoping to talk the mob into dispersing. But the rioters would not listen to reason.

Top, a young soldier watches as the city burns. Above center, tanks had to be called in to protect Detroit firefighters. Above, police and troopers arrive on the riot scene.

In late afternoon, when sporadic sniping was reported, Governor George Romney proclaimed a state of emergency and called in 400 state police and some 7,300 national guardsmen. But the riot was now spreading almost unchecked. By Sunday evening, Detroit's inner-city was out of control.

Although police and national guardsmen were now on the scene, it was soon obvious that they could not control the rioters. So at three a.m., Monday, July 24, Governor Romney called for federal troops. However, there were several delays, so it was not until early Tuesday morning that the first of 4,700 airborne troops in full battle dress arrived in the riot area.

During the day on Monday, fires reached their peak when the fire department received a staggering 617 alarms. Yet when they arrived at a fire, the firefighters were driven off by the rioters. By week's end, more than 1600 fires were reported and damage from fire and looting edged past $50 million.

Monday was also to witness the riot's first victim. A white man was killed by gunfire while running from a looted store. He was the first of 44 killed.

By Tuesday night, federal troops (many of them veterans of the war in Vietnam) had brought a tense calm over the east side. Yet the riot raged out of control on the west side.

On Wednesday, more than 3,000 arrests were made (7,331 arrests were made by the time the riot was over). This resulted in prisoners being housed in Jackson State Prison, Milan Penitentiary, county jails, city buses, police garages, the police gymnasium, and even the public bathhouse on Belle Isle.

Early Thursday, the riot finally began to subside. On Friday, the last major fire was reported.

As the fearful city began to return to some form of stability, the people of Detroit were left to talk about what had happened. They had not endured a battle between white and black like that which had torn the city in 1943. What they had been a part of was a new type of rioting, a battle against authority, whatever its skin color.

During the riot, more than 1,600 fires were reported, top. Above, a meeting of the Board of Trustees of New Detroit, the nation's first "urban coalition." From left, Walter Douglas, Stanley Winkelman, William T. Patrick, Jr., Rev. Malcolm Carron, Lawrance Doss, and Max M. Fisher.

Although Detroit had endured a horrible disaster, there was one tentative answer — a new beginning. As Father Richard was heard to have spoken 162 years earlier, *Speramus meliora; resurget ceneribus* — "We hope for better things; it will arise from the ashes."

On Thursday, July 27, the first step towards the new beginning was taken. That afternoon, Mayor Cavanaugh and Governor Romney invited 500 Detroiters, a cross-section of the community including block club leaders, militant blacks, union officials, the heads of major companies, and a special committee from the Greater Detroit Chamber of Commerce, to meet in the auditorium of the City-County Building. Never before had the city seen such a gathering. The leaders of the automobile industry were there: Henry Ford II; James M. Roche, president of General Motors; Lynn Townsend, president of Chrysler; and Roy Chapin, Jr., president of American Motors. UAW President Walter Reuther pledged the help of his hugh union in the clean-up task and Roche offered the "facilities, skills, resources, and people" of the giant General Motors.

Out of the meeting came the decision to establish a "New Detroit Committee," composed of all elements of the community, to channel private resources into the city, and to chart its future. Its staff would come largely from manpower loaned by various corporations. Department store president Joseph L. Hudson, Jr. was chosen chairman. William T. Patrick, who had been the city's first black councilman, was named executive director. Hence, Detroit became the first city to organize an "urban coalition."

Over the next 10 years, New Detroit not only endured but contributed significantly to the city's renewed vitality. During that period, more than $28 million was allocated for its programs. By 1977, New Detroit's board of trustees had grown to 66 members. These board members along with other volunteers were engaged in 10 special program areas which included: education, employment and economic action, housing and neighborhood stabilization, health, drug abuse, community self-determination, minority economic development, public safety and justice, anti-racism, and the arts. Much of the success that Detroit and its people have experienced since 1967 are a direct result of the work of New Detroit.

159

More than a dozen foreign language or ethnic newspapers are printed today in Detroit; among them: The Jewish News, Dziennik Polski (The Polish Daily News), the Gazette van Detroit ("the only Belgian newspaper in America"), The National Greek Tribune, first published in 1920, the Detroiter Abend-Post, celebrating its 125th anniversary in 1979, and La Tribuna del Popolo (The Italian Tribune). Below, the tailoring shop of Walter J. Steyskal (at right) in 1907. Founded by his father in 1868, the elder Steyskal was originally from Bohemia.

The peoples' city

Out of the unrest of the 1960s and the civil rights movement came a renewal of interest in ethnic-American culture. This was particularly important for Detroit as it has the largest multi-ethnic population of any city in the United States. Detroit has the largest Arabic-speaking population outside of the Middle East, the second largest Polish population in America (only Chicago has more), the largest U.S. concentration of Belgians, Chaldeans and Maltese.

The interest that has grown in cultural heritage can be seen through the more than 10 million visitors who have attended Detroit's annual weekend riverfront ethnic festivals since their start in 1970. More than a dozen major daily or weekly foreign language or ethnic newspapers are printed in Detroit. More than 150 ethnic radio and television programs are available in more than 30 languages. Several movie theaters regularly show features in Spanish, Greek and Arabic.

Today, Detroit's largest ethnic group is, of course, the black community and its story is found throughout the pages of this book. Here we turn to the story of the city's other ethnic groups.

Although there has been an important revival in ethnic heritage in the last decade, Detroit has had, as we have seen, a cosmopolitan flavor since its earliest days. In the mid-19th century, the first large wave of immigrants came to the city — the Germans, the Irish, the Poles. But the big influx of immigrants arrived in the early years of the 20th century to work in the automobile factories. They came by the thousands from Armenia and Syria, from Greece and Hungary, from Belgium and Italy, from Russia and the Ukraine. When Henry Ford announced his $5 a day wage, the waves of immigrants grew to the tens of thousands, and Detroit was to see the arrival of Austrians, Bulgarians, Croatians, Finns, Lithuanians, Norwegians, Rumanians, Serbs, Slovaks and Swedes. From 1910, Detroit's foreign-born

Music was an important part of life for Detroit's Belgians; below, an early view of the Belgian American Band, organized in 1912.

The Belgian influence: the Detroit Archery Club, "Willem Tell", top, in 1900; it was founded in 1884. Above, a Cornillie Brothers Moving and Storage wagon about 1900; one of the early Belgian community's leading businesses, it is still in existence. Below, a month before dedication of Our Lady of Sorrows Church in June 1911; located at Meldrum and Berlin, it was for years the leading Belgian church in Detroit.

population of 150,000 nearly doubled to 289,000 in 1920. This growth continued at such a rate that by 1925, the foreign-born accounted for nearly 50 percent of the city's population of 1,242,000.* Detroit, which in 1900 had ranked as the 13th largest city in the United States, now ranked fourth.

The first Finns to arrive were skilled metal workers from Massachusetts, who came to work as auto body makers for Packard Motor Company. When Ford announced his high wage, many Finns moved to Detroit from upper-Michigan's copper country.

A small group of Dutch also arrived at this time and the auto industry is indebted to one of these immigrants, Jan Reef. He developed a gear process which was widely used by early car makers.

One of the largest groups to settle in Detroit at this time was Hungarian. The majority settled in the Delray area on the city's southwest side, and by 1930, it was considered to be the center of Michigan's Magyar (Hungarian) culture.

The Armenian community that first grew in Detroit differed from the other ethnic settlements in that it was comprised almost entirely of single young men. Living in boarding houses, their social life was centered around the local coffee houses. The men worked in the auto plants, and when they were able sent for their wives and intended brides back home. Many took their savings from their factory jobs and went into business for themselves. These included rug retailing, restaurants, coffee houses, shoe repair, dry cleaning and hotels. So many Armenians settled in the West Jefferson and South Solvey area of Delray that street car conductors on the West Jefferson Line would call out "Armenian Boulevard" for the South Solvey stop. Other important Armenian communities grew in Highland Park and on Detroit's east side.

The first Belgians began to arrive in Detroit about 1890, settling on the east side where they found employment in area brickyards. When World War I began in Europe, the immigration from Belgium to the Motor City increased substantially. By that time, "the City" as they called Detroit, had become the largest Belgian community in the United States.

---

*In 1904, on the eve of Detroit's manufacturing boom, there were 13,000 Poles, 1,300 Russians and 900 Italians living in the city. By 1925, there were 115,000 Poles, 49,000 Russians, and 42,000 Italians.

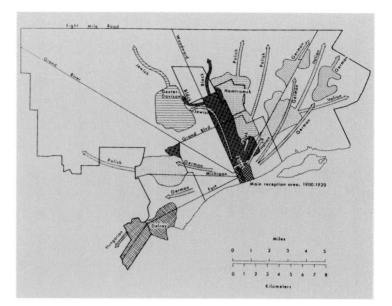

A source for Belgian employment was the Enterprise Foundry, above left, in 1908; it was started by Emiel Van Wanseele. Above right, Detroit's ethnic communities in 1950, and major migration paths, 1900 to 1950.

Founded in 1888, the St. Charles Beneficial Society continues to be one of the more important organizations in Detroit's Belgian community.

Two of the largest groups to settle in Detroit were the Italians and the Greeks. The first Greek families began arriving in the late 1880s and settled on Monroe Street between Beaubien and St. Antoine. Later, the settlement moved onto Macomb Street where the first Greek coffee house was opened. Because many Greeks were merchants, they lived near their stores and in many cases above their shops.

The Greek Orthodox Church has been especially significant in the life of Detroit's Greek community. By 1909, when no more than 250 Greeks had settled in the city, a campaign was begun to raise money to purchase space for a church. Within a year, sufficient funds were available to rent a second floor of a hall on Broadway Street and the Annunciation Church was founded.

The first large numbers of Italians began arriving in Detroit in the 1880s (the first families had arrived here as early as the 1850s) and settled on the near east side in the area of Mullett, St. Antoine, and Orleans Streets. These first families came from northern Italy but were soon joined by people from the other parts of their country. In 1883, a group of Sicilian immigrants arrived in Detroit from Cleveland where they were fruit merchants, they soon opened similar businesses. Detroit was unique in that the Italians who settled here had come from all parts of Italy. Most other large U.S. cities had Italian colonies but these were made up only of Italians from one or two regions of the country. As would be expected, many Italian settlers in Detroit found employment in the city's factories, but many others established their own shops and markets. In 1930, the Italo-American Commercial Guide listed more than 120 retail groceries owned by Italians.

As was mentioned earlier, the city's Polish citizens began to move from Detroit's lower east side into Hamtramck about 1910. As the Dodge plant grew, so grew that city's Polish population, and Polish street names began to appear in Hamtramck in the early 1920s. It is interesting to note that settling with the Poles in Hamtramck were peoples from Russia, Austria, Lithuania and Czechoslovakia. All these are people whose homelands are contiguous to Poland in Europe.

Another important group to settle in the Hamtramck area were the Ukrainians. Like so many other nationalities, they first came to Detroit to work in the automobile factories. Today approximately 50,000 to 60,000 Ukrainians live in the Detroit area, many arriving by way of Canada following World War II.

The pressures for Americanization of the new arrivals began earlier in Detroit than in the nation generally. The initial stimulus was the high unemployment rate during the winter of 1914-15, when it was discovered that more than 60 percent of the applicants for work or aid at the Detroit Board of Commerce employment service were non-English speaking. As a result, English language instruction was undertaken in night schools conducted by the Detroit Board of Education. Then in 1919, as the number of immigrants continued to grow, a group of concerned citizens opened a "cottage" in downtown Detroit to serve as a center of identity and service for newcomers to the city. The workers, primarily employees of the YMCA, gave assistance to the thousands of new residents who needed instruction in the language and rudiments of living in "the new world." From this beginning in the small brick building at the corner of Adams and Witherell grew the International Institute.

Czech culture: On May 2, 1914, Detroit's Czech community gathered to lay the cornerstone for its new cultural hall at Butternut and Tillman Avenues. The building, above, called the Czech National Building, served for many years as a center for social life, language classes, political organizations, singing and theatrical groups.

Today, located in its own building on East Kirby in the city's cultural center, the International Institute continues to serve Detroit's foreign-born residents with advice and help with immigration and naturalization matters, individual and family counseling, English language classes, interpreters and translations of documents.

Several of the larger companies in the city had also begun classes in English language instruction. One of these, Ford Motor Company, went a step further than simply imparting a new language to foreigners.

At the beginning of the 20th century it was generally accepted that America was the great melting pot into which diverse immigrant groups entered. Their foreign cultures, languages, customs and values would melt and the resultant broth would be "an American" — a product of a new and uniform consistency devoid of the character of any of the individual ethnic ingredients. The Ford Motor Company carried this theory to an extreme. The graduation ceremony at its school included a large replica of a steaming pot on a stage. Into this pot would walk the graduates in their immigrant clothing. The pot was stirred by the English instructors and the graduates would emerge in American suits waving American flags.

Although the melting pot theory was a strong force in American life, a large number of the new immigrants continued their old world customs. Fortunately many survived and are still practiced today. Hungarians still celebrate "Locsolodas" or Easter Monday, and "Disznotor" a ceremonial feast following the butchering of a pig.

Above, the Sokol Palacky Hall at Michigan and Beecher; it was here, right, that members of the Czech physical fitness society met for fellowship and to practice gymnastics; this picture was taken during World War I.

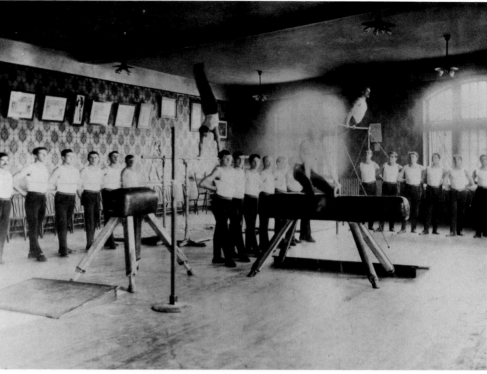

The Detroit Finnish Education Association opened a hall on 14th Street in 1924, right. In 1974, the Finnish people opened a beautiful Cultural Center on West Eight Mile Road in Farmington Hills, above.

Musical societies have always played an important role in Detroit's German community, below. The Harmonie Society was founded in 1849 and the Concordia Singing Society in 1865; pictured are the founding members of Concordia, an organization still in existence.

Many Polish still practice the Christmas customs of breaking and sharing the Christmas wafer among relatives, placing hay underneath the tablecloth, serving 12 varieties of dishes for Christmas Eve supper, and going around from house to house with "Christ's Crib" and caroling. The Greeks have shared with Detroiters their music and their dancing, the Lebanese and Syrians their fine food, the Irish, St. Patrick's Day — when every Detroiter is an Irishman-for-a-day.

Sports were always an important part of Belgian life and the new residents brought with them their love of bicycle racing (Belgium's national sport), archery, darts, bowling, and pigeon raising and racing. The Ukrainians brought their holiday customs of "Sviat Vechur" (the holy supper), the "Korovaky" (wedding bread) and the gaily colored "Pysanky" (specially decorated Easter Eggs).

Special festivals also continued to be celebrated, such as the Hungarian Fall Festival of the Grape, the Mexican Feast of Our Lady of Guadalupe, the Polish Strawberry Festivals, and Chinatown's Moon Festival.

Through the years, Detroit's many ethnic groups have preserved these traditions and customs through not only a number of excellent specialized restaurants but also through their social and civic organizations. For example, the Danes meet at their Danish Club of Detroit on Grand River; the Finns at their Cultural Center on Eight Mile Road; the French-Canadians at the Societe de St. Jean Baptiste. Many Germans are still active in the German-American Cultural Center on East Outer Drive; the Hungarians at their Magyar Haz (Hungarian House) on West Jefferson; and the Poles at the Polish Century Club. The center of Irish culture will be found at the Detroit Gaelic League. The focal point of cultural, social and fraternal activities for the Italians is the Italian-American Cultural Society. The Scots still gather at the St. Andrew Society Hall on East Congress.

165

Italian groceries: Many Italians who settled in Detroit entered the grocery business; typical was Giglio's Market on Mitchell and Illinois, top left, in 1926, with owner Frank and Frances Giglio, son Joe Giglio and an employee. Top right, in 1915, Angelo Bonaldi opened a book and newspaper store, "Libreria Bonaldi" at 2740 Rivard Street on the city's east side; Louis Bonaldi and family are in the car. Above left, in 1912, the Detroit Italian community crowned its first "Miss Columbus Day." Above right, members of Detroit's Italian community still participated in many of the old world religious festivals and traditions.

As the city grew, many of the original ethnic communities disappeared or moved to other areas of the city. From their first settlement on the lower east side, the Italians moved out Gratiot. They have tended to remain east siders and today their homes extend all the way into the Grosse Pointes and St. Clair Shores. The German community, also originally centered on the city's near east side, has now largely disappeared and German-American families will today be found throughout the metropolitan area.

During the early 1900s, Detroit's Jewish community, made up largely of Russians who were fleeing the pogroms and persecutions of their Czarist homeland, was located on the lower east side along Hastings Street. By the 1940s the Jewish Community was to be found in the 12th Street, Linwood and Dexter area. Later it transferred to the Livernois-Seven Mile area, then into the suburbs of Oak Park, Southfield and West Bloomfield.

The English and Scots, once heavily concentrated in the northwest between Woodward and Grand River Avenues, have now spread throughout the metropolitan area. The Greeks are also scattered now, although there is still a thriving and colorful Greek Town located around Monroe and Beaubien Streets.

In the fall of 1978, one of Detroit's oldest ethnic communities, Corktown, was placed on the federal governments National Register of Historic Places. Corktown is notable not only for its age and Victorian architecture, but for being a workingman's neighborhood; a reminder that history is not written only in mansions and public buildings.

To most Detroiters, Polish sausage means Kowalski, above; located in Hamtramck, the company is owned and managed by the family's third generation. Below, an example of old world customs, a Christmas tree decorated with handmade ornaments.

During his visit to Detroit in the summer of 1976, Polish Cardinal Wojtyla (later named Pope John Paul II) celebrated mass at the historic St. Albertus Church.

Originally the home for the city's Irish, Corktown was later a Maltese community, and is today the center for Detroit's Latinos. Made up primarily of Mexican-Americans, this community also includes Puerto Ricans, Cubans, and many from Central and South American countries. The Latinos began building their community here in the early 1920s, though the area's principal growth has come within the last 10 years. Bounded roughly by the Detroit River to the south, Trumbull Avenue on the east, Michigan Avenue on the north, and Woodmere Cemetery on the west, the community has grown to include parts of the old Hungarian Delray area as well as Corktown. The center for today's Latino community is the Latin Americans for Social and Economic Development Inc. (LASED) on West Venor. Another important organization is H.O.P.E. (Hispanos Organized to Promote Entrepreneurs). Formed in 1975, H.O.P.E. is forceful in Hispanic economic development.

Another ethnic group that has grown in recent years is that of the Arabic-speaking peoples. The first Arabs came to Detroit as early as the 1890s from Lebanon and Syria. The largest influx, though, occurred in the last 30 years, with most coming as refugees fleeing the Middle East.

The various nationalities making up this ethnic group in addition to the Lebanese and Syrians include people from Jordon, Yemen, United Arab Republic, Saudi Arabia and Iraq. Many of these people have settled in Dearborn in an area called

The citizens of Krakow, Poland, gave to Detroit a statue of Revolutionary War hero Gen. Thaddeus Kosciuszko, above; dedicated August 13, 1978, it stands at the intersections of Michigan, Third and Bagley. Right, Dix Avenue, one of the centers of Detroit's Middle Eastern community; a mosque is on the left, Ford's Rouge plant on the right.

167

Every summer, American Indians from Detroit gather on weekends throughout Michigan and Canada to celebrate their heritage, culture and tradition, above and above right. It is estimated that 30,000 Indians live in the metropolitan area.

Center right, children from Detroit's Jewish community learn the traditions and heritage of their culture. Below right, Arab men play pinochle at the Beit Hanina Club, located in the south end of Dearborn. The sign behind them spells out the name of the village outside Jerusalem from where the members came.

During the last 50 years, tens of thousands of immigrants from all over the globe have come to Detroit and made the city their new home.

168

Walk along the streets of Greektown top, and you may hear more Greek than English. The area draws crowds of evening diners. A short distance from the Renaissance Center, visitors discover what Detroiters have long known: Mediterranean food, Continental bakeries and quaint shops. Above, the Irish working class once inhabited homes such as this in Corktown (named after the Irish county of Cork). Today, many such homes have been renovated.

the South End, or Salina. Here the center of Arab life is the Arab Community Center for Economics and Social Services (ACCESS) on Salina Street. Other large concentrations of Middle Eastern people will be found on Detroit's east side, in Highland Park, Hamtramck, and in Detroit's eastern suburbs.

Today it is estimated that there are upwards of 100,000 Detroiters of Middle Eastern descent, making Detroit the largest Arabic-speaking community in North America. Most are of Eastern Orthodox faith with only about 30 percent being Moslems. The Moslems, however, were some of the earliest Arabic-speaking people to settle in Detroit and the first Mosque in America was built in Highland Park in 1919.

Another large group of Middle Eastern Detroiters are the Chaldeans, the first of whom arrived here just before World War I. Centered in the Seven Mile Road-Woodward Avenue area, their principal social and religious centers are Sacred Heart Roman Catholic Church and the Chaldean Education Center.

uring the last 50 years, tens of thousands of immigrants from all over the globe have come to Detroit and made the city their new home. This influx is not a thing of the past, it continues to the present day. In 1975, for example, more than 8,400 legal immigrants settled in Detroit. Although from a variety of countries, these new residents came principally from Yugoslavia, Korea, Mexico, Greece, Italy and Germany.

Detroit can boast proudly of more than 100 ethnic and nationality groups. Yet, while they represent a variety of languages, customs and traditions, Detroit's ethnic communities have worked hard during the last decade at creating a feeling of respect and harmony. Ethnic conferences have been conducted, an ethnic study center has been established at Wayne State University, the Michigan Ethnic Heritage Studies Center has been established, and a new awareness of the importance of our diversity is being taught in area schools. Detroit is indeed fortunate, for the renewed interest in its ethnicity has resulted in not only a better life for the peoples of these various cultures, but for all the city's residents.

"Where Life is Worth Living"

At the end of the 19th century, the old Board of Commerce coined a phrase to describe the prosperous Victorian community of Detroit. The slogan "Where Life is Worth Living" told of a proud and growing city that provided many of the best things of life for its residents. Now, more than 80 years later, it is a phrase that could very well once again be used to describe this city. For today Detroiters are experiencing not only a renaissance of their physical city, but of their quality of life as well.

This resurgence of quality of life has spread into virtually every sector of the community.

Detroit, for example, has long been recognized as a center for music. The Detroit Symphony Orchestra enjoys a reputation of undisputed excellence. The Michigan Opera Theatre has emerged into national prominence. Blues and jazz can be heard at any number of the city's fine clubs. The Music Hall Center is becoming a focal point of the performing arts. The Fisher Theater is playing to full houses and the community theater is growing.

There is also a growing awareness of art and creativity. The Art Institute, in addition to its own superb collections and to hosting outstanding touring exhibits, has launched a series of solos and group shows to feature Michigan painters and sculptors. The number of local art galleries is growing, and the Center for Creative Studies and Wayne State University have developed fine art schools.

In the cultural center, the Detroit Public Library houses special reference and research collections available to students and scholars. The Library's new TIP (The Information Place) service is answering questions and providing information for residents throughout the metropolitan area. The Historical Museum and the new Detroit Science Center are also attracting visitors from all over metropolitan Detroit to view their quality exhibits.

There is Eastern Market, that great open-air bazaar just a mile from downtown with its stalls filled with fresh produce and its wholesale shops of meat, fish, poultry, produce, cheese and nuts; Belle Isle, which is experiencing its own renaissance with its new nature center and fishing piers, with its lakes, canals, baseball fields, children's zoo, carriage paths, aquarium* and botanical gardens; and Greek Town, with its bakeries, restaurants and shops.

Detroiters have at their doorstep the world's busiest waterway, the Detroit River, and Lake St. Clair with its power boat racing, yachting, fishing and other water sports. In this area is one of the largest number of pleasure boats per capita in the nation. Throughout the downtown area are excellent shops and outstanding restaurants. Right across the river is the world's second largest country, Canada — a friendly land whose shores offer one of the finest views of Detroit.

Detroit's colleges and universities have growing enrollments, and are today some of the nation's most qualified centers for education. The new Detroit Medical Center is expanding into one of the leading medical complexes and provides advanced health care.

Finally, at the water's edge, the great towers of the Renaissance Center have permanently transformed the city's skyline, symbolizing the renaissance of the city and of an increasing quality of life.

---

*Operated by the Detroit Zoological Commission, the Belle Isle Aquarium is the oldest public aquarium in the western hemisphere. The building was begun in 1901 and opened to the public on August 18, 1904.

Left, the Detroit city skyline, 1973. Insets, from left: Eastern Market's Big Chicken supergraphic; Sanders' old delivery wagon on Belle Isle; Renaissance Center.

Above, the Orchestra Hall at the time of its opening in 1914. Left, Azalia Hackley became a leading authority and promoter of black music in the early part of the 20th century. Right, Ossip Gabrilowitsch was the leading figure in the development of Detroit's Symphony Orchestra.

The Orchestra Hall, reopened as the Paradise Theatre in 1941, became "home" to such greats as Duke Ellington, Dizzy Gillespie, Billie Holiday, The Mills Brothers, Lionel Hampton and Dinah Washington.

Mary Dale Clarke

During the last half of the 19th century and the early years of the 20th, Detroit was a leader in the music publishing business, second only to New York City. They included such nostalgic hits as, from left, "Detroit Skating Polka" published by Weiss & Van Laer in 1858; "Harmonica Polka" published by D.S. Amsden in 1859; "We Are Coming Father Abram" published by J. Henry Whittemore in 1862; and "Effie May" published by Whittemore in 1864. Jerome H. Remick, above, invested $10 in "The Dance of the Brownies" and subsequently became one of the largest music publishers in the world.

While today Detroit is indeed experiencing a physical and humanistic revival, many of the activities which contribute to the quality of life have long played a significant part in the history of the city. In 1854, a Detroiter named A. Couse wrote and published a song entitled *The Detroit Schottisch.* It was not long before Couse's little tune became one of the nation's most popular songs. Thus began Detroit's music publishing business, a business that for the next 75 years was to flourish and grow, ranking Detroit second only to New York City in the publishing of music.

In the 40 years that followed *The Detroit Schottisch,* Detroit's published music was largely for the local market. But with the 1890s, ragtime and Detroit rose to the top of the musical scene. Such tunes as *At A Georgia Camp Meeting* and *Dark Town Strutters Ball* began pouring from the presses of Whitney-Warner, Belcher & Davis and other Detroit publishers. One of these tunes, *The Dance of the Brownies,* was bought by Jerome H. Remick for $10, and his investment set him on the way to becoming one of the largest music publishers in the world. From 1905 until he retired from the business in 1928, Remick's firm published more than 60,000 pieces.

While Detroit was busy publishing popular music, one of its citizens was becoming a leader in the field of black music. Her name was Emma Azalia Hackley. Born in 1867, reared and educated in Detroit, this concert singer, choral director and humanitarian devoted herself to the musical education of black people. Azalia Hackley traveled throughout this country and abroad raising funds for scholarships and working to revive interest in genuine black music. She died in Detroit in 1922 and in 1943, her private papers and memorabilia were presented to the Detroit Public Library by the Detroit Musician's Association, the local chapter of the National Association of Negro Musicians. Today the E. Azalia Hackley Memorial Collection, housed at the Library, is one of the nation's most valuable collections of research materials which document the achievements of blacks in the performing arts.

On the evening of November 19, 1914, Detroit's new symphony orchestra gave its first concert at the Detroit Opera House. The leading figure in the development of the orchestra was Ossip Gabrilowitsch, who became conductor in 1918 and was one of the leading pianists of his day. In 1919, the symphony was moved from temporary quarters into the beautiful new Orchestra Hall, one of the acoustically finest auditoriums ever to be built in this country. In 1939, three years after Gabrilowitsch's death, the Detroit Symphony left Orchestra Hall and moved to more economical quarters.

In 1941 Orchestra Hall was reopened as the Paradise Theater and became "home" for many famous black performers in jazz, blues and vaudeville. Among the performers who played the Paradise were Duke Ellington, Dizzy Gillespie, Billie Holiday, The Mills Brothers, Lionel Hampton and Dinah Washington. But in 1951, economics forced The Hall to close once again. Thereafter it was used occasionally as a concert hall and recording studio. In 1971 Orchestra Hall was scheduled to be torn down, but at the last minute was saved from the wrecker's ball. Today it is being restored, and once again beautiful music is heard from its stage.

After leaving Orchestra Hall, the symphony gave its performances in the Music Hall or in the Masonic Temple Auditorium. In 1956, the symphony once again had a permanent home when the Henry Edsel Ford Auditorium was opened in the civic center.

The year was 1961, and Berry Gordy presented Motown's first million seller gold record to William "Smokey" Robinson and the Miracles, Motown's first recording artists. Left, jazz star Marcus Belgrave; below, jazz guitarist Earl Klugh.

Berry Gordy, Motown's founder.

Diana Ross, right, and the Supremes with Florence Ballard, left, and Mary Wilson.

Marvin Gaye

Stevie Wonder

Hitsville U.S.A.: it was where it all started, the first home of Motown Record Corp. on West Grand Boulevard. From left, Edward Holland, Diana Ross, Mary Wilson, Lamont Dozier, Brian Holland and Florence Ballard.

No account of music in Detroit would be complete without the sound of Motown. In 1959, a young black man, Berry Gordy, Jr., borrowed $800 from his family and founded the Motown Record Corporation. Located in a house on West Grand Boulevard, Motown began as one of a number of small rhythm and blues record companies which sprang up in Detroit during the 1950s, partly in response to a demand for such music by black-oriented radio stations.

For his performers, writers and producers, Gordy turned to Detroit's black community, the same environment in which the music itself had its roots. Motown's first success was a song called *Shop Around* by William "Smokey" Robinson and The Miracles. Released late in 1960, the record quickly became a smash, selling more than a million copies by February 1961.

Motown went on to develop such artists as Stevie Wonder (a blind boy who at the age of 12 recorded *Fingertips* and went on to win numerous Grammy Awards as producer, writer and performer), Marvin Gaye, The Temptations, The Marvelettes, The Four Tops, and Martha and The Vandellas. Their songs included such hits as: *I Second That Emotion, How Sweet It Is, My Girl, Up Tight (Everything's All Right)*.

But it was really three young girls that brought success to Motown. They were Diana Ross, Mary Wilson and Florence Ballard, better known as The Supremes. They were the most successful singing group in the 1960s and had more number one hits in a row than any other group in the history of popular music. Their songs, all of which were written by successful composers Brian Holland, Lamont Dozier and Eddie Holland, included the hits *Where Did Our Love Go, Baby Love,* and *Stop In The Name Of Love.* By 1967, company sales topped $20 million and Motown was the second largest vondor of single records in the United States.

In the early 1970s, Gordy expanded operations and moved his headquarters to Los Angeles. There the company continued to grow at such a rate that by the end of 1972, Motown was the largest black-owned business in the country, with sales of $40 million. In addition to records and tapes, Gordy entered the movie industry, producing the favorite "Lady Sings the Blues," then "Mahogany" and in 1978 "The Wiz," all staring Diana Ross.

To most, however, Motown meant, and continues to mean music. It is a special sound, born on the streets of Detroit, listened to and enjoyed the world over by all who know the Motown Sound.

Above, the south wall of the court at the Detroit Institute of Arts showing one of the four frescoes by Diego Rivera. Left, a detail from the north wall. Above right, the Detroit Institute of Arts shortly after its opening in 1927.

Beginning in the 19th century, Detroit was the home of several prominent artists; the Detroit Art Association was formed in 1875 and Detroit's first public gallery opened in 1888.

There was little interest in art in early Detroit, but during the first half of the 19th century, the city was home to several prominent portrait painters. James C. Lewis, who came to Detroit in 1824, was noted for his portraits. John Mix Stanley won recognition for his landscapes and portraits. T.H.C.P. Burnham, understandably nicknamed "Alphabet Burnham," is best remembered for his portrayal of crowds and street scenes. Robert S. Duncanson, a black artist from Ohio whose training was financed by anti-slavery societies, had a studio in Detroit during the 1840s and lived in the city permanently after the Civil War. Alvah Bradish, in addition to being a fine portrait artist, frequently gave lectures in art appreciation.

During the later years of the 19th century, Detroit produced a number of other notable artists: Robert Hopkin, Gari Melchers, Julius Rolshoven, Lewis T. Ives and his son Percy Ives, and Joseph W. Gies.

The Detroit Art Association was formed in 1875 to provide art exhibitions, but there was no public art gallery in the city until 1888. In that year, the Detroit Museum of Art was opened at Jefferson near Hastings. In 1919, the new city charter established an Arts Commission and the Art Museum became the Detroit Institute of Arts. In 1927, a magnificent new museum designed by Paul Cret was opened on Woodward. It was substantially enlarged in the 1960s with the addition of two wings.

One of the museum's most notable holdings is a series of four murals by the noted Mexican artist Diego Rivera. When they were completed in the 1930s, they created bitter controversy. Powerful in their depiction of Detroit's industrial life, the paintings led some to accuse Rivera of injecting Communist ideology into his portrayal. There was even talk of whitewashing the murals. They remained intact, however, and may be viewed today.

Two other organizations made important contributions to the history of art in the Detroit area. In 1907, the Arts and Crafts Society (today the Center for Creative Studies) was founded and was soon established as an art school of major importance. In 1930, the famous Cranbrook Academy of Art was founded in suburban Bloomfield. The Cranbrook complex, consisting of the art school, a church, a science museum and private school, was established by *Detroit News* publisher George G. Booth and his wife Ellen Scripps Booth.

Renaissance cleanup at 2nd Avenue and Holden.

Outdoor stabile at Detroit Institute of Arts, right. Environmental sculpture on the grounds of Cranbrook Art Academy, middle right. Inside the Detroit Institute of Arts, lower right.

Theatre has been significant in Detroit's history, as today's large number of professional and community theatre groups attest. Above, the Majestic Theater on Woodward near Willis Avenue, in 1922 looking south, before Woodward was widened. Inset, Detroit's famous Opera House, built in 1869, was consumed by fire on October 7, 1897. The Opera House was rebuilt, served for a time as a department store, and was razed in 1963. Left, the Garrick Theater on Griswold near State Street in the 1930s.

180

Left, the Lyceum Theater on Randolph Street just north of East Lafayette Avenue in 1900. Center, the Detroit Civic Theatre in 1931, now the home of Wayne State University's Bonstelle Theatre. Right, the woman who formed the Bonstelle Players in 1910, Jesse Bonstelle.

Although theatre had a difficult beginning because of antagonistic Protestant attitudes, Detroit today has a thriving community and professional theatre environment.

Like art, the theater had little success in early Detroit. This was due in large part to the antagonistic attitude towards the theater on the part of most of the city's Protestant churches. However, as early as 1830, a barn near the Steamboat Hotel was used by traveling theatrical troupes. During the following years, a number of buildings were used as theaters. Then in 1869, the Detroit Opera House was opened, and for 30 years it remained the center of Detroit musical and theatrical life. Destroyed by fire in 1897 and immediately rebuilt, it was located on Campus Martius just east of Woodward. The Opera House was remodeled into a department store in 1937 and finally torn down in 1963.

During the late 1800s and early 1900s, a number of other fine theaters were built, including the Lyceum and the Garrick. These were followed by the Washington, the Shubert-Lafayette, and the Cass. However, competition of motion pictures and then television brought dark days to the theater in Detroit. Eventually all these theaters were closed. Today the successful Fisher, remains as the city's only professional, legitimate theater. Opened in 1963 in the remodeled motion picture house of the Fisher Building, the Fisher Theater boasts the largest full-season subscription audience in the country.

Along with professional legitimate theater, Detroit has had its share of community theaters. The most important of these was the Bonstelle Players, formed by Miss Jesse Bonstelle in 1910. After 1924, the group had its own theater, the Bonstelle Playhouse, in the reconverted Temple Beth El on Woodward Avenue. Known as the maker of stars, among the great figures of the theater Miss Bonstelle encouraged include Katharine Cornell, Ann Harding, Frank Morgan, Melvyn Douglas and William Powell.

In 1928, the Bonstelle Players were reorganized as the Detroit Civic Theatre. Four years later, however, Miss Bonstelle died, and the theater closed its doors the following year. Thereafter the facility was used as a movie house and for vaudeville until it was taken over in 1951 by Wayne State University as its undergraduate theater.

Today, community theater thrives in Detroit through Wayne State University's Hilberry (the only graduate repertory theater in the country), Bonstelle Theatre, Studio Theater, The Detroit Youth Theater at the Institute of Arts, "The Theatre" at Marygrove College, and the Detroit Repertory Theater. One of the newest playhouses is the Attic Theater in Trapper's Alley located on Monroe Avenue in Greek Town. More than 100 years ago, the building was the home of one of Detroit's leading companies. Traugott Schmidt & Sons, fur traders and leather tanners. Today, the Trapper's Alley complex of buildings, in addition to the Attic Theater, house a variety of stores, shops, restaurants and entertainment spots.*

---

*In addition, there are more than 100 other community theatre groups in the Detroit area, making this one of the largest community theatre centers in the United States. Detroit, incidentally, has the second largest number of cultural arts organizations in the United States, second only to New York.

181

Below, modern dancers perform at the Horace E. Dodge and Son Memorial Fountain. Far left, the Hillberry Theater production, "Of Mice and Men," on the Wayne State University campus. Left, ballerina on pointe at a St. Mary School of Dance recital. Right, the world famous Detroit Public Library showing the Cass Avenue entrance and wings which opened in 1963.

182

Along with art, music and the theater, Detroiters have long had an interest in reading and in books. The city's first library was a private organization known as a subscription library. Incorporated in 1817, the City Library Association, sold shares of stock to raise funds and only shareholders could borrow books. The Association had rooms in the old University of Michigan Building on Bates Street.

It was not until after the Civil War that Detroiters had their own free public library. In 1865, the Board of Education established the Detroit Public Library with a reading room at the rear of the city high school in the old capitol building, and in 1877, the library moved to its own building. The present main library was opened in 1921. The design is Italian Renaissance; the architect was Cass Gilbert. The library was substantially enlarged when its wings were opened in 1963. Today the Detroit Public Library is one of the nation's finest. With holdings of more than two million volumes, it has extensive reference and research collections in the fields of technology, music, cartography and literature. It also houses the nationally known Burton Historical Collection and the National Automotive History Collection.

The life expectancy of a newspaper in Detroit during the last half of the 19th century was frequently short and changes in ownership were numerous. Up to 1885, for example, 253 newspapers had been started in Detroit. At the turn of the century, four major papers were being published in the city. The *Free Press* and the *Tribune* were the morning dailies, while the *Detroit Evening Journal* and the *Detroit News* were the leading afternoon papers.

The *News* had been founded in 1873 by the colorful James E. Scripps and over the years took control of several other papers, including the *Advertiser, Tribune,* and *Journal.* In 1960, the *News* purchased William Randolph Hearst's *Detroit Times.* Today only the *News* and *Free Press* remain.

Detroit's largest black-owned newspaper, the *Michigan Chronicle,* was established in 1936 by Louis E. Martin. Under editor Longworth M. Quinn, Sr., the paper has become an active voice in the community with a circulation of 33,000. Prior to the *Chronicle,* the city's leading black newspaper was the *Detroit Tribune.* The first issue appeared on April 14, 1933. James E. McCall was the paper's editor holding that position until the mid-1940s. Other important ethnic papers being published today include: the German *Abend Post,* founded in 1854; *Dziennik Polski* (Polish Daily News), founded in 1904; and the *National Greek Tribune,* founded, 1920.

In addition to publishing Detroit's leading afternoon newspaper, the *Detroit News* was also a pioneer in the field of electronic communications. On the evening of August 20, 1920, a radio station owned by the *News* broadcast the first regular radio program in the United States.* Condenser dials were adjusted, generator brushes were cleaned, and strains of *Annie Laurie* and *Roses of Picardy* went out over the

---

*Although this was the first regular broadcast, KDKA in Pittsburgh was the first commercially-licensed station.

Early electronic media: top left, a staged picture shot a few days after the August 20, 1920 inauguration of the Detroit News' makeshift studio; on that date, the station 8MK (WWJ) went on the air for the first time. Top right, WWJ radio studio four years later, on November 19, 1924. Above left, spectators watch Detroit's first on-the-air television broadcast October 23, 1946. Above right, Detroit's first TV broadcast; WWJ-TV at Convention Hall, November 22, 1946.

air waves. Originally known as 8MK, the station was later named WBL, and finally in 1922, WWJ. That year it initiated broadcasts of University of Michigan extension courses and Sunday services from St. Paul's Episcopal Cathedral. The first Tiger baseball game was broadcast in 1927 with Ty Tyson at the microphone.

Another early station, WCX, later WJR, signed on May 4, 1922. WXYZ, founded October 10, 1925, as WGHP, was bought by George W. Trendle in 1929. He changed its name, moved its studios to the Maccabees Building (now the School Center Building) and in three years sent forth the cry of "Hi, Yo, Silver" to join the immortals of radio. "The Lone Ranger," "The Green Hornet" and "Sgt. Preston of the Yukon" thundered out of the Maccabees Building across the country and made Detroit rank with New York, Chicago, and Hollywood as a radio center.

In the fall of 1946, the *Detroit News'* WWJ-TV produced the city's first television broadcast at Convention Hall. On March 4, 1947, the station introduced the first commercial television program in Detroit from its studios on West Lafayette at Second. The *Detroit News* still operates radio station WWJ, but in 1978, WWJ-TV was sold by the *News* to the *Washington Post*. The new owners renamed the station WDIV-TV. In return for WWJ-TV, the *News* assumed control of the *Post* owned WTOP-TV in Washington.

Detroit is also the home of the first privately-owned black radio and television stations in the country, WCHB and WGPR-TV. Other ethnic radio programing is heard on stations WIID, which carries 33 programs in 20 languages, and on WMZK, with 48 programs in 25 languages.

Top, the University of Detroit's McNichols campus. Above, the university's dental school complex on East Jefferson, and the student center, right.

Wayne State University is the city's largest: top, "Old Main" at Cass and Warren. Center, McGregor Center. Above, the university's College of Education building.

Detroiters have access to several excellent colleges and universities. Wayne State, the city's largest university, is an outgrowth of the merger of several separate colleges maintained originally by the Detroit Board of Education. Although the university did not come into official existence until 1933, some of its colleges had been in existence for many years. The medical college was established in 1868 as the privately-owned Detroit Medical College, and it is from the founding of this, its oldest college, that the university dates its origin. The college of education was founded by the city in 1881 as the Detroit Normal School. The liberal arts college is the outgrowth of post-graduate high school training offered at the old Detroit Central High School (now Wayne's "Old Main") beginning in 1915. Wayne University, as it was first named, remained under Board of Education control until 1956, when it came under state control and support and received its present name of Wayne State University.

Detroit's other major university, the University of Detroit, was founded in 1877 as the Detroit College by priests of the Jesuit order. First housed in a two-story residence on Jefferson Avenue near downtown, new colleges such as law, engineering, business administration and dentistry were added over the years. As a result, the school was reorganized in 1911 and renamed University of Detroit. The school continued to grow at such a rate that in 1922, a 42-acre site for a new campus was obtained at West Six Mile and Livernois. In 1927, this became the school's main campus. It was later named the McNichols campus in honor of Fr. John McNichols, the university's president from 1921 to 1932. Today U of D is Michigan's largest independent university. Three other smaller liberal arts colleges were also established by other Roman Catholic orders: Marygrove, Mercy and Madonna colleges.

Other important area schools include the Detroit Institute of Technology, founded by the YMCA in 1891; the Detroit College of Law, also established by the YMCA, opened in 1892; the Lawrence Institute of Technology, originally occupying a building at the Ford Highland Park Plant, opened in 1932; and Shaw College at Detroit. Founded in 1936, Shaw College at Detroit is one of the few predominately black colleges in a major northern city.

186

The LaSalle window at the Dossin Marine Museum on Belle Isle.

Detroit Science Center. Above, the escalator tube at the Center.

Detroit Historical Museum.

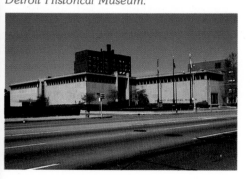

During the early 1950s, at the time the city was developing the civic center, an important new addition was being made to the city's cultural center. On July 24, 1951, the new Detroit Historical Museum was opened at Kirby and Woodward across the street from the Public Library. In 1968, the museum was substantially enlarged with the opening of the Kresge Wing. The city historical department is now comprised of the main museum in the cultural center, the military museum at Fort Wayne, and the fine Dossin Marine Museum on Belle Isle.

Today, the cultural center has grown to include not only the Historical Museum, Public Library, and Institute of Arts, but also the Rackham Memorial Building, the Children's Museum, Your Heritage House, Merrill-Palmer Institute, the Scarab Club, the International Institute, the Center for Creative Studies (formerly the Soceity of Arts and Crafts), and the impressive new Detroit Science Center. Currently plans are being formulated for the development of a cultural campus setting for the various institutions that comprise the cultural center.

187

Greenfield Village and the Henry Ford Museum, below, were founded in the late 1920s by Henry Ford, and today is one of the most unique museums in the world. Far left, an old steam locomotive at Greenfield Village; left, Cotswold Cottage. Inset, the front of a Bugati automobile in the Henry Ford Museum.

Top, Henry Ford, left, and Thomas Edison lay the cornerstone for the Edison Institute, September 27, 1928. Above, in the mid-19th century, the Clinton Inn, now in Greenfield Village, was the first overnight stagecoach stop on the Great Sauk Trail (now U.S. 12) from Detroit to Chicago.

Along with the institutions of the cultural center, Detroiters are fortunate in having in nearby Dearborn one of the finest museum complexes in the world, the Greenfield Village and Henry Ford Museum. Collectively known as the Edison Institute and founded in 1929 by Henry Ford, visitors tour the nearly 100 historic buildings that have been brought here and placed in a village setting of 19th century America. The museum adjacent to the village contains historic collections representing nearly all areas of human enterprise, including outstanding groupings of furniture and transportation vehicles.

During the early 1950s, as development of the cultural and civic centers were well underway, plans were being made for yet another important center. On May 23, 1956, the front pages of Detroit newspapers announced plans for what was to become one of the nation's largest medical complexes, the Detroit Medical Center.

Originally the center was to include Harper, Grace, Woman's (now Hutzel), and Children's Hospitals and the Wayne State University Medical School. To that group has since been added the Rehabilitation Institute and Detroit General Hospital.

Bounded by Woodward, the Chrysler Freeway, Warren and Mack, the center has seen the construction of a new medical school campus (Wayne now has the second largest medical school in the country), modern hospitals, office buildings and housing for medical personnel. Among the highly specialized services provided are care for children with sickle cell anemia and other blood related problems, chemo and radiation care for cancer patients, cardiac care including open heart surgery, special

One of the city's most exciting contributions to the renaissance movement is the "Young Detroiters," left, youth who sing and dance the praises of a city that is coming alive; the Greater Detroit Chamber of Commerce sponsors the group, which developed a musical revue entitled "My Detroit — Welcome to It." Below, an aerial view of Fort Wayne, reconstructed. Bottom, Mariners Church in its new home.

190

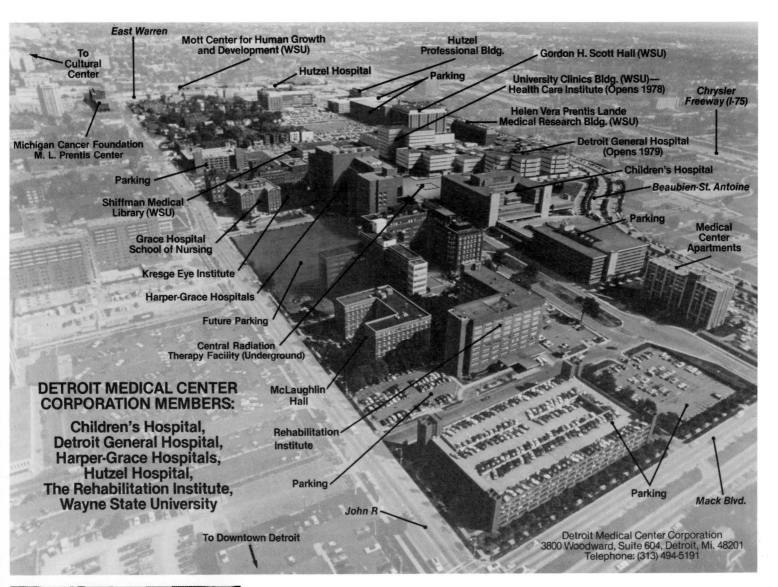

East Warren

To Cultural Center

Mott Center for Human Growth and Development (WSU)

Hutzel Hospital

Hutzel Professional Bldg.

Parking

Gordon H. Scott Hall (WSU)

University Clinics Bldg. (WSU)— Health Care Institute (Opens 1978)

Helen Vera Prentis Lande Medical Research Bldg. (WSU)

Chrysler Freeway (I-75)

Detroit General Hospital (Opens 1979)

Children's Hospital

Beaubien-St. Antoine

Michigan Cancer Foundation M. L. Prentis Center

Parking

Parking

Medical Center Apartments

Shiffman Medical Library (WSU)

Grace Hospital School of Nursing

Kresge Eye Institute

Harper-Grace Hospitals

Future Parking

Central Radiation Therapy Facility (Underground)

DETROIT MEDICAL CENTER CORPORATION MEMBERS:

Children's Hospital, Detroit General Hospital, Harper-Grace Hospitals, Hutzel Hospital, The Rehabilitation Institute, Wayne State University

McLaughlin Hall

Rehabilitation Institute

Parking

Parking

Mack Blvd.

To Downtown Detroit

John R

Detroit Medical Center Corporation 3800 Woodward, Suite 604, Detroit, Mi. 48201 Telephone: (313) 494-5191

Top, an aerial view of Detroit's expanding Medical Center. Above, construction of a tunnel connecting Detroit General Hospital and Harper-Grace Hospital.

prenatal care for mothers with acute or chronic pregnancy-related problems, renal (kidney) dialysis and surgery, neonatal (intensive care for infants), modern ambulatory care facilities concentrated at the new Health Care Institute, emergency and trama care through Detroit General Hospital, and a unique program for rehabilitation of the physically handicapped.

Today, the most spectacular physical change to the city is, of course, the new Renaissance Center. When Henry Ford announced his plans for this $500 million riverfront development in the fall of 1971 he stated:

"The revitalization is a task for the business community here. There are more than enough human and financial resources to undertake a job of this kind, and what we have been lacking is a solid first step to get something started. The size of the development is such that no single company can handle it by itself. We want and will need the participation of other companies to bring the plan to reality."

It was not long before Henry Ford's call to action was heeded. In less than six months, 51 companies, which were either located in Detroit or which were based elsewhere and did extensive business in the city, joined in a partnership to get the

191

The Renaissance: Top, from left; the Plaza Hotel rises above the completed office towers July 13, 1976; skaters enjoy the skyline view at the Hart Plaza ice rink which opened to the public December 8, 1978; the new Horace E. Dodge and Son Memorial Fountain designed by Isamu Noguchi. Left, the new symbolically rises from the ashes of the old. Above left, University of Detroit's Dowling Hall, Renaissance campus. Above right, buildings on the east side of Woodward after renovation.

Scott Fountain on Belle Isle.

project rolling. They put up $114 million in equity capital, and they guaranteed another $12 million in loans. A consortium of 28 banks around the country underwrote a $200 million mortgage, which in turn, was backed by four major insurance companies and the Ford Motor Credit Company. In addition, $11.5 million in unsecured debt rounded out the $337 million first-phase financial package.

The area selected for the development was immediately to the east of the civic center, bounded by the Henry and Edsel Ford Auditorium, Jefferson Avenue, St. Antoine Street, and the river. To design the Renaissance Center, Henry Ford called upon famed Atlanta architect John Portman. The plans that Portman prepared were breathtaking. The first phase of the project was to consist of a 70-story 1400-room luxury hotel and four 39-story octagonal office buildings surrounding the hotel. When completed, the five buildings would employ about 20,000 people. The hotel would be the tallest building in Michigan and the tallest hotel in the world as measured from the lobby level to the top of the building.

Renaissance Center was to be the catalyst for changing the image of downtown Detroit. And, indeed, within a short time, the stabilizing influence of this vast undertaking was felt. The University of Detroit law and dental schools, located across Jefferson Avenue from Renaissance Center, were planning to vacate their premises when the massive project was announced. The schools not only stayed but launched a $7 million modernization program. Nearby Saints Peter and Paul Roman Catholic Church changed its mind about moving. Neighborhood stores began sprucing up in anticipation of the many visitors and workers who were soon to be flocking to the new hotel and four office towers.

Finally, on May 27, 1973, ground was broken and this great project was underway. In October, just as the heavy equipment was being moved into the area, a team of archeologists appeared on the site. Sponsored by the Michigan Archeological Society, the team was funded by a grant to the Detroit Historical Society from the Ford Motor Company Fund.

Working around — and with the complete cooperation of — the contractors and workmen, the team of archeologists, bundled up against the cold, began sifting out bits and pieces of 19th century Detroit from the mud. The Renaissance Center was located on one of the oldest sections of Detroit. The hotel itself was going up directly on the 1820 site of the Brush Farm House and eastern stockade wall of the old city. By the time their digging was completed, the archeologists had uncovered more than 20,000 artifacts representing a complete cross-section of life in Detroit of the 1820-1850 period. The artifacts salvaged from the site included dishes, glassware, bottles, pewter forks and spoons, scissors, spools of thread, pieces of clothing, children's toys, and even a fragment of an April 3, 1833 edition of the town newspaper, the *Detroit Advertiser.*

As the items were uncovered, they were taken to the Historical Museum, where the long and tedious process of reconstruction and cataloging was begun. The variety and number of artifacts uncovered was so extensive that one member of the team called it, "the richest early 19th century urban archeological dig in this country." In May 1974, the archeologists completed their work on the site, and the bulldozers began their work in earnest.

On March 15, 1977, less than four years after groundbreaking, the hotel, named Detroit Plaza, was opened. The first two office towers opened in 1976; the third in late spring 1977; and the fourth in the fall of 1977. Thus, the first phase of Henry Ford's daring project was completed.

These great towers stand today as a symbol of the rebirth of Detroit and of the quality of life of its citizens.

Detroit — indeed a city, "where life is worth living."

Far left, Calvary Baptist Church, award-winning architecture by Gunnar Birkerts. Top center, interior mall of Fairlane Shopping Center. Below, Ambassador Bridge at sunset. Right, a night view of the Masonic Temple. Below right, fireworks over the river.

Above left, the skyline of Detroit from Lafayette Park in 1975. Below left, staging of a strike scene while filming "The Betsy" in Detroit, 1977. Top, a "salty" oceangoing vessel at the new federal dock. Above, a Bicentennial visit of the Christian Radich, a Norwegian tall ship. The training vessel first docked at Detroit in 1954, and 12 years later returned to commemorate the Bicentennial.

The Renaissance is alive and well in Detroit, right. Below right; sidewalk cafe; Belle Isle playscape; Afro-America-77 celebration.

Partners in economic progress

Free enterprise has played the dominant role in Detroit, from the earliest days when French traders counted their take from the sale of beaver skins to the thriving manufacturing center and headquarters city that is the Detroit of today.

Organization has been the key to much of the success of this enterprise. Although the Detroit Board of Commerce was founded just three years after the turn of the century, the organizations responsible for its creation date back to 1856, when the Board of Trade was founded.

The directors of the Detroit Merchants and Manufacturers Exchange and Chamber of Commerce met with representatives of the Board of Trade and other organizations in early 1903. They discussed the formation of a common organization that would eliminate duplication of effort in several programs, yet was broader in scope than any existing group.

A canvas for 100 members to pay $100 each was recommended and a target date of January 1904, was set. By the end of June 1903, 238 members had been signed. The formal organization of what is now the Greater Detroit Chamber of Commerce was completed on June 30, 1903.

The first year's program of work, which attracted the participation of 142 members, included the organization of a convention bureau, now the Metropolitan Detroit Convention and Visitors Bureau, and the Adscript Club, now the Adcraft Club.

Shortly after its organization, the Chamber began a campaign to bring more business into Detroit. During one year, the campaign attracted 109 new manufacturing corporations with $6 million of authorized capital and projections of 77 new industrial buildings.

In 75 years since the beginning, Detroit Renaissance, Inc., New Detroit, Inc. and the Economic Club of Detroit all emerged from Greater Detroit Chamber of Commerce activities.

In 1906, the Chamber's efforts to attract new business resulted in a growing pain — smoke and soot. The Chamber proposed an ordinance that was later

In 1973 construction was started on a new Federal building, seen here with the Michigan Bell Telephone Building in the background.

adopted by the Detroit Council for the control of pollution.

In 1910, the Chamber responded to an all-time high incidence of typhoid fever. The cause was traced to Detroit's milk supply, and the Chamber immediately stepped in to work with the Detroit Board of Health and later with the U.S. Department of Agriculture for a solution.

Another early assignment was improved transportation, especially to the coast-to-coast railroad lines that ran 60 miles south of Detroit. The Chamber urged and supported the construction of the Detroit-Windsor Tunnel, completed in 1912, providing an open trade route for Detroit freight to reach the eastern seaboard through Canada.

The Chamber has supported other citizen interests throughout the years: public education millages and financing; auto traffic safety; finding jobs for immigrants and unemployed (which reached a peak in 1969 with a JOBS contract from the U.S. Department of Labor and 2,100 job placements); lower coal costs for heating purposes during the Depression; vaccinations for school children; a city clean-up program (now

Project PRIDE), and more.

The Chamber has consistently been involved in programs relating to the defense of the country. World War I inspired such programs as Chamber-sponsored French lessons for soldiers gearing for Europe. Edwin Denby, 1916 Chamber president, enlisted in the Marines as a corporal (he finished the war as a major); the Adcraft Club financed an enlistment campaign; the Chamber's lounge was converted into a Red Cross office, and the Chamber was the first Detroit organization to meet its Liberty Loan goal.

After the war, the Chamber urged the hiring of veterans and the retraining and hiring of disabled veterans. Immigration continued its pace, and the Chamber aided in the naturalization of citizens. Among the employees of the Chamber's Alien Information Bureau, 17 languages were spoken.

The Chamber's interest in retailing was always high, and the Retail Merchants Bureau was formed in 1919 with a nucleus of 100 downtown stores. In 1922, the Chamber initiated a shoplifter-curbing program by circulating photographs of shoplifters caught in the act. The present Retail Merchants Association's STEM (Shoplifters Take Everybody's Money) program is doing the same thing today with shoplifting awareness communication.

The St. Lawrence Seaway was another idea that drew active Detroit Chamber support. The Chamber's Washington, D.C., representative established the basis of an effort to build the Seaway after talking to other Washington reps.

The first St. Lawrence Waterway Convention was held in the Board of Commerce Building in 1920. Although the Seaway was openly opposed by railroads, the Chamber continued its support until the merits of the waterway were recognized.

The Chamber's efforts brought a foreign trade bureau branch to Detroit in 1924, and in 1925, the Chamber began a national air tour featuring Detroit pilots serving as ambassadors to Detroit, flying 4,000 miles around the country.

Another effort, which took more than ten years, culminated in completion of the Ambassador bridge to Windsor in 1929, and the motor vehicle Detroit-Windsor tunnel, completed in 1930.

After the 1929 stock market crash, the Chamber began a speed recovery campaign, consultations and clinics that made Detroit the only large city in the nation with a financial recovery program, and the municipal debt was soon cleared. By 1935, all but 24 of the 300 factories that were vacated during the Depression were occupied.

During World War II, the Chamber surpassed its quota of war bonds by selling $18 million worth, and urged the hiring of women workers.

In 1949, the owners of the Detroit City Airport wanted to sell their land for commercial development. Chamber representatives appeared before the Detroit Common Council and played a major role in saving the airport. Through the years, the Chamber has been the city's official representative to the Civil Aeronautics Board for increased and improved air service.

The Greater Detroit Chamber of Commerce today conducts comprehensive government relations, economic development, consumer/marketing, community development, communications and member services. Affiliate organizations include the Retail Merchants Association, the Food Industry Council, the Wholesale Distributors Association and the Business/Education Alliance.

The Greater Detroit Chamber is supported by the voluntary investments of more than 4,000 southeastern Michigan member business firms.

Because free enterprise has been the catalyst for Detroit's growth and development, this chapter presents the histories of a representative number of those Chamber-member companies which have witnessed Detroit's growth along with their own. Some have been growing with Detroit for a great many years. Others, relatively new to the city, have already made their mark and are betting on a strong future. They have confidence in the Renaissance. All of these book sponsors, no matter what their age, are proud of their contributions to Detroit and of their own history. With the publication of this book, the stories of these companies are presented to relate their part in the growth of Detroit.

Barton-Malow Company

State's leading construction firm blends new techniques, old traditions

The Barton-Malow Company, Michigan's largest construction firm, used mule teams in some of its early projects more than half a century ago. More recently, in building the world's largest domed stadium, it used a giant helicopter to place the supporting cables for the 10-acre fabric air-supported roof.

The latter structure, known as the Pontiac Silverdome, is typical of the projects which have brought Barton-Malow industry-wide recognition for its development of new techniques to cut costs and expedite job completion. The Silverdome, home of the Detroit Lions Football team, was hailed by *Engineering News/Record* as "one of the great design and construction achievements of our time" and by the National Society of Professional Engineers as "one of the ten outstanding engineering feats in the U.S. in 1975."

At a time when other stadium projects were experiencing huge cost overruns, Barton-Malow completed the

Burton Historical Collection

Excavating a Detroit construction site a little over half a century ago required a lot of hand digging. Mules and draft horses did the hauling.

Silverdome "on schedule and within budget", an achievement which was recognized by the coveted "Build America" Award presented by the Associated General Contractors of America and Motorola Communications, Inc.

Now into its second half-century, the firm looks ahead eagerly to the special challenges of such projects as hospitals, research centers, complex industrial plants, filtration and other ecological installations while looking back proudly at a distinguished body of work for distinguished clients, including a number who have been customers throughout Barton-Malow's entire career.

The company was started in 1924 by Carl Barton, a young engineer from the University of Michigan. A few years later he was joined by Arnold Malow. Both young men had substantial background through work with major Detroit contractors and both remained with the company through long and distinguished careers prior to retirement.

In spite of the lean years of the Depression, the company steadily built a solid record of achievement. Prominent among its largest clients was the Great Lakes Steel Corporation (now a division of National Steel), but major jobs were offered with increasing frequency by other companies until the list of Barton-Malow customers resembled an industrial *Who's Who*.

An important part of the Barton-Malow tradition lies in the fact that all the top executives have had a thorough grounding in practical field experience in addition to their technical preparation. The career of Board Chairman Ben. C. Maibach, Jr., is an example. He went to work as a Barton-Malow laborer after graduating from high school in 1938. Even this was a matter of tradition. His father, a young carpenter from the Bay City area, had

Barton-Malow used a Sikorsky S-64 Skycrane Helicopter to erect the steel cables which support the 400,000 square foot Pontiac Silverdome fiberglass roof.

joined the company in its infancy and had become its No. 1 superintendent.

President Rolland M. Wilkening started with the firm in 1950 as a construction laborer, just after graduating from Purdue University as a civil engineer. Ben C. Maibach III, Executive Vice President, spent his summers working as a laborer while earning his engineering degree at Michigan State University, a pattern which has been followed by many of the firm's engineers.

When Ben Maibach, Jr., went to work for the company in 1938, he considered entering college in the fall as a full-time student — but the firm's annual volume had reached $1 million and he found himself so busy that he enrolled in night classes at the University of Detroit and continued to work in the field as laborer, engineer's helper, timekeeper and in any other capacity where he was needed. Then he

undertook training as a carpenter's apprentice — ordinarily a four-year stint — and within a year rose to the position of foreman. Meanwhile, at night school, he studied reinforced concrete design, a subject which had been long neglected because of the increasing emphasis on structural steel. As the nation girded for World War II, the subject took on new importance because of the shortage of steel. At the age of 21, he was made a superintendent and placed in charge of major jobs, beginning an ascent up the executive ladder which saw him become president in 1960 and chairman in 1976.

The tradition of community service is strong within the organization. In addition to numerous civic and cultural responsibilities, both top officers are active in their religious faiths. Maibach was ordained a minister in the Evangelical Baptist Church in 1949 and as secretary-treasurer of the Mission Committee has made several journeys to the orient to assist in development of a missionary program. Wilkening is President of the Detroit Area Council, Boy Scouts of America. He is a former President of Cross of Christ Lutheran Church and past chairman of its board of education; he also served as a member of the board of management for the Lutheran School for the Deaf for 19 years.

According to the 15th annual *Engineering News/Record* report of leading construction contractors, Barton-Malow ranked first in Michigan with a 1977 volume of $172.3 million, and ranked 70th nationally among the top 400 companies listed.

In a recent survey of U.S. construction management firms by *Building Design & Construction,* Barton-Malow ranked third nationally and first in Michigan construction management volume.

BASF Wyandotte Corporation

Wyandotte: a company and city that grew together

The name "Wyandotte" usually means two things to most Detroit area residents — the chemical company, and the bustling city of some 40,000. They are almost synonymous, because they grew up together. The company has

been an important part of the community almost since it was founded in 1890 by Captain John Baptiste Ford. He conceived the idea to supply raw materials to the plate glass industry, which he had introduced earlier in the United States.

The principal product was synthetic soda ash, a major ingredient in glass manufacture.

In 1891, when the first brine well was sunk, the frame buildings erected and the kilns lighted, Captain Ford was 80 years old, an age when most men are well into something else. But, the Captain and his son, Edward, were determined to master the process involved in making soda ash, and together with experts from England, they succeeded.

The buildings were destroyed by fire the following year, but Captain Ford was not a man to quit. To prevent a similar disaster from wiping out all his facilities, he rebuilt on two sites about two miles apart. The North Works location, which he accquired after the fire, includes 197 acres with nearly a mile frontage on the Detroit River. The old South Works property is 52 acres.

In 1894, the Captain formed the Michigan Alkali Company with $1 million capital, and the following year the first buildings of the North Works complex were built. In 1896, twelve brine wells were drilled; the bicarbonate of soda plant was established in 1897, and in 1898, when the Captain was 87, the J. B. Ford Company was organized to sell cleaning compounds for the retail trade.

By the turn of the century, Michigan Alkali was an integral part of the city. An 1889 editorial in a local paper said, "Busy hives of industry are the Michigan Alkali Works…manufacturing products that reach every corner of the earth. Giving employment to over 1,200 men, the Ford industries are a blessing to the city."

In its early years, the company added production of other inorganic chemicals such as chlorine, caustic soda, calcium carbonate and calcium chloride.

In 1943, the two Ford enterprises, Michigan Alkali and the J. B. Ford Company, were consolidated under the name Wyandotte Chemicals Corporation. The company entered the organic chemicals field in 1947 with the produc-

The first general office of the Michigan Alkali Company at Works No. 2. (North Plant). The cornerstone was laid September 15, 1895, and the building occupied in 1896.

tion of ethylene oxide and ethylene glycol. In 1958, it added production of urethane polyols, and in 1967, toluene diisocyanate, the two principal ingredients in the cellular plastics family.

In 1970, BASF Wyandotte Corporation was formed through the merger of BASF Corporation into Wyandotte Chemicals Corporation. It operates as an American member of the BASF Group of chemical companies, with headquarters in Parsippany, New Jersey. The parent company, BASF Aktiengesellshaft, is headquartered in Ludwigshafen, West Germany.

Today, BASF Wyandotte Corporation employs more than 6,000 people at 19 locations throughout the United States and in Canada. Net sales in 1977 amounted to more than $816 million. Since the merger, BASF Wyandotte has had a sustained pattern of planned growth and plant expansions. Successful new plant start-ups and selective capacity improvements in existing production facilities increased the number and vol-

This is a 1924 Research Laboratory at Wyandotte Chemicals with researchers testing various formulations for possible development into new products.

ume of products manufactured and sold.

Since that day in 1890, when Captain John Baptiste Ford first conceived the idea of founding the Wyandotte soda ash plant, both the company structure and the city have changed. When he drilled his first brine well in 1891, Captain Ford probably had no idea of the size the company was to become, but the city of Wyandotte and its people are grateful he drilled it.

The Bendix Corporation

Diversified supplier provides high technology products worldwide

The Bendix Corporation today is a diversified worldwide manufacturer providing thousands of products to the automotive, aerospace-electronics, shelter and industrial-energy markets. Bendix is among America's top 100 industrial manufacturers, with annual revenues in the late 1970s of more than $3 billion

and net income of more than $100 million.

In true storybook fashion, Bendix grew from humble beginnings. Success was hard-earned, built on the ideas and will of a young man in the Midwest. Vincent Bendix, who ran away from his home in Moline, Illinois at the age of 16,

was a tinkerer with mechanical "things." Little wonder he was attracted to the fledgling automotive industry. In 1907, he formed an automobile company which assembled and sold a few vehicles under the name of Bendix. The idea was good, but Bendix' timing couldn't have been worse. Ninety-four

201

Based in the Detroit area since 1942, Bendix' world headquarters are in Southfield.

new automobile makes were introduced that year and the Bendix model, like many others, didn't survive the competition.

Undaunted, Bendix sought a niche in advancing the mechanical state of the art in the infant industry. For one thing, the hand crank by which one started a car was inconvenient. Bendix thought about it, and in 1910 conceived the idea of the starter drive which would start a car's engine electrically with the push of a button. After a three-year search, he found a company in Elmira, New York which agreed to manufacture the device. The first Bendix starter drive was installed on Chevrolet's "Baby Grand" touring car in 1914 and 5,500 drives were produced that year. By 1919, production had soared to 1.5 million and soon, nearly every vehicle produced in the United States was equipped with the Bendix starter drive. Finally for Bendix, now in his mid-30s, came the payoff for his resolve in the face of repeated frustrations. He was launched as an automotive supplier.

With capital in hand from the starter drive venture, Bendix set out to repeat his success. In 1923, at the Paris Auto Show, he renewed his acquaintance with the French engineer Henri Perrot who was working just then on a four-wheel brake system. A master bargainer, Bendix secured the rights and persuaded Perrot to return to South Bend, Indiana and set up shop with him. The four-wheel brake system first appeared on cars in 1924. Over the next four years, production volume increased fivefold to 3½ million brakes a year and plant capacity was increased from 20,000 to more than a million square feet to meet the demand.

With the fortune Bendix had gained came the opportunity to explore new fields. His instincts drew him into aviation, for which he saw great business potential. Even though he was personally uneasy about flying, and probably never flew more than a half dozen times in his life, Vincent Bendix tried to borrow some of the glamour of the Lindbergh era. In 1929, at a time when only 8 percent of his company's sales were in aviation products, he renamed it the Bendix Aviation Corporation. Two years later he established the Bendix Trophy transcontinental air race which attracted the famous names among aviation's pioneers: Jimmy Doolittle, Amelia Earhart, Roscoe Turner. The race was discontinued in 1962, as the aviator's leather cap, goggles and scarf were overtaken by the supersonic military jets.

Just as Vincent Bendix was committed to technological leadership and diversification, so is the modern Bendix. While his personal interests often led Vincent Bendix into new fields, the several generations of management who succeeded him pursued a policy of diversification in the interest of building a stronger corporation.

While Bendix no longer makes starter drives, it continues to build automotive brakes. In fact, Bendix makes more brakes, for more different types of vehicles than any other manufacturer in the world, over 16 million each year for more than 400 different applications from golf carts to jumbo jets.

Brakes, while an important part, remain only a part of the Bendix story, however. Today, as Vincent Bendix may have envisioned in 1929, the company is a major producer of aviation and space equipment. Bendix equipment flies on today's military, commercial and private aircraft just as it has flown on virtually every program of the space age, including lunar landing missions. Bendix is also very much involved in helping meet the down-to-earth challenges which confront society every day. It helps answer the nation's need for more housing, through building materials and manufactured homes subsidiaries. It builds machine tools and other equipment to help keep industry running and provides geological services throughout the world in search of natural resources.

A lot has changed since the day Vincent Bendix was inspired to create "the mechanical hand that cranks your car." But much remains the same. The committment to technological leadership and diversification. And the vision of the future that The Bendix Corporation will help create.

Blue Cross and Blue Shield of Michigan

Budgeting for sickness brought about major health plan

The 1930s are remembered by many as a time of breadlines, unemployment, and such immortal phrases as, "Brother, can you spare a dime?"

But they also marked the birth of a new group sharing concept of paying for health care before you got sick. For the first time, people could budget for sickness.

The idea that made this all possible was prepayment.

Blue Cross and Blue Shield of Michigan has since become one of the giants in the prepayment field. Today it provides health care coverage for 5.4 million persons in the state— about 60 percent of the population. It pays out more than $2.5 billion each year in benefits for regular and government programs, and handles more than 40 million claims.

It is the largest Blue Plan in the country in terms of benefits paid, and is second in enrollment, behind the New York Plan.

Its beginnings were humble. In 1939, the Michigan Society for Group Hospitalization, later known as Blue Cross of Michigan, was established with a $10,000 loan from three Detroit hospitals.

A year later, the Michigan State Medical Society began Michigan Medical Service (later Blue Shield of Michigan) to pay for medical service to complement the hospital payment plan.

The Plans' first major customer was Ford Motor Company. In 1940, Ford asked them to develop a contract for its employees. They came up with a hospital contract providing 21 days of hospital care annually for 60 cents a month, and surgical/obstetrical, x-ray, and anesthesia services provided in the hospital for 40 cents a month.

Chrysler Corporation and General Motors Corporation signed similar contracts the next year.

Today the "Big Three" auto companies comprise about 40 percent of the Plan's customers.

The early days of the Plans were not without difficulties. In 1941, the State sent a deputy insurance commissioner to help shut down the Blue Shield Plan because income was only half the actual cost of services. However, support by the United Auto Workers, led by Walter Reuther, and acceptance by doctors of a cut in Blue Shield payments put the Plan back on its feet.

Health care benefits today for Blues' subscribers, compared to the early coverage, stagger the imagination.

They range from 365 days of hospital care for general illness, to a wide scope of special benefits — prescription drugs, out-patient psychiatric care, dental services, vision and hearing benefits. The ability to deliver this coverage to auto employees nationally has been a major reason for the Plan's growth.

The corporation has also recognized

The 21-story Blue Cross/Blue Shield Service Center with its connecting two-story computer facility and adjacent five level parking structure is located on an 11-1/2 acre plot in downtown Detroit.

This building served as headquarters for the Blue Cross and Blue Shield Plans in Michigan from 1954 to 1971 when the 21-story Service Center was built just two blocks away. The corporation still uses the building.

changing trends in health care. The original intent of covering only hospital care has been expanded over the years to include outpatient care, care in extended care facilities, and care in the home, helping to prevent greater escalation of costs.

At the Plans' inception, physicians

dominated the Blue Shield board and hospital representatives were in the majority at Blue Cross. Each acted voluntarily — Blue Cross in 1964 and Blue Shield in 1971 — to create a public majority.

In 1974, the boards voted to consolidate as one corporation. Today, as then, rising costs are the major health care problem, increasing at almost twice the rate of other costs.

The Michigan Plan has been aggressive in alleviating the problem. In 1977, it operated 69 cost control programs that saved $429 million in payments, primarily through reviews of professional charges, facility costs, medical necessity, and benefit eligibility.

Working with hospitals, physicians, and community representatives, the Plan trailblazed new reimbursement concepts for hospitals and physicians, implemented in 1978.

The Michigan Plan, aware of its community responsibilities, made a commitment to Detroit's future during the 1960s and built its needed Service Center on a downtown site. The firm today employs 5,600 persons, most of whom live within the city.

The Plan is also involved in community activities such as: health education, paid health career experience for high school students, enabling high school dropouts to earn a diploma, designing a traveling exhibit on life styles and health care costs, and providing a wide scope of health information through special telephone lines.

"The changes of the past are prologue for the changes that lie ahead," says President John C. McCabe of the corporation's future. "We will continue to draw that balance between mirroring and molding what goes on in health care in order to maintain our objective of providing the best possible health care at the lowest possible cost."

Burroughs Corporation

Industry leader grows from adding machine to total information processing

Some observers predict that the rapidly growing information processing industry will be the largest in the world by the year 2000. Detroit-based Burroughs Corporation is growing right along with it, doubling sales volume every five years and consistently leading

the industry in terms of technological progress.

Just a century ago, however, information processing was beyond the grandest dreams of William Seward Burroughs. A bank clerk with a passion for precision mechanics, Burroughs

wanted to remove the drudgery of manual addition from the lives of thousands of clerks and bookkeepers. He was determined to build a machine that could quickly and accurately record long lists of figures. He formed the American Arithmometer Company in St.

Everyone showed up for photo day at the Burroughs plant in 1906.

Louis in 1886 and in 1891 he introduced the first practical adding and listing machine.

By 1903, the American Arithmometer Company's need for greater production capacity and a larger source of skilled labor prompted the company to select Detroit as its new headquarters. A site was chosen near the northern limits of the city and construction of a new plant began in the summer of 1904. In October, a unique train pulled out of a St. Louis depot. On board were the foremen and factory employees, their wives and children, family pets, household furnishings, office and factory equipment, and the inventory of adding machines.

In 1905, the company took on the Burroughs name. It was employing 1,200 people and selling almost 8,000 machines a year. Over the next 15 years, its product range expanded to include the company's first calculator and first "duplex" adding machine which had two separate totalling mechanisms and featured both subtotals and grand totals. By 1920, Burroughs had sold 800,000 machines, and was employing 12,000 people.

Burroughs machines became standard instruments in banks and offices on every continent during the 1920s and 1930s. The company product line grew to some 450 models, including a "Pass Book Machine" for savings bank bookkeeping, a "Burroughs Portable" adding machine, the first electric key-actuated calculating machine, and the Burroughs Standard Typewriter.

During the early 1940s, Burroughs was engaged in volume production of Norden bombsights at the Plymouth, Michigan plant. This program was a forerunner to the extensive contributions the company would make to major scientific, space exploration, and defense programs in the 1950s and 1960s.

As early as 1940, Burroughs began its research into electronics and by 1949, permanent facilities were opened in the

The Burroughs world headquarters.

Philadelphia area for electronic research and development.

Burroughs growth accelerated in the 1950s with many significant product developments. Its huge UDEC (Unitized Digital Electronic Computer) was delivered to the Wayne State University Computation Laboratory in Detroit, and the E 101 desk-size electronic digital computer was introduced. The company's research and development center was working to develop a series of computers for business problem solving.

During the 1950s and 1960s, the company participated in a variety of specialized defense and space exploration projects. In 1958, Burroughs delivered the world's first operational transistorized computer, which was used to guide the launch of the Atlas Intercontinental Ballistic Missile (ICBM). The company's development of the Atlas computer system represented a major technical achievement. The Atlas system and its successors were used

over the next 20 years in support of the country's historic space program to guide all Mercury and Gemini manned orbital launches, all Ranger and Mariner lunar exploratory missions, and several other earth satellite missions. Burroughs computers were also being developed and installed during this period for the Navy's POLARIS program and for the Air Force's SAGE, ALRI, and BUIC continental air defense systems.

Great advances in technological development were made during the 1960s as Burroughs established itself as a major force in the emerging electronic data processing industry. Burroughs B 5000 solid-state, modular data processing system was considered to be a decade ahead of its time, and featured concepts which have since become industry standards.

Rapidly changing technology has taken the company through two complete new series of computers in the 1970s with additional major advancements in circuitry, system architecture, data storage, and communications.

In 1970, the company introduced its '700' Systems family of computers, which further strengthened Burroughs position in the worldwide electronic data processing market. In late 1975, the company began introducing an even more sophisticated series of systems, the '800' Systems family. The series covers every sector of the computer market from the small-scale B 80 to the very large-scale B 7800, giving Burroughs the strongest product position in its history.

Maintaining its leadership in applied computer technology, Burroughs today offers a complete and exceptionally advanced range of computer systems and equipment, augmented by a growing family of office automation products, business forms and supplies. Its success has brought Burroughs to second position in the computer industry in terms of electronic data processing shipments and revenue, and total profits. Revenue reached the $1 billion milestone in 1972 and only five years later, in 1977, exceeded $2 billion.

Burroughs now employs more than 50,000 people. Its products are produced in 60 engineering and manufacturing centers in nine countries, and are marketed in more than 120 countries. Its new world headquarters complex stands on the site of the original Detroit plant, marking three quarters of a century of growth, progress and contribution to this diverse, dynamic city.

Campbell-Ewald Company

Detroit ad agency and Chevrolet began ride to top in 1922

With two accounts, a staff of six, and a wealth of advertising experience, Frank J. Campbell and Henry T. Ewald founded their advertising agency on February 7, 1911. Today, Campbell-Ewald is one of the top 20 agencies in the country and the largest based in Detroit.

When Campbell retired in 1917, he sold his interest to Ewald, who became sole owner and head of the agency until his death in 1953.

In 1944, Henry G. Little joined the agency as general manager and became president in 1952. After Ewald's death, Little served as both president and chairman of the board until 1958 when Thomas B. Adams became president. At 38, Adams was the youngest top executive of a major advertising agency. Little retired in November, 1966, and Lawrence R. Nelson, a 40-year veteran of the agency and vice chairman of the board, was elevated to board chairman.

Nelson retired January 31, 1968. At the same time, Adams left his presidential post to become Campbell-Ewald's new chairman of the board and chief executive officer. His entire working career spent with the agency, Adams joined Campbell-Ewald in 1945 after his release from the Naval Air Corps at the end of World War II. During his rise to the chairmanship, Adams served as a copywriter-contact man, Chevrolet account executive and account supervisor, vice president and assistant to the president, and president.

In February 1968, Adams' presidential vacancy was filled by Hugh M. Redhead. Redhead joined Campbell-Ewald from the Mellon National Bank in Pittsburgh, where he had been a senior vice president. Prior to Mellon, Redhead spent 12 years with an advertising agency — Fuller and Smith and Ross — in Pittsburgh. Redhead was chosen for Campbell-Ewald's presidency because of his extensive background in both advertising and finance. An unfortunate accident in the fall of 1975 took the life of Redhead.

In January 1976, Richard D. O'Connor was elected president to replace Redhead. O'Connor rose to the presidency from a 1956 start as a

The Campbell-Ewald Copy Department in 1949. The department co-director, L. T. Robinson (standing) is seen with (clockwise around the table) W. H. Gage, Jr.; W. B. Booth; E. M. Mulock, Jr.; J. C. Stephan; M. S. Charlton; R. S. Field, department co-director; R. J. Mauer; J. M. Bonbright; R. I. Warren; and J. N. A. Rawlins.

Frank J. Campbell (left) and Henry T. Ewald reminisce in 1951 when their company observed its 40th anniversary.

Campbell-Ewald trainee on the Chevrolet account. During the following 20 years, he held almost every Chevrolet account administration position, including a tour in the agency's Chicago office, and culminating in a January 1963, appointment as executive vice president and Chevrolet account director. In August, 1975, O'Connor was appointed executive vice president and chief operating officer of the agency.

Serving over 38 clients, Campbell-Ewald today maintains division offices in New York and Los Angeles. In addition, the agency maintains branch offices in Atlanta, Chicago, Cincinnati, Dallas, Kansas City, Phoenix, San Francisco and Chevy Chase, Maryland. It employs 600 people.

Campbell-Ewald offers a full range of skilled communications and marketing services, with particular emphasis on transportation, food, and industrial product accounts. It also operates Ceco Publishing Company, which publishes controlled-circulation magazines and produces specialized custom print and videotape communications programs.

The agency's three oldest accounts are AC-Delco (formerly United Motors Service), Delco-Remy and Chevrolet Motor Division. In 1922, Campbell-Ewald acquire the Chevrolet account, which it has maintained continuously. Chevrolet has grown from a pioneer automobile manufacturer to the world's largest, and the Chevrolet account has grown to be the world's largest single advertising account.

Campbell-Ewald takes a leading position in encouraging young men and women to educate and train themselves for positions in advertising. The agency helped found Northwood Institute at Midland, Michigan, where a school of advertising operates.

In 1955, Campbell-Ewald initiated one of the most liberal profit sharing retirement plans in the industry. The plan promotes economic security previously unknown among employees in the advertising business.

The agency is well known for its civic and community involvements. It has offered its talents to police recruiting campaigns, statewide water pollution projects, New Detroit, Inc. (an urban coalition), and such diverse organizations as the Urban League, Salvation

Army, Chamber of Commerce and Junior Achievement.

Management of Campbell-Ewald is vested in a seven-man executive committee of the board of directors and a three-man finance committee as well as the board of directors.

In November of 1972, Campbell-Ewald became part of The Interpublic Group of Companies, and part of the largest communications combine in the world.

In July of 1976, the formation of Campbell-Ewald Worldwide, with Thomas B. Adams as chairman, was announced by The Interpublic Group of Companies, Inc., parent company of Campbell-Ewald.

DETROITBANK Corporation

Michigan's oldest major bank — a tradition of strength

Only one major bank in Michigan has been serving its customers continuously for almost 130 years. That bank is Detroit Bank & Trust, the principal subsidiary bank of DETROITBANK Corporation. Founded in 1849 as the Detroit Savings Fund Institute, it had only 56 depositors with total assets of $3,287 at the completion of its first year of operation. As Detroit grew and prospered, so did the bank and later its parent company, DETROITBANK Corporation. Today, its assets approach $4.5 billion and it serves hundreds of thousands of customers throughout Michigan, the nation and the world. With equity capital of more than $250 million, DETROITBANK Corporation has one of the strongest relative capital positions in the banking industry today and ranks among the nation's leading regional bank holding companies.

From the beginning, Detroit Bank & Trust has exhibited concern for the city and its people. The following statement, from the original bank charter in 1849, exemplifies the underlying philosophy which has guided the bank throughout its history:

"It is intended to encourage the industrious and prudent and to induce those who have not hitherto been such...to save and lay by something for a period of life when they will be less able to earn a support."

Among the first directors of the Detroit Savings Fund Institute were some of Detroit's most respected leaders representing a wide range of businesses, industries and the professions. Men such as Elon Farnsworth, an attorney and first president of the bank, and directors Solomon Sibley, John Palmer, Shubael Conant and Benjamin Kercheval formed the base of tradition from which the bank has grown and prospered.

While one other bank in Michigan is larger than Detroit Bank & Trust, none can claim its tradition of uninterrupted service to customers. It is the only major bank in the state to weather successfully every financial crisis in its history — including the great Depression of the 1930s. From Elon Farnsworth to the present, the bank has had only 12 presidents. This constancy of leadership is also reflected in the directors, many having served in that capacity for 20 years or more.

Throughout, these have been men who sought to preserve and protect the assets of the customer, while keeping pace with the demands of modern technology and modern society in a planned and orderly way.

The name of the bank has changed only slightly since its beginnings. From the Detroit Savings Fund Institute in 1849, the name was changed to the Detroit Savings Bank in 1871 — and still under the direction of Elon Farnsworth. In 1933, while Joseph M. Dodge was president, the name was changed to the Detroit Bank in order to reflect the fact that customers could obtain checking and other services from the bank in addition to savings. At the time of the merger with the Detroit Trust Company in 1956, the name was changed to Detroit Bank & Trust.

Today, the traditions of Detroit Bank & Trust are carried forward by its parent company, DETROITBANK Corporation. It now operates Detroit Bank & Trust and seven other banks in Michigan, including the oldest and largest bank in Muskegon — Hackley Bank & Trust. DETROITBANK Corporation banks have a total of more than 120 offices to serve customers. While retail banking activities are concentrated in southeastern Michigan, there are nine banking offices in Muskegon and two in metropolitan Grand Rapids, Michigan. Lending activities are national and international in scope. Customers range from the paper boy to the company president, and from the corner store to the multi-national conglomerate. Individuals, companies and governments both in the United States and abroad are served by the banks of DETROITBANK Corporation.

Among the subsidiaries and affiliates of the Corporation is an equipment leasing company. Detroit Bank & Trust also operates a full-service banking office in London, England, a Canadian financial services subsidiary and a large and experienced international banking division. The trust department of Detroit Bank & Trust is the oldest and one of the largest in Michigan with trust assets under management in excess of $3.5 billion.

The traditions and history of the city are also reflected in the bank's locations and facilities. In 1849, the Detroit Savings Fund Institute opened in rented quarters in the rear of the Mariner's Church — now an official historical landmark which is part of the riverfront

Main banking room, Bank Chambers, 1890. To the right of the column stands bank president Sidney D. Miller.

renaissance in Detroit. From that location at the corner of Woodbridge and Griswold streets, the main office building was later to be erected on the site of the famous "Underground Railroad" at Griswold and State streets. During the Civil War, this was a key location in the transportation of slaves from the South into Michigan and Canada. In 1965, the present main office building was constructed on a site which was discovered to be the southwest corner of historic Fort Lernoult, which protected the City of

Detroit in the late 1700s. During excavation, remains of the fort's bastion and other relics were uncovered and are now on display at the Detroit Historical Museum. Ever mindful of its unique relationship to the history of the city, in 1974 — on the occasion of its 125th anniversary — Detroit Bank & Trust funded the publication of *Detroit and Its Banks,* the only comprehensive history of banking in Detroit.

In 1978, DETROITBANK Corporation had banks serving Michigan residents under its name in not only Detroit but

in Livonia, Southfield, Sterling, Troy, and Warren. Also part of the corporation are Hackley Bank & Trust in Muskegon, and Kentwood Bank in Kentwood.

DETROITBANK Corporation and its principal subsidiary, Detroit Bank & Trust, have built upon the traditions of the industrial heartland of America to serve the community and the nation and the world with quality and excellence in banking. During the last 130 years, it has come to represent the best that banking has to offer.

Detroit Edison

A young 75, alive and well and looking forward

Detroit Edison is as close to its customers in Detroit and Southeastern Michigan as the nearest electric switch, but most people take the company's services pretty much for granted — an indication that Detroit Edison is doing its job, just as it has since 1903.

During 1978, Detroit Edison reached its Diamond Jubilee year. In those 75 years the growth of Detroit Edison has paralled the growth of the communities it serves.

Within the lifetimes of many of its customers and retired employees, Detroit Edison has grown from its January 17, 1903 founding with 220 employes and a few thousand customers in Detroit to nearly 11,000 employees providing electric energy for more than five million people throughout 7,600 square miles of Southeastern Michigan.

During that time Detroit's population of nearly 300,000 grew to 465,000 by 1910, to nearly a million by 1920, and today is more than 1-1/3 million. Another three million people live in its suburbs. More people meant more electricity.

This growth has been generally steady but at times the pace has quickened dramatically. Shortly after 1903, for example, several new manufacturing corporations with $6 million of capital located in the Detroit area, with a promise of 77 new industrial buildings. During a single year, 1915 to 1916, industrial production in Detroit rose from $600 million to $900 million.

Newest operating electric generating facility in the Detroit Edison system is the Monroe Power Plant located near Monroe, Michigan. One of the largest coal-fired generating stations in the world, its 800-foot high stacks are the tallest concrete structures in Michigan. This plant can produce three million kilowatts.

A replica of Detroit Edison's first electric generating plant, Station A, once located at Washington Boulevard and State Street, is now located at Greenfield Village. It was the first building in the U.S. built specifically for housing electric generating equipment. Henry Ford, who worked at the original plant, had this replica erected in 1944. The original plant produced about 400 kilowatts of electricity.

Even before the turn of the century, Detroit's rapidly-increasing demand for electricity resulted in the early formation of the Edison Illuminating Company. That company's chief engineer was Henry Ford, who founded The Ford Motor Company in 1903, the same year that Edison Illuminating became Detroit Edison.

Back in 1903, total plant investment of Detroit Edison was $7.5 million. In its 75th anniversary year, 1978, Detroit Edison was a $4 billion-plus corporation.

Southeastern Michigan set many records in production during World Wars I and II, with production continuing at a rapid rate during peacetime. In the 1920s, the Buhl, Fisher, Penobscot (now City National) and Guardian buildings were completed. The Detroit-Windsor Tunnel and the Ambassador Bridge were also completed in the 1920s.

In the 1950s, Detroit completed the Ford Auditorium. And, in the 1960s, Cobo Hall, the Arena, Detroit's Civic Center and numerous other building projects were completed.

As growth continued in the Detroit area, the demand for electricity increased, and Detroit Edison grew as it kept ahead of the demand.

A frequent innovator in meeting customers' needs, Detroit Edison is credited with research bringing about the use of infrared heat for drying lacquers, development of a low-cost electric range, electric substations which operate unattended and installation of the world's largest power plant boilers.

One of the company's more recent programs assures a steady supply of low-sulfur coal from Montana for its power plants in Michigan. Over a 26-year period this new source of coal, which travels about 1,700 miles, is expected to save Detroit Edison customers about $1 billion.

The company's concern for protecting the environment goes back many years, too. As early as the mid-1920s the world's first electrostatic precipitator was installed in a Detroit Edison power plant. The device dramatically reduced particulate matter entering the air from power plant stacks. By 1982, this and other environmental protection efforts at Detroit Edison will have cost nearly $1.6 billion.

During its first three-quarters of a century Detroit Edison, like the Detroit area itself, has had its up and downs. Today, as the area enjoys a renaissance, the company too is keeping pace.

In a recent statement, Detroit Edison's Chairman and Chief Executive Officer William G. Meese noted company progress in such diverse but important areas as "customer service, environmental matters, employment of women and minority group members, plant construction, research, fuel supply, supervision, employee and retiree benefits.

"The real history of Detroit Edison," concluded Chairman Meese, "is, of course, people. I feel that our customers, employees past and present, shareholders, suppliers and others associated with Detroit Edison deserve a hearty salute for helping make it possible for the company to have grown and prospered as it has during the past 75 years.

"Yes, Detroit Edison is proud to be a young 75, alive and well and looking forward!"

The Detroit Free Press

Pace-setting morning paper produces timely innovations

In 1979 the *Detroit Free Press*, which has been responsible for many new trends in its history, enters a new era in American journalism.

In a new plant on the riverfront, the roar of the first of 42 press units is launching the *Free Press* on its way to becoming the largest newspaper in America printed entirely by the offset method. And it features news that's minutes old.

Almost 150 years earlier, on a day in May, the paper's first edition came off a press that was manually operated and contained news that was as much as four months old.

Yet, for all the mechanical and editorial progress, the paper's basic approach to serving the great Detroit and Michigan community has never varied. It was stated first by Sheldon McKnight and restated scores of years later by John S. Knight.

Said Publisher McKnight in his first edition of *"The Democratic Free Press and Michigan Intelligencer"* on Thursday, May 5, 1831:

"The Democratic citizens of this territory, having found the two newspapers already established here completely under the control of the city aristocracy, we have been compelled to set up an independent press."

One hundred and nineteen years later in May, 1940, John S. Knight and his associates bought the paper. He outlined what his policy would be in these words:

"We do not operate in the interests of any class, group, faction or political party...we are ourselves free and our

On election night. Nov. 5, 1929, politicians flocked to the Detroit Free Press news room to get results.

An early (1859) home of the Detroit Free Press at the northwest corner of Griswold and Woodbridge.

paper shall be free...free to the truth, good manners and good sense...we shall be for whatever measure is best adapted to defending the rights and liberties of the people and advancing useful knowledge."

Success resulted in each instance. Within months, McKnight's weekly had grown to such stature that he was able to convert it into the first daily newspaper in Michigan by 1835, and by the early 1960s, with Lee Hills as publisher, the *Free Press* had become the fifth largest morning paper in the United States.

In the process, it had also taken the lead in the Detroit circulation race, until *The News* recaptured first place with the purchase of the *Detroit Times* in November, 1960.

In between, the *Free Press* had managed to add luster to itself and to American journalistic history, on the one hand by winning several Pulitzer Prizes and on the other with many innovations.

It led the fight to gain statehood for Michigan (secured in 1837), and with a new owner, Wilbur F. Storey, it gave impetus to the tradition of factual and objective reporting of both local and national news.

Storey expanded telegraph and correspondent services to cover events all over the country and he created a city staff, which included one reporter who walked the length of the riverfront each day to get the latest shipping news. He also introduced the interview and the printing of testimony in important trials, and he put out Michigan's first Sunday newspaper.

Early in the Civil War, a group of newspapermen gathered at the *Free Press* to organize the Western Associated Press, which subsequently merged with the New York Associated Press to form the world's greatest news-gathering organization.

William E. Quinby succeeded Storey

as editor, and the newspaper achieved an international reputation when it established a branch in London and began printing the London edition of the *Free Press* in 1881.

It was the first American newspaper published in the Old World, and it sold more than 90,000 copies a week, a large circulation for those times.

Quinby also introduced feature writers, among them the famed Edgar A. Guest, the people's poet, and he presented the first Washington columnist to appear in a Detroit newspaper. In 1878, Quinby put together the first newspaper supplement designed especially for women. He called it "The Household."

The paper has outgrown several plants. The most recent was built in the

1920's at 321 W. Lafayette, but by the early 1970s circulation had soared to well over 600,000, dictating still another move. Plans were completed for a $48-million production plant on 22 acres at the foot of Eighth Street.

As Lee Hills, who came to the *Free Press* in December, 1951, and who played a major role in its subsequent growth into a strong, home-delivered morning newspaper, has said: "Paying attention to the readers means doing something for them, giving them information they can put to use immediately, in short, providing them the instant opportunity to improve the quality of their daily lives."

Today, the *Free Press* continues to build on these traditional concepts.

Detroit International Bridge Company

Bridge links two countries and handles over five million vehicles a year

The Ambassador Bridge, the world's longest suspension bridge when it opened in November 1929, joins the United States and Canada at their busiest international crossing point.

This two-mile-long bridge which joins Detroit, Michigan and Windsor, Ontario, has a span of 1,850 feet across the Detroit River, with a clearance of 152 feet to accommodate St. Lawrence Seaway and lake traffic shipping.

In 1977 this bridge carried more than 5,200,000 vehicles and about 10 million people across the border. Owned and operated by the Detroit International Bridge Company, which is a public stock company with about 1,600 shareholders, the bridge observes it 50th birthday in 1979.

The Detroit-Canada Tunnel opened in 1930 and the two cross-river facilities handle about 10 million vehicles a year. Passenger ferries operated until the late 1930s.

Constructed at a cost of $23.5 million and financed privately, the Ambassador Bridge was the culmination of several years of effort by the late Joseph A. Bower who had the financial ingenuity and skill to develop a plan and make it succeed.

Shortly after World War I, Charles Evan Fowler, consulting engineer for the City of New York developed plans for a combined railway and vehicular bridge across the Detroit River. He organized

The Ambassador Bridge

the American Transit Co. and the Canadian Transit Co. and in early 1921 obtained government authorization to proceed with his plan.

Fowler's plans never materialized, mainly due to lack of financing and the problem of land acquisition. Because a bridge had to be built with enough height to allow shipping to pass underneath, it meant very long and expensive approaches to provide grades suitable for locomotive operation.

In the early 1920s Joseph Bower came on the scene and in 1924 he took options on the rights of the two companies formed by Fowler, and retained the services of McClintic-Marshall Co. of Pittsburgh, to handle the engineering and construction of the bridge. It took Bower another three years of planning, approvals and financing before actual construction began in 1927.

Bower, who died in August 1977, at the age of 96, came from an impoverished background centered in Detroit. With only a grade school education, he

managed to pass the State Bar examinations after bypassing law school, and later he learned accounting. In 1899, at the age of 19, he went to work for the Detroit Trust Co.

He developed an ability to make poor loans productive and used many innovative methods to achieve success. This ability subsequently led him into the New York banking circles where in 1916 he became vice president of the Liberty National Bank, assigned to save the "soured loans" made to troubled companies, including Mack Trucks and Ford Motor. By 1924 he was a vice-president of the New York Trust Co.

A practical businessman, Bower saw

in the bridge idea a profitable enterprise which he believed could be achieved with private funds.

Bower negotiated the purchase of all private property needed for the vehicular bridge approaches, and as a private venture he circumvented political entrapments.

Physical work on the bridge started on September 20, 1927 and construction progressed rapidly and smoothly with the 363-foot-high steel tower piers and concrete anchorages in place.

Suspension cables were strung and work had started on hanging the bridge floor platforms, when suddenly on March 5, 1929, only a few months before the planned completion date, all work stopped.

Engineers learned that identical high tensile cable being used on a Rhode Island bridge was deteriorating quickly, so they decided to replace the Ambassador Bridge cables with proven cold drawn steel wire.

This involved removal of the original 19-inch cables, which was an unprecedented piece of work. New cables were strung, with a loss of only four-and-a-half months.

Despite these handicaps, construction on the bridge finished on November 6, 1929, two years and three months after the contract became effective, and at a cost one percent less than budget.

The bridge was formally dedicated on November 11, 1929, with nearly 200,000 people crowding onto the structure to mark its completion. It was opened to traffic on November 15.

The cash fare for a car and driver in 1929 was 50 cents, and the same rate is in effect today if tickets are purchased.

Bower relinquished sole ownership in 1939, but he continued to serve as chairman of the board for 20 years and was honorary chairman until his death.

Today, his son, Joseph W. Bower of Florida, is chairman, while Roy G. Lancaster of Windsor serves as president and general manager.

The Detroit Lions, Inc.

A transplanted lion's roar has been heard since '34

They come from all over the Midwest, and points elsewhere, to watch the Detroit Lions battle NFL rivals in the architectural wonder called the Pontiac Silverdome. And why not?

It is perched in almost the exact population center of the three major counties which make up the Detroit metropolitan area... Wayne, Oakland and Macomb.

Covering 10 square acres, it seats an awesome 80,638 fans under a glass-impregnated teflon roof which is kept up there with air pressure while the Lions ply their muscular trade in a style which attracted just a shade under 2 million fans for their first three seasons as Silverdome tenants.

But it wasn't always that way.

The seeds of professional football were first planted in Detroit way back in 1920 and called the Heralds. Nice sounding name. But they wouldn't grow.

In 1925 more seeds were dropped and named the Detroit Panthers. No fans. So long, Panthers.

Three years later, another variety called the Detroit Wolverines were sprinkled in the area which then was... and still is... a hotbed of collegiate football. They didn't even finish the '28 season.

But six years later, in 1934, a new approach was tried. Instead of planting seeds, an entire pro football team was dug up in Portsmouth, Ohio, and transplanted to Detroit. They were named the Lions.

Pro football with all its thrills was in Detroit to stay.

They played at the University of Detroit stadium in those early days, some 10 miles from the heart of the city. Led by Hall of Famer/Earl "Dutch" Clark and the likes of stars such as Ernie Caddell, Ox Emerson, Ace Gutowsky, Glenn Presnell and big George Christensen, they won their first

Earl (Dutch) Clark was the Lions' first super-star back in the early days of the Detroit franchise, a charter member of pro football's Hall of Fame.

10 games including seven consecutive shutouts, their first season.

But their first championship had to wait until 1935 when they dropped the New York Giants in the title game, 26-7.

The man who brought them to the Motor City — George A. Richards — also brought along the idea of having the Lions play a game on Thanksgiving Day. The first one was in 1934. It still is being played now as the Lions look at the calendar and find they are not far removed from their 50th season as a Detroit-area institution.

Like the game of pro football itself, the Lions were, are and probably always will be controversial, argumentative and sometimes violent both on the field and off.

After averaging around 15,000 fans a game at U-D, they decided to move downtown in 1938 to the baseball park called Briggs Stadium with its 50,000 capacity. They attracted 198,000 fans that first year, but then started skidding on the gridiron and at the gate.

Owner Richards sold out in 1940 to Fred Mandel, a Chicago department store tycoon. Coaches came — and went in almost predictable order. In 1942, they were winless in 11 games. They rallied a little from year to year, then slipped back again. Mandel finally gave up the effort and sold the club to a group of Detroit businessmen brought together by Edwin J. Anderson and D. Lyle Fife in 1948.

Then along came Bobby Layne, a cocky Texan with a drawl with not much of a throwing arm but with the flair of a riverboat gambler. He was *the* leader and quickly he was given talent to lead. Like li'l Doak Walker out of SMU. Big Leon Hart of Notre Dame, receiver Cloyce Box, Lou Creekmur, Fum

The Lions' first NFL championship trophy was won in 1935.

Bobby Layne (No. 22) quarterbacked the Lions to fantastic seasons in the 1950s after coming out of Texas.

McGraw and Tulsa Bob Smith were the nucleus.

They broke even in 1950 with a 6-6 mark to end red marks on the victory side of the page but in 1951 they caught fire under Coach Raymond (Buddy) Parker, another Texan who was moody and superstitious but who was a brilliant football analyst.

Parker led the Lions into dominance

during the 1950s. Six times in seven straight seasons they either won — or lost — a title on the final weekend of the season. They won the championship in '52 and won it again in 1953, and when they didn't win they were close.

Layne's magic on offense, plus the defensive skills of a rookie named Joe Schmidt, who joined the team in 1953, kept the fans coming, and they came in bigger numbers as pro football hit the television screen and made even stay-at-homes stand up and cheer.

After a 9-3 record in 1956, Parker suddenly quit as coach. His top assistant, George Wilson, replaced him and in 1957 the Lions were again

crowned champions.

Then, as Lion fortunes fluctuated, controversy swirled among the large group of club owners until it threatened to explode. William Clay Ford, grandson of the automotive pioneer and a top official of the Ford Motor Company, was persuaded to puchase control of the franchise, and he did in 1964.

The NFL began expanding and the Lions were placed in a division in which Green Bay (under Vince Lombardi) ran off a string of titles until Minnesota (under Bud Grant) took over where the Pack left off.

The Lions hit the Playoffs in 1970 under Coach Joe Schmidt but restlessly ran off a string of finishes as runners-up while coaches came and went.

In 1975, the Pontiac Silverdome was ready and the Lions made their move. It shifted them only 20-odd miles from their former base but it opened up an entirely new area of fans stretching up into the sports-minded state of Michigan.

The 1934 "transplant" had become a success. And the roots of pro football are growing deeper each year.

The Detroit News

A newspaper that enraged and enriched a great city

When James E. Scripps founded his newspaper in 1873, he had $5,000 in cash, high hopes, and some odd notions. The cash went fast and the high hopes plummeted. But the odd notions about newspapering worked — and they helped shape a great city as well as a big, expanding news organization.

Scripps, 38 at the time, a tall man with large eyes, black hair and full beard, called his new paper The Evening News. It was a four-page tabloid that sold for two cents, three pennies less than the price of four rival papers. The paper reflected Scripps' opinion that newspapers of the day were too expensive, too big, terribly dull, and mostly useless.

"I believe," said Scripps in his first editorial, "that a wide diffusion of wholesome literature is a public good, and that this might be very greatly promoted by placing the subscription price of the newspaper so low as to bring it within the means of everyone."

James E. Scripps, founder of The Detroit News

Critics might carp that daily journalism is hardly "wholesome literature." (There is, however, a certain charm in reading, 105 year later, items in that first News about a "lunatic on a locomotive," the low-born dog who played the piano, and a woman named Rice who fell from a wharf.) Still, Scripps wisely put the paper on a course of doing

Peter B. Clark, president, The Evening News Association and publisher, The Detroit News.

great good for the greatest number.

He had other ideas, equally odd at the time but refreshingly perceptive even today. He argued that newspapers ought to be made to be read by everybody, not just the educated, the rich, the influential. He insisted that newspapers ought to "convey intelligence" to

211

the mass of people.

Although it got off to a slow start (losing nearly $5,000 the first year), *The News* attracted a loyal and broad readership. By the end of its second year, the paper could post a respectable profit; within five years, its circulation had leaped to 36,000 daily.

It was, of course, only the beginning. Scripps' newspaper, renamed *The Detroit News* in 1905, grew to become the centerpiece of an independent communications company that today includes television stations in Tucson, Arizona; Oklahoma City; Mobile, Alabama; Austin, Texas; and Washington, D.C. It also owns an AM-FM radio station in Detroit, a daily newspaper in Palm Springs, California, and a graphics company with printing operations and five smaller newspapers in New Jersey. Revenues of the corporate parent, The Evening News Association, topped $175 million in 1977.

With current circulation of more than 630,000 daily (and over 820,000 on Sundays), *The News* ranks as the nation's largest afternoon daily and the fifth largest newspaper in the United States. It boasts one of the most modern newspaper plants in operation, a $40-million-plus marvel of automation completed in 1973.

The News and the city enraged and enriched each other as they grew apace. Over the years, the newspaper mounted crusade after crusade against corrupt people and practices, both public and private. Feisty and tenacious, the paper allied itself with causes popular with common people — and won an uncommon number of readers.

Today, there is a "renaissance" in the community. It is neither a place nor a symbol but a good feeling, and it affects a broader community encompassing 4.5 million people in southeastern Michigan — a community whose activities still are mirrored by its leading newspaper.

The newspaper company which James E. Scripps started remains today in the hands of his descendants and heirs. The president is Peter B. Clark, a great-grandson, who earned a doctorate in political science at the University of Chicago and taught at Yale University before joining *The News* in 1961. In an era of corporate amalgams and diffused control, especially in media companies, *The News* remains among the few independent, privately owned communications companies.

The Detroit News, like the city, thrives on challenge. Both grew up under the stimulation and excitement of fierce competitiveness and occasional chaos. That, perhaps more than anything, forged a confidence that energy and enterprise made things work.

Ex-Cell-O Corporation

Philosophy of 1919 still valid 60 years later

In 1919, on the second floor of a small two-story building on downtown Beaubien Street, a group of men with the philosophy, "Quality and precision on a mass production basis," founded Ex-Cell-O Tool and Manufacturing Company and began making drill jig bushings and supplying the automobile industry with various production parts.

The company produced a precision ball bearing in 1922, which, when incorporated in a grinding spindle in 1923, determined to a great degree the direction of the company's development. This spindle enabled Ex-Cell-O to achieve speed, accuracy and long life in its own manufacture of precision parts and was basic to the design of most of the machine tools subsequently developed.

At about that time, commercial aircraft companies began developing the airplane into a reputable mode of travel. Aircraft require precision parts, and, in 1925, Ex-Cell-O pioneered in the mass production of those parts. When Charles Lindbergh made his famous solo flight to Paris in 1927, Ex-Cell-O aircraft parts helped to power the engine of "The Spirit of St. Louis". Ex-Cell-O's involvement in aircraft parts

Ex-Cell-O Corporation had its beginnings as Ex-Cell-O Tool & Mfg. Co. on the second floor of this building at 184 (now 1214) Beaubien in downtown Detroit.

production became so deep that, in 1928, the company was renamed Ex-Cell-O Aircraft and Tool Corporation.

The Depression marked a renaissance for Ex-Cell-O, for it was then that the company's program of growth through research, development and acquisitions was born.

As Ex-Cell-O moved into the 1930s, Continental Tool Works, a cutting tool manufacturer, was acquired. New product developments followed one after another.

The company introduced a special purpose machine for multiple drilling — a precision boring machine it had been developing for several years. New models of the machine and new cutting tools were brought out almost annually during the subsequent years. And, in 1935, the first commercial precision thread grinder was marketed by Ex-Cell-O.

During that period, Ex-Cell-O began replacing glass milk bottles with paperboard cartons. Through the development of its Pure-Pak® packaging machine, Pure-Pak paperboard milk containers (another Ex-Cell-O development) could be automatically formed, filled and sealed. The world began pouring milk from paperboard containers and continues to do so today, using more paperboard cartons than any other milk container.

The company's expanding product line called for a less confining name, and, in 1937, Ex-Cell-O Aircraft and Tool Corporation became Ex-Cell-O Corporation.

World War II saw the corporation gear for war. Ex-Cell-O was one of the first companies to anticipate the effects of national defense on its production, and it initiated research on aircraft parts, shell-turning machines and other products.

During the war, Ex-Cell-O produced millions of aircraft parts, and other Ex-Cell-O-built equipment played a major role in helping other industrial concerns meet the demands placed on them by a wartime economy.

Peace brought prosperity and a continuing desire to grow. Following the war, Ex-Cell-O acquired Robbins Engineering, Accurate Bushing, Michigan Tool, Cadillac Gage, Bryant Grinder, Remex Electronics, Willey's Carbide Tool, Micromatic Hone, Amco, Beaver Tool and Engineering, Kent-Owens Machine Tool Works, Conveyor Specialties, Greenlee Bros., A. E. Parker & Sons and, most recently, McCord Corporation.

Foreign expansion included the formation of Ex-Cell-O Corporation of Canada, Ltd., Ex-Cell-O Corporation (England) Ltd. and Ex-Cell-O GmbH in West Germany.

Today, Ex-Cell-O is one of America's major industrial corporations. With eight locations in the Detroit area alone, including its executive offices in Troy,

Ex-Cell-O Corporation today has its executive offices in this sleek, modern structure in Troy. Its 15,000 employees produce thousands of different products in more than 60 plants, offices and developmental facilities in the United States, Canada and overseas.

the corporation has more than 60 plants, offices and developmental facilities. Its 15,000 employees produce thousands of products in more than 30 broad lines. These range from packaging machines that fill the world's milk containers, to impact-absorbing bumper systems for lighter cars, to advanced machine tools and tooling concepts for industry.

"Since its recent merger with McCord (a Detroit-based company since 1908), Ex-Cell-O has become an all-new corporation," said Edward J. Giblin,

chairman and chief executive officer. He noted that the success of Ex-Cell-O has been due primarily to its ability to identify opportunities for growth and to successfully develop and/or acquire products with advanced technology or of a highly proprietary nature. Mr. Giblin stated, "We believe that such opportunities offer even greater potential for growth in the future, and we are committed to research and development efforts within our sphere of expertise to achieve continuing profitable growth in the years ahead."

First Federal Savings of Detroit

State's largest savings & loan has many 'firsts' to its name

Walter Gehrke was a discouraged man when he picked up his *Detroit Free Press* on June 10, 1933. The small real estate and mortgage company he headed in those Depression days had almost nothing but delinquent accounts on its books. As Gehrke recalled later, "All sources of credit for any purpose, including saving one's home, had completely dried up. Home-owners were facing the catastrophe of eviction. Trying to do one's duty under these desperate conditions was a sad and difficult experience."

When he tossed the paper down, that discouraged man had been transformed into a hopeful man, a man galvanized into action. For in it was a small article announcing passage of the Home Owners Loan Act by Congress, for the relief of people who were about to lose their homes. The Act also provided for the organization of savings and loan associations by federal charter, with the assistance of government funds.

First Federal's first home was at 150 West Fort Street. The small office opened for business in 1934, with furnishings and fixtures valued at $54.72.

That bit of newsprint, combined with Walter Gehrke's courage and persua-

siveness, generated the birth of First Federal Savings and Loan Association of Detroit — a multi-billion-dollar concern that Gehrke always believed was the first savings and loan association in the country started under the new act of Congress.

Gehrke boarded the next train to Washington to find out what the new law was all about. Later, he confessed it was rather a wild-goose chase, since the Act was so new that nobody could explain it. But someone in Washington did suggest getting up a petition requesting a charter for a savings and loan association.

Upon returning to Detroit, Gehrke managed to get 60 friends to sign a hand-written petition — the petition believed to be No. 1 — only to learn after filing it that the government had printed standard petition forms, and that it had to be done over.

Getting responsible signers was no easy task, for nearly all of Detroit's business people had money problems and had lost confidence in financial institutions. But eventually, Gehrke got 104 signatures on the new petition, and promises for a total of $8,000 in contributions. First Federal was on its way.

A charter was granted in December, 1933. Shareholders met for the first time on January 10, 1934, to adopt by-laws

In 1965, First Federal moved into this 23-story, twin-towered skyscraper at Woodward and Michigan, in the heart of downtown Detroit, where it is now a landmark.

and elect directors. The association applied for membership in the Federal Home Loan Bank in Indianapolis the next day. Minutes of the April board meeting proudly noted that mortgage loans totaling $15,800 had been approved.

By the following October, assets had climbed to $100,000 — thanks to new deposits and U. S. Treasury funds — and First Federal was ready to open its first office. Quarters were in a small room at 150 West Fort Street (the site is now part of the Federal Reserve Bank Building), with furnishings and fixtures valued at $54.72.

In 1942, First Federal moved into its own home at the corner of Lafayette and Griswold. The association continued its steady growth, and when Walter Gehrke died in December, 1963, First Federal had passed the half-billion dollar milestone.

Meanwhile, it had again become time to move to larger quarters. Reaffirming its faith in, and commitment to, downtown Detroit, First Federal decided to build a landmark edifice at Woodward and Michigan, on the site of Detroit's first skyscraper, the Majestic Building.

First Federal's 23-story, twin-towered skyscraper opened in August, 1965. Built of faceted dark granite and glare-refracting glass, the towers have indeed become a contemporary Detroit landmark and have won national honors for the architectural firm of Smith, Hinchman and Grylls.

First Federal has compiled many "firsts" in its history. It was one of the first lending institutions in the metropolitan Detroit area to make FHA and VA loans, and was principal mortgagee for Detroit's first urban renewal project, the Lafayette Pavilion Apartments. It was the first savings association in the area to open neighborhood branches, and the first Michigan S & L to install computer systems and 24-hour automatic teller service.

Under the direction of Hans Gehrke, Jr., chairman of the board and nephew of First Federal's founder, and James A. Aliber, president and chief executive officer, the association has adhered to its original goals: Encouraging thrift by providing a secure place to save, and encouraging home ownership by providing mortgage funds.

From its humble beginnings with a home-made petition and a few thousand dollars, First Federal Savings of Detroit has grown to become the largest savings and loan association in Michigan — indeed, the largest outside of California — with offices in Southeastern Michigan, the Saginaw Valley and Grand Rapids.

Ford Motor Company

From one man and his dreams to a global enterprise

Ford Motor Company joined the business world at a time when automobile companies were making fast starts — and even faster fades. In 1903 alone, more than 80 new auto companies were started.

Most of them soon disappeared, but Ford thrived and has developed into a mainstay of the domestic economy in the United States and an important force in international trade.

The company started with just 10 employees in a small, converted wagon factory on Detroit's Mack Avenue on June 16, 1903. Its assets consisted mainly of some tools, blueprints, plans, patents and $28,000 in cash scraped together by 12 investors.

The first Ford Motor Company car — the 1903 Model A — was advertised as "the most perfect machine on the market" and "so simple that a boy of 15 can run it."

When he introduced the Model T in October, 1908, Henry Ford was on the way toward achieving his goal "to build a motor car for the multitude." The light, durable Model T had a base price of $825, which was cut sharply in later years thanks to mass-production cost reductions. Shown here is the Model T Touring Car.

The car may have been perfect and simple, but business wasn't. In about a month, the new company had all but run through its cash. Then, on July 15, a check arrived from a Chicago dentist — the first person to buy a car from the company. The stockholders, who had seen the bank balance dwindle to $223.65, breathed a collective sigh of relief as Dr. Ernst Pfennig's check for $850 was deposited.

Shaky start notwithstanding, Ford Motor Company has grown into one of the world's leading industrial concerns.

Its products are sold in more than 185 countries and territories, and in 1977, it had record worldwide car, truck and tractor sales of 6.5 million units. It employed an average of 479,000 men and women in nearly 300 manufacturing, assembly, engineering and research facilities. Its assets were valued at nearly $11 billion and there were 335,000 stockholders around the world.

It all started with Henry Ford's dream of building a simple but durable car priced low enough to be within financial reach of virtually any working man. The Model T — introduced in the fall of 1908 — was the essence of that dream, and it became the symbol of low-cost, reliable transportation. Model T production topped 10,000 units in its first year, an industry record at the time. But even that didn't satisfy the demand. Building each car by hand was too slow.

Henry Ford began to subdivide the

In the spring of 1902, a year and a half before Ford Motor Company was established, Henry Ford (right) hired bicycle racer Barney Oldfield to drive Ford's huge "999" race car in the famed Grosse Pointe, Michigan, auto race. Oldfield won, setting an American speed record and launching a legendary career.

When his only son, Edsel, died prematurely at the age of 49 in 1943, Henry Ford resumed the presidency of the company until the end of World War II. His eldest grandson, Henry Ford II, now chairman of the board, became president in September 1945.

Even as Henry Ford II drove the industry's first postwar car off the assembly line, he was making plans to reorganize and decentralize the company, which was losing money at the rate of several million dollars a month. Henry Ford II's postwar rebuilding program has been called the most phenomenal comeback in U.S. industrial history.

Today, Ford is one of the largest industrial corporations in the world and the oldest automobile company in the United States. In addition to automobiles, trucks and tractors, the company produces steel, glass, vinyl, paint and automotive radios. Through a subsidiary, it produces sophisticated electronic components for use in worldwide communications, space exploration and national defense. Ford also operates financing, insurance and automotive replacement parts businesses.

As it completes its 75th year, Ford Motor Company has grown from one man and his dreams into a global enterprise making an important contribution to international economic stability.

work, bringing parts to employees and scheduling the parts to arrive at the right spot at the right time. In 1913, after nearly three years of development, he and his staff devised a moving assembly-line system for automotive assembly. This mass-production system eventually made it possible to provide all the cars the public wanted, at affordable prices.

On January 5, 1914, Ford startled the world by announcing that he would pay his employees $5 for an eight-hour day. That was twice the existing rate for a nine-hour day, and it caused a sensation. The next morning, 10,000 job applicants lined up at the Highland Park (Michigan) plant.

By 1919, Henry Ford had bought out all outside stockholders — at a cost of over $105 million. (Ford Motor Company became a publicly owned corporation again in 1955 and today Ford stock is listed on major stock exchanges throughout the world. Company stockholders reside in all 50 states, the District of Columbia and in 80 foreign countries and territories.)

General Motors Corporation

Leadership and redimensioned cars revolutionize the auto industry

The automobile was still largely regarded as a sport in 1908 and few people could afford one. But William C. Durant was a man of vision, and, better than most, he foresaw the future of automobiles.

Durant had first made a name for himself as the leading wagon and carriage producer in the United States. When he reorganized the failing Buick Motor Company, it, too, became an industry leader.

But in 1908, Durant took a step that would establish his business credentials as nothing he had done before. He formed a company called General Motors — today General Motors Corporation, the world's largest industrial corporation.

Other automakers had built their businesses by expanding existing facilities. Durant built General Motors by bringing together many small automobile producers and component and parts manufacturers in a single holding company. It was an idea that worked very well. By 1919, GM was already the fifth largest industrial enterprise in the world.

That same year, the corporation began building the General Motors Building in the New Center area of Detroit. The first tenants began moving into the 15-story Albert Kahn-designed office structure the following year. It has served as corporate headquarters ever since and was named a National Historic Landmark in 1978.

In the post-World War I slump of 1920, the bottom dropped out of the automobile business. Durant was forced to resign as president of General

The General Motors Building on Grand Boulevard in the New Center area of Detroit is the headquarters and administrative offices of General Motors.

Motors. Operating control passed to Pierre S. du Pont of the du Pont Company, a substantial GM investor.

In 1923, GM executive Alfred P. Sloan, Jr., was named president of the

215

corporation. He was to be part of top GM management for 33 years until his retirement in 1956, and his brilliant innovations in management have been adopted by businesses around the world.

One of the most important things Sloan did was establish the product policy of producing cars "for every purse and purpose." This was the idea that a variety of cars would be sold in different price areas, one for each car division. Sloan also developed the system in which each division is an integrated business selling a separate group of products. The concept of management by committee was also produced under Sloan's guidance. This concept links decentralized operating divisions with policy coordination from corporate committees at the top.

Management by committee is the system that still governs GM today — along with a board of directors composed largely of "outside" directors — men and women not part of corporate management. Among the top committees are the executive committee, the finance committee, and the administration committee. Another is the public policy committee, established in 1970, to give matters of broad national concern a permanent place at the highest level of management.

During World War II, GM halted civilian production completely and converted its plants to an all-out war

The 1979 Cadillac Eldorado, one of GM's redesigned personal luxury cars.

effort. Car-making resumed after the war, and postwar expansion saw production soar.

GM entered the small car field in 1959 with Chevrolet's rear-engine Corvair. Other small cars followed.

More important than individual small car models was the plan GM adopted in the early 1970s to redimension its entire auto line-up for better fuel economy. Weight and exterior size would be reduced while interior room and comfort were retained. GM Chairman Thomas A. Murphy called it "the most comprehensive, ambitious, far-reaching, and costly program of its kind in the history of our industry."

The first "downsized" cars were GM's 1977 full-size autos — about a foot shorter and 700 pounds lighter than their predecessors. They proved an instant hit and were followed in 1978 by redesigned intermediates.

GM established records for worldwide factory sales of passenger cars and

trucks in 1977, selling a total of 9,068,000 units. Besides Chevrolet, Pontiac, Oldsmobile, Buick, and Cadillac cars — and other overseas models — the corporation also manufactures such products as trucks, buses, locomotives, diesel engines, construction and earth-moving equipment, and household appliances.

GM is owned by 1,245,000 stockholders. Worldwide employment averaged 812,000 people in the first quarter of 1978. The corporation has 121 plants in 21 states and 77 cities in the United States plus additional facilities in 35 other countries.

Extensive testing facilities are maintained at the GM Proving Ground at Milford, Michigan, and the Desert Proving Ground in Mesa, Arizona. Staff work in research, design, manufacturing development, engineering, and environmental activities is done at the General Motors Technical Center in Warren, Michigan.

Giffels Associates, Inc.

Dedication to quality service built design firm's reputation

Ernest R. McCamman, president of Giffels Associates, Inc., believes the architectural-engineering and planning firm of 700 professionals has indeed fulfilled the dreams of its founders, Raymond Francis Giffels and Victor Emil Vallet.

In its 54 year history, Giffels has designed over $10 billion of construction work.

But its beginnings were on a more humble scale. In digging through company archives, when the company celebrated its golden anniversary in 1975, a ledger was uncovered that recorded the firm's first jobs. In scrawled penmanship, a bookkeeper noted proudly under the heading "Job" the

first project, for Vulcan Iron works — State Theatre. The fee was $24, promptly paid.

Today, global assignments yield annual fees totaling just under $30 million.

It all began in 1925 when the firm was founded by a partnership agreement between Giffels and Vallet, both engineers employed at that time by the Albert Kahn organization. Their first office was in Detroit's Lincoln Building (no longer standing), but because of growth a move was made within a year to larger quarters in the Marquette Building, maintained until 1978.

In 1928, the firm was incorporated as

Giffels & Vallet, Inc., the year Louis Rossetti joined the organization to further architectural design capability. A year later, the growing volume of such work led the company to adopt the name, "Giffels & Vallet, Inc., L. Rossetti, Associated Engineers and Architects."

It was also in 1928, that a Windsor, Ontario office was opened. Today, Giffels Associates, Ltd., independently owned, is headquartered in Rexdale, Ontario, a Toronto suburb.

On Vallet's retirement, in 1956, Raymond Giffels was elected president and held the position until his death in 1963. He was succeeded by his brother, Carl A. Giffels. Shortly, thereafter, the assets of the company were purchased by 15 of the principals and today there are 111 shareholders. All are actively engaged in the day-to-day activities of the firm. It was during this period that the staff peaked at 1270 and the company name became Giffels and Rossetti, Inc. and remained so until

1969 when Louis Rossetti retired.

Carl Giffels retired in December of 1972 and Alfred M. Entenman, Jr. was elected president, who was succeeded by McCamman in December 1978.

Giffels' staff of 700, one of the largest in the design profession, takes pride in the fact that even though the firm's billings have increased from an initial $24 fee to millions, it is more satisfying that repeat assignments from clients represent as much as 70 percent of the workload.

And to accommodate an anticipated increase in project volume, Giffels headquarters was relocated in 1977 to a five-story, 200,000 square foot building in Southfield, Michigan, a northern suburb of Detroit. The Detroit office is now at 333 W. Fort Street serving as a vital and permanent branch. Giffels also has offices in Frankfurt, Germany and Washington, D.C.

Diversification of assignments has always been Giffels' forte. McCamman recalled a 1955 *Saturday Evening Post* article titled, "The Boys with the $5,000,000,000 Brains." The sidebar read in part... "when they aren't playing with paper dolls, they (Giffels-Vallet-Rossetti) will draw you plans for anything, to do anything; factories, atomic reactors, baseball stadiums, race-track grandstands. But houses? Not a chance — too difficult." One of the firm's vice presidents said at the time, "The average home is a hotel, restaurant, factory, utility plant and a clubhouse all in one miniature package with a price limit on it. That's too tough."

Another bygone recollection pertains to Raymond Giffels, who liked little pranks. The *Post* article cites, "On a visit

Co-founders of Giffels, left to right, the late Raymond F. Giffels and Victor E. Vallet. At right is Louis A. Rossetti, who joined the design organization in 1928.

to Paris last summer he discovered gleefully that his draftsmanship enabled him to change the lettering on post cards of the Eiffel Tower so that the alteration would be almost unnoticeable. This enabled him to present pictures of a little job he did in Paris, the Giffels Tower."

Since 1925, the firm's philosophy has not varied... "The personal pride that all of our employes have in their work is the key to what is called the Giffels' Attitude. It is the dedication and determination to provide a truly meaningful service; it is the combination of our creativity and expertise directed toward providing our clients with any single phase of the many services we offer — any combination of these services — or the complete range of our total capability. No project is too big. Just as importantly — no project is too small...and...each project is handled as though it is the most important one in the office."

The big and small projects designed by Giffels in Detroit have been an important stimuli to Detroit's stature and growth. They include Cobo Hall, the headquarters for Blue Cross and Blue

Giffels President Ernest R. McCamman

Shield, Wayne State University's Scott Hall and Clinics Building, the new Detroit General Hospital, Wayne County Jail, Detroit Edison assignments, the Fort Street Post Office, Jeffersonian Apartment, expansion of Briggs Stadium (now Tiger Stadium), Chrysler's Huber Avenue Foundry, St. Martha's Episcopal Church, a downtown branch of the Manufacturers National Bank of Detroit, WDIV-TV Studio, Cadillac Motor headquarters, an office for Chevrolet Gear and Axle, Henry Ford High School, assignments for Detroit's Water and Sewerage Department and, on a smaller scale, the remodeling of Detroit's Press Club.

Giffels is proud of its contributions in making Detroit a better place to live and work.

Frank B. Hall & Co. of Michigan

Original service concepts prevail as company grows with Detroit

April, 1939 saw Detroit, the industrial giant of transportation, emerging from the Great Depression — surviving a period when because of the nature of its prime industries, it was probably harder hit than any other city in the United States.

During that month, three men of long experience in the insurance industry decided to stake their fortunes and

futures on their own competence as an independent insurance agency. These three — Robert J. Byrnes, M. Frank McCaffrey and William Price — established their business as Byrnes-McCaffrey, Inc. The fourth partner, Frank Dimond, joined the group shortly thereafter and together they set out to establish what was to become one of the country's leading

independent insurance agencies.

The new firm soon found itself in the midst of a resurgent Detroit as the city and its industries stretched to maximum capacity to meet the challenges of World War II. The end of the war found Byrnes-McCaffrey, Inc. well established and prepared to embark upon a solid and prolonged period of growth.

During this period, the company's outstanding reputation, established in such a short space of time, enabled it to first provide services for the Automotive "Big Three," headquartered in Detroit.

Continued growth necessitated the construction of a new building at 1534 East Jefferson Avenue and operations at this site were started in 1953. This

Before moving into the Renaissance Center, this building at 1534 East Jefferson Avenue was the Michigan headquarters for Frank B. Hall & Co.

period also saw the establishment of separate Life and Accident, Aviation, Bonds and Surety and Boiler and Machinery Departments, to complement the existing Fire, Casualty and Marine Departments. This growth was in line with the original concept of the founders that customers were entitled to the full services of experts in every field rather than merely the contact of a generalized account executive.

During the 1960s, the solid base established in the '40s and '50s enabled the firm to continue its growth in every line of insurance. The list of customers now included a large share of the automotive giants and many principal automotive industry suppliers. Also among the valued clients by this time were the major public utilities and leading financial institutions.

The 1960s era also visited some serious catastrophes upon Detroit and surrounding areas. In 1964, a tornado wrought havoc upon the Anchor Bay area of Lake St. Clair, leaving hundreds homeless and many homes and businesses totally or partially destroyed. The need for prompt and equitable assistance from the insurance industry was immediately recognized by then Governor George Romney, and he appointed M. Frank McCaffrey as Special Deputy Insurance Commissioner to coordinate and expedite the recovery of the storm devastated area.

When the City of Detroit was stricken with massive property losses as a result of the "1967 riot," Frank McCaffrey's experience in the earlier disaster was again recognized and he was again appointed to aid in resolving the

problems caused by the overwhelming number of claims made against virtually all segments of the property-casualty insurance firms.

By the time Byrnes-McCaffrey, Inc. celebrated its 30th Anniversary in 1969, many changes had occurred in the insurance industry and in the type of business serviced by the agency. Many of its customers operated on a national and international scale and thus it became increasingly necessary to deal with an ever-widening range of insurance markets to properly service the company's accounts. It was becoming more apparent that what had begun as a highly specialized local organization, would have to seek broader affiliation in order to continue to provide effective service to its customers.

In 1971, Brynes-McCaffrey, Inc. merged with Frank B. Hall & Co., a prestigious New York brokerage firm, and thus greatly increased its abilities to provide expertise in every area of insurance services. At the same time, it retained its strong identity with Detroit and its principal industry. Since the merger, unprecedented growth necessitated a move to the Renaissance Center. This is a natural move, for as partners in the Renaissance Center Partnership and as its insurance agents since the earliest stages of planning, Frank B. Hall & Co. has been closely involved in the revitalization of Detroit.

Moving into the 1980s, the agency looks forward to continued growth while still maintaining its well-established roots in Detroit. Today, Frank McCaffrey continues to serve as chairman of Frank B. Hall & Co. of Michigan and vice president and director of the parent company.

The J. L. Hudson Company

Hudson's continues to grow with a stronger Detroit

On April 2, 1881, when Joseph Lowthian Hudson first opened a men's and boys' clothing store in Detroit to the accompaniment of a band concert, the four-page program of events stated: "We aim to make our store popular by keeping always a full stock of the most desirable goods obtainable, selling them at low prices, and dealing fairly and

squarely with our customers."

As business grew, prospered and expanded according to this "revolutionary" concept of retailing, Hudson augmented his merchandise by including home furnishings.

In 1891, he moved to the present Woodward Avenue site, a location judged by friends to be too distant from

Detroit's business core. But people came anyway. In fact, by 1892, the new store rang up sales of close to one million dollars. And, in ten years, Hudson had achieved a name respected for integrity and civic interest, fairness and competence as a merchant.

From 1911 on, section after section was added to the building until, with the purchase of the Newcomb & Endicott property and the erection of a new unit, capacity was doubled. The final section was completed in 1946, making Hudson's downtown store twenty stories high and a full block square.

Upon his death in 1912, Hudson's four nephews assumed the management of the business their bachelor uncle had

Hudson's first Detroit location was the old Detroit Opera House on Campus Maritus, opened in 1881.

founded. The Webber brothers led Hudson's into its second phase of growth as an emerging giant in the retail field, adopting as their slogan: "Growing with Detroit."

In response to suburban growth, Hudson's opened its Northland store in 1954, in what was billed as the largest regional shopping center in the world. Hudson's now totals fifteen stores, with an anticipated opening of at least one store per year well into the 1980s.

In 1961, Joseph L. Hudson, Jr., a grand-nephew of the founder, was named Hudson's chief executive officer. At thirty, he was the youngest president of a major store in the history of retailing.

Hudson's and the Dayton Corporation of Minneapolis, had a similar merchandising philosophy and had grown in parallel style. Both desired expansion beyond their respective states. In 1969, Hudson's and Dayton's merged to form the Dayton Hudson Corporation, the eighth largest non-food retailer in the United States.

Hudson's is more than a giant mercantile operation whose most current annual revenues passed a half-billion

Hudson's moved to its present site on Woodward Avenue in 1891.

dollars. It is a public institution that has always maintained leadership in the civic life of the community.

Such leadership won its founder, Joseph Lowthian Hudson, recognition as one of Michigan's prominent philanthropists. In fact, through his personal efforts, the main building of the Detroit YMCA was made possible.

Also, as chairman and one of the organizers of Detroit's Associated Charities, the senior Hudson helped create an organization which served as a model for Detroit's present day United Foundation. He gave leadership and support to the acquisition of the State Fairgrounds, the Detroit Museum of Arts (now Detroit Institute of Arts), the Detroit Board of Commerce, prison reform, and to other social and economic concerns.

Hudson's and the Dayton Hudson

Corporation continue to be one of the twenty largest corporate philanthropists in America.

Emphasis is focused on community-based social action programs which are innovative in developing new solutions to community problems, such as the Inner City Sub-Center, a community organization on Detroit's east side, and arts institutions and organizations such as the Detroit Institute of Arts, the Detroit Symphony, and the Detroit Renaissance Foundation.

Annually observing the International Freedom Festival, Hudson's co-sponsors a spectacular aerial fireworks display from barges moored in the Detroit River.

Hudson's Santa Parade, always held on Thanksgiving Day, officially marks the beginning of the Christmas season for many Detroiters. The first parade in 1924 consisted of horse-drawn lumber and milk wagons and boasted ten to twelve floats. Today, the planning of the parade is fulltime, and parade floats are built by a crew of five Hudson's employees working year round.

Until recently, Hudson's possessed the world's largest American flag. The 235 feet by 104 feet, three-quarter ton flag was recently donated to the Smithsonian Institution.

As Hudson's continues to grow, so does Detroit. Bolstered by its burgeoning "renaissance," Hudson's downtown store shares in this growth by showing sales increases, part of a welcome trend.

According to Joseph L. Hudson, Jr., "…we continue to seek ways in which the future of this store can be strengthened…A renovated Hudson's Downtown store…could be the renaissance of retailing in downtown Detroit and would serve our community for the next 50 years."

Hughes & Hatcher

Major menswear chain started with a dream and a small Detroit store

In 1902, Jacob Pincus left his struggling little hometown in Russia and came to America where he went to work for his uncle in a small clothing factory. Finding America truly the "land of opportunity," Pincus sent for his four brothers and together they opened a clothing factory of their own in Philadelphia.

Meanwhile, in bustling Detroit in

1910, two friends — Fred Hughes and Leslie Hatcher — opened a men's clothing store, catering to the carriage trade with which they were already familiar. Its location — a handsome little building just north of downtown Detroit on fashionable Woodward Avenue.

Both businesses, hundreds of miles apart from each other, prospered for many years. But the going got tough

during the Depression, and Detroit was particularly hard hit. Hughes and Hatcher's little store on Woodward Avenue was in deep financial trouble. Its principal creditor was a clothing factory in Philadelphia — Pincus Brothers.

Pincus offered to assume ownership of Hughes & Hatcher, with Hughes (who was then sole owner) continuing as manager just as if the business had not changed hands.

How a little store in Detroit became a big chain is partly a matter of business acumen, timing, and luck, with all three playing major roles in the years of Hughes & Hatcher's phenomenal growth.

Jacob Pincus had two sons: Bernard

and Max. In 1938, Bernard joined the company and in 1941 became its head. His brother Max joined him in 1952.

In 1959, the Pincuses purchased Harry Suffrin's chain of four stores. In the meantime, a Hughes & Hatcher store was opened in Pittsburgh.

The shopping center phenomenon was emerging, and shopping patterns were changing all over the country. Between 1959 and 1978, the company opened 43 stores, becoming the largest independent men's fashion chain in the country. Today there are 27 Hughes & Hatcher stores in Michigan, 10 in Pennsylvania, five in Ohio, one in Illinois and five in Wisconsin.

The company's center of activity continues to be Detroit. In 1964-65, the company opened its corporate headquarters just west of downtown Detroit: a 100,000-square-foot complex consisting of executive offices and a warehouse/distribution center/tailoring shop. (The tailoring shops alone employ 400 people and alter a million suits a year.)

And the company maintains, uniquely, two stores in downtown Detroit. The original store at Woodward and Montcalm, and another which opened in 1969.

The latter was the largest retail development to be built in downtown Detroit in many years and was constructed prior to the building of Renaissance Center.

During this Hughes & Hatcher expansion period, the company went public and became listed on the American Stock Exchange. Ten years later, its performance and annual sales gained it placement on the New York Stock Exchange.

H&H continued to solidify its image, and to expand its merchandise line. In 1974, it purchased 20 retail outlets from Hart Schaffner & Marx, one of the nation's most respected clothing manufacturers. Some of these stores took the Hughes & Hatcher name. But in several instances the acquisition included stores of distinct and impressive personality. Jacob Reed's Sons in Philadelphia. B. R. Baker in Cleveland. Small's in Lansing. These stores were allowed not only to keep their names and identity, but also to operate as semi-autonomous divisions of H&H. By 1978, there were 66 stores in the Hughes & Hatcher family.

In 19 years of expansion under its present management, Hughes & Hatcher became the most exciting menswear chain in the nation, combining tremendous buying experience and world-wide contacts, extraordinary selections of merchandise, and the individuality, friendliness and personality of a hometown store.

How does this translate into figures? Impressively. In 1959, H&H did $8,913,248 in business. In 1978, H&H's gross figures had soared to almost $100 million.

The final scene to these events, is, perhaps, oddly appropriate. In 1977, a large chain of retail stores and broadcast facilities — the Outlet Company, of Rhode Island — became interested in Hughes & Hatcher. Would the Pincuses, after all those years of personally guiding the company into its great success, be willing to part with it? The answer was yes. In August, 1977, the assets of Hughes & Hatcher were sold to the Outlet Company; and Max Pincus signed a long-term contract to continue the management of H&H.

And the stock of Hughes & Hatcher? It was converted to an investment fund, in which most of Hughes & Hatcher's stockholders continued to keep their investment. The name of the fund has its own special connotation. It's called The Widener Place Fund, which is the name of the street on which the Pincus family — its brothers and uncles and cousins — lived in the days of their first prosperity in America: when the promise of the new land came so wonderfully true.

The original store at Woodward and Montcalm.

Johnson & Higgins

Oldest U.S. insurance broker has served Detroit since 1914

In many ways, the story of Johnson & Higgins is the history of business insurance and the broker/agent's function in America.

Johnson & Higgins is the country's oldest insurance brokerage firm, having begun as marine average adjusters in 1845 on Wall Street, when New York was the greatest port in the country and, with the opening of the Erie Canal, the "gateway to the West."

For most of its first 55 years, the firm's business was chiefly that of average adjusting and marine insurance brokerage. When the Civil War put an end to the boom days of the Merchant Marine, Johnson & Higgins had reached a stage of national recognition. On May 13, 1862, following an attack by the Confederate gunboats, Secretary of the Navy Gideon Wells "directed Messrs. Johnson & Higgins of New York to send one of their agents to New Orleans in the steamer Connecticut to examine the sunken steamer Varuna with a view of raising her."

Before the turn of the century, Johnson & Higgins — recognizing the needs of the growing industrial revolution — already had opened seven strategically located branch offices.

The San Francisco earthquake occurred on April 18, 1906, and the ensuing fire raged for three days. The San Francisco J&H office staff, aided by the firm's senior fire adjuster dispatched from New York, was able to settle all claims of J&H clients satisfactorily within six months.

The Detroit office of Johnson & Higgins was established in October 1914 to serve not only the growing automobile industry but also its support and supply industries. When war came that year the merchant fleets of all nations became the focus of attack. Congress established a Bureau of War Risk Insurance, calling for the appointment of an advisory board to the Secretary of the Treasury. A senior Johnson & Higgins executive was one of the three named to the board. To the credit of this board, of the entire list of claims reaching the Bureau, only one went to litigation.

During the Depression, insurance suffered with the commerce of the country, and Johnson & Higgins bore its share of trouble. Nevertheless it was able to keep its staff intact.

World War II ushered in a new era for American business and for the insurance industry as well. Group insurance and pensions, an insignificant percentage of payroll before the War, developed into the employee benefit programs of today that often represent as much as 30 to 40 percent of payroll costs. The War also gave rise to added marine insurance requirements. When the government began importing strategic war materials, leading marine brokers were selected to serve as an Insurance Committee to handle all such insurances. From this group, Johnson & Higgins was selected to act as the servicing brokers. In addition, J&H was called upon repeatedly by its clients to solve many unusual problems connected with a variety of government contracts.

With the 1950s the pace of acquisition, conglomeration, and multi-nationalism accelerated. Anticipating many of these developments, Johnson & Higgins created new offices and expanded its overall service base. Perhaps nowhere was this more dramatic than in the international area. Johnson & Higgins became the first broker/agent to create a worldwide network of wholly-

J&H loss control specialists Bart O'Brien and Jim Frederick at an automotive stamping plant.

Robert L. Hannon, Jr.

owned offices where national broker/agents did not exist. Today the firm has more people and more offices outside the North American continent than any other similar firm.

Johnson & Higgins also strengthened its correspondent network situated not only in Europe but in other strategic areas of the world where the firm does not have its own offices. Today, Johnson & Higgins is one of the largest insurance broker/agents in the world, with 33 offices in the U.S. and Canada, and an additional 34 offices overseas in 17 countries. Together with the company's exclusive correspondents, J&H serves business in all commercial centers of the free world.

The Johnson & Higgins office in Detroit, in its almost 65 years of existence, is a full-service office with a current staff of more than 100. It includes property loss control consultants as well as safety and security specialists in every area of business insurance, not only in the Detroit area but throughout the state.

The Detroit office had 21 employees in 1963 when Richard T. Henshaw, Jr., succeeded W. B. Tigue as manager. There were 37 employees when Henshaw was elected a director of Johnson & Higgins and moved to New York where he became executive vice president of the parent firm.

Robert L. Hannon, Jr., succeeded Henshaw as president of Johnson & Higgins (Michigan) in 1966 and became the first manager of the Detroit office to serve on the board of directors of the parent company.

Johnson & Higgins remains today a privately held company, owned entirely by its directors. Unlike other major insurance broker/agents, Johnson & Higgins has no outside shareholders. To all clients in Michigan and elsewhere J&H can say, "We answer only to you."

K mart Corporation

'Satisfaction always' policy wins consumer loyalty

To know the K mart Corporation you must understand the man who founded it and the man who changed it.

Founder Sebastian S. Kresge was born on a poor and rocky farm near Scranton, Pennsylvania, two years after the Civil War. Frugality was a necessity in this area; these people paid their bills, wasted nothing, and practiced a rigid

code of honesty. And it was this philosophy that made Kresge and his company successful.

After graduating from Eastman's Business College, he got a job as a traveling tinware salesman. He managed to save $8,000 which he used in 1897 to buy a partnership with J. G. McCrory in a dime store in Memphis. A year la-

ter, they bought a store in Detroit. In 1899, Kresge bought out McCrory's interest in the Detroit store and his company was on its way.

Kresge learned every aspect of the retail business, took many financial risks and made numerous personal sacrifices. He chose his personnel carefully, and sought associates with initiative and integrity.

Once in the 1920s, one of his district managers in New York was told by a contractor that a new store could not be ready in time for the advertised opening. He sent a wire to Kresge asking for advice. Kresge's return wire said "Sorry

221

Company founder Sebastian S. Kresge (right) with Harry B. Cunningham when he was elected president on May 8, 1959.

The first Kresge store, 1899

to hear of your trouble — but glad to know you are there to take care of it."

When Kresge retired as president in 1925, there were 304 Kresge stores in the U.S. and his company's sales were $106 million. Kresge remained chairman until 1966. He died that year at 99.

For nearly half a century, the company was one of the most successful variety store businesses. But by the mid-'50s, retailing in America was swiftly changing. Company management selected a young, aggressive general vice president to spend 1957 and 1958 studying consumer needs and current methods of retailing. Management was not to know then that this young executive, Harry B. Cunningham, was to be the catalyst that would catapult a multi-million dollar variety store chain into a multi-billion dollar mass mer-

chandising firm. The name of the firm was changed from S. S. Kresge Company to K mart Corporation by shareholders in 1977.

Cunningham did not set out to be a retailer. After studying journalism for two years at Miami University in Ohio, he became a newspaper reporter. He met a company executive and saw more of a chance of advancement in retailing. In 1928, he started as a stock boy working up to 90 hours a week. He became a store manager, a district manager, assistant sales director, sales director and then general vice president. He was elected a member of the Board of Directors in 1956.

After his two years of travel and study, Cunningham was convinced that

discounting was the new direction for the company. When he became president in 1959, Cunningham and his management team prepared for the corporation's entry into the discount department store field — an unproven business. However, management reasoned, discounting would succeed if someone did it with top quality merchandise, real discount prices and eliminated the shopper's risk with a "satisfaction always" policy. These conditions had been the company's policies since 1899. K mart would just continue this tradition. Sebastian Kresge said: "Good for you. I want you to know I am behind you one hundred percent."

Cunningham chose a senior vice president, C. Lloyd Yohe, as the architect to create his dream and to establish the character of K marts. The first K mart opened in 1962.

When Cunningham retired as chairman in 1972, K mart Corporation's sales were $3.1 billion.

In the ensuing years, three new prototype K marts — 68,000, 55,000 and 40,000 square feet — were added to the original 84,000 square-foot prototype. They were designed to suit the needs of smaller cities and to give K mart flexibility when expanding in heavily-populated urban centers.

By the end of 1977, the company was operating 1,367 K marts, 329 Kresge units and 86 Jupiter units in the U.S., Canada and Australia producing $9.9 billion in sales — well on the way to the $16 billion volume projected for the company's 1981 fiscal year by Chairman Robert E. Dewar who succeeded Cunningham.

K mart Corporation was born of innovation courage...and continues to prosper because of it.

Macauley's Office Products

Office products industry leader family owned for 109 years

Macauley's most recent addition in Twelve Oaks Mall, Novi, Michigan

James F. Macauley was only 22 years old when he moved from Rochester, New York to Detroit in 1869, but in May of that year he established what was to become one of the most successful and progressive office products dealers in the country.

The first Macauley store was located in the Old Union Depot Building on East Jefferson, across the street from the

Old Biddle House, which was then the city's leading hotel for commercial travelers. Sales of stationery, magazines and books were made in the store as well as on trains as passengers boarded. It was a modest beginning for James Macauley, but success was soon to follow.

In 1872, W. T. Macauley joined his brother to form Macauley Brothers;

Booksellers and Stationers. In addition to books and stationery, the Macauleys branched out into novelties, fireworks, and even bicycles.

The business continued to prosper and in 1883, when larger quarters were needed, the store relocated to Woodward Avenue. This new location included such modern conveniences as a railway cash carrier and electric lights.

Due to the expansion of the J. L. Hudson Co., the Macauley's Woodward Avenue store was then relocated on Library Street. It was at this point that Roy H. and Ward Macauley, the second generation of the Macauley family, succeeded in continuing the family business. This store produced some lighter moments for Macauley's, as well as some of the city's more noted citizens. It was recalled, that in 1912, Henry Ford brought his son Edsel into the store to purchase fireworks. Ford then paid for them with a $100 bill. The young clerk in the store, Arthur Macauley, son of Roy and eventually the third generation successor, had to scurry around the city to other merchants to get the large bill changed.

The Library Street store was eventually relocated to Farmer Street in 1924 to become the main office. About this time, Macauley's was heavily involved in supplying text books to the Detroit Public Schools.

After surviving the Depression, Macauley's began to divorce itself from bicycles, fireworks, and books to strengthen its position in office products.

In 1954, with expansion in mind, and an invitation from J. L. Hudson's, Macauley's became a tenant of the Northland Shopping Center, which at the time, was the largest shopping mall in the country. Macauley's continued to expand into regional shopping centers with stores in Eastland, Wonderland and the Sears Shopping Center in Lincoln Park.

In 1961, John L. Macauley became the fourth generation Macauley to head the firm, succeeding his father, Arthur, who remained active in the company until 1969. And while Jack remains as

Macauley's, 172 Woodward in 1907

president today, his son Mark is likely to become the fifth generation to be at the helm.

From quill pens and bicycles to word processing and micrographics supplies today, Macauley's has paid close attention to the needs of its customers. The continuous changes in the company, and policies towards servicing the customer, has created a strong base on which will rest the future growth and development of the company.

Today, Macauley's has developed into a multi-faceted operation in order to serve all businesses regardless of size. For the smaller businesses there is the "Tele-Serve" Department, an automatic ordering system. The customer simply requests a convenient time when they wish to be called, and Macauley's then does it automatically, on a scheduled basis.

The scope of Macauley's business is not limited to retail stores and telephone

sales. There is also an experienced staff of sales representatives that make "in-person" sales calls to larger commercial office supply users. Their size is growing as rapidly as the retail stores. Macauley's has also instituted a new automated system to solve the ordering problems of a large business. The computerized systems help control the cost, distribution, inventory, and internal charge-back procedures of large corporations.

Macauley's offers only the best of office supplies, furniture, and machines, while incorporating only the most innovative and convenient ways of purchasing these items. Therefore, Macauley's continues as it has for over 100 years, being the most progressive office products dealer in Detroit. Growing to eleven retail outlets as of July 1978, and plans for greater growth in the future, Macauley's is assured of continuing success for years to come.

The standard of business that James F. Macauley advanced in 1869 remains intact today, "your needs of tomorrow is our business today".

Maccabees Mutual Life Insurance Company

Once a small benevolent society company now ranks at top in its field

What is Maccabees? If you were to stand on a street corner in downtown Detroit and ask that question of the first 100 people you saw, most would recognize the name. But, how many, do

you suppose, would know that (1) It is the largest domiciled life insurance company in the state of Michigan, (2) It ranks 31st in insurance in force (nearly $5 billion) among all mutual life

insurance companies in the United States and Canada, and (3) It ranks 43rd in assets among these same companies.

These numbers are impressive, of

The Home Office of Maccabees Mutual Life Insurance Company, 25800 Northwestern Highway, Southfield, a Detroit suburb.

course, but more important is the rich tradition of service and innovation which lies behind them. Today, perhaps more than ever before in our nation's history, our society needs organizations such as Maccabees Mutual — organizations which are dedicated to making positive contributions to the common good while maintaining a respectful custodial role toward our common heritage.

Now, this may sound somewhat presumptuous, but let's take a brief look at how Maccabees Mutual has played and continues to play, such a part.

- Judas Maccabeus was a great Jewish warrior. His tribe, the Maccabees, was the first known society in history to care for widows and orphans.
- Several thousand years later, a handful of men met in the backroom of a jewelry store in London, Ontario to form a benevolent society to provide for widows and orphans. They called themselves The Order of the Knights of Maccabees of the World.

It is interesting to reflect that a group of Scot Presbyterians in Canada took a Jewish name out of a Catholic Bible (the Book of the Maccabees is found in the Douay, not the King James, version) and, three years later, moved the organization to Michigan. Maccabees Mutual has always thrived on and still welcomes complexity and diversity.

The early growth of the society was remarkable. Within a few years, it claimed more than 10,000 members. By World War I, there were 600,000 representing every state and every Canadian province and the Society was the largest of its kind in the world. Such explosive growth did not come by accident. On the contrary, it came because the organization did more than simply react to the needs of society; it anticipated them. Thus, the Maccabees was one of the first insurance organizations to offer disability income and endowment policies. It established homes for the aged and cared for

disaster victims. As a fraternal society, it also took a special interest in the young and sponsored numerous social, educational and recreational activities. The Society prospered throughout the first half of this century and included among its ranks mayors, governors, legislators and numerous famous personages, such as Franklin D. Roosevelt, Bing Crosby and Eddie Rickenbacker.

However, World War II changed more than the world's political map. The needs of society had changed irrevocably. The Maccabees was no longer equipped to meet those needs as a fraternal society. Consequently, its leadership decided to convert the Society to a mutual life insurance company.

The wisdom of that decision has been justified many times over. Today, Maccabees Mutual is one of the fastest growing life insurance companies in the country. It is a recognized leader in both the individual and group insurance fields. This was achieved by building a strong home office staff, a professional sales force dedicated to offering quality life, disability, and pension insurance products to both the personal and the business professional markets.

These achievements are remarkable, considering the relatively short period since Maccabees became a purely mutual life insurance company. Nonetheless, it expects even greater successes in the future. Foundation has been laid and the company now looks forward with confidence to a second century of progress, during which it will continue to be of service to policyholders and the general public.

Manufacturers National Bank of Detroit

A tradition of service and progress: "That's my bank!"

Manufacturers Bank was established in a time of adversity — the 1930s Depression. Opened on August 10, 1933, Manufacturers National Bank was founded by Edsel B. Ford and seven associates including John Ballantyne, the bank's first president.

Like the city it serves, Manufacturers Bank was able to meet the difficulties of the thirties and to emerge stronger and

ready to handle the challenge of World War II. Only ten years after it opened, the bank was deeply involved in helping industries and consumers in the war effort.

The institution started its operations with headquarters in the Penobscot Building and three branch offices — two in Dearborn and one in Highland Park. By the 1940s it had greatly expanded

and required larger facilities. The new main office was located in a historic building at Fort and Shelby, designed in 1898 by the famed New York architect Stanford White.

By 1952, Manufacturers Bank had ten offices and a merger with United States Savings Bank had increased its assets to $586 million. Consolidation with Industrial National Bank in 1955 brought Manufacturers Bank actively into the consumer finance field. More diversified services were consequently made available to the bank's customers.

Along with the continuing expansion came new technology which greatly changed banking operations. Tedious jobs once done manually could now be handled more efficiently with new machines and computers.

For example, in the early years, checking account statements were posted by hand and all of the branch employees came downtown to help mail them. Today customers can receive a combined computerized statement indicating all of their checking, savings and loan transactions.

Payroll methods have also changed greatly. Until 1946 Ford Motor Company paid employees in cash. The payroll was made up, put in a box and cranked by conveyor through a tunnel to the Ford payroll clerk across the street from the bank. Today, corporate customers can arrange to have their employees' paychecks deposited directly in their checking accounts — saving time and paper work for all concerned.

In 1956, William A. Mayberry, who had been with Manufacturers Bank since 1933, was named president, and in 1959 he was named chairman of the board. Under his leadership, Manufacturers became a billion dollar bank by 1963, its 30th anniversary year. That same year, the federally chartered Manufacturers-Detroit International Corporation was formed to supplement the services of the International Banking Department.

Only three years later, deposits exceeded $1.5 billion and the number of branch offices totalled 64. To consolidate operating departments housed in separate buildings, plans were announced to construct a 55,000 square foot operations center at 411 West Lafayette in downtown Detroit. Dedicated in 1971, the Manufacturers Bank Building is both efficient and attractive to employees, customers and pedestrians alike.

Having grown to more than 70 offices by 1969 the branch system also underwent change. It was organized into geographical regions, increasing the bank's flexibility and strengthening customer relations.

That same year, Roland A. Mewhort was named chairman of the board

The interior of Fort-Shelby Bank Office, formerly the main office of Manufacturers National Bank of Detroit.

and continued as chief executive officer. He was succeeded as president by Dean E. Richardson, formerly executive vice president.

As it did in the 1930s, Manufacturers Bank again invested in Detroit's future in 1972, this time through its participation in the Renaissance Center Partnership.

A year later, Manufacturers National Corporation, a bank holding company, was formed and Manufacturers Bank became one of its subsidiaries. Since then, the corporation has acquired three banks (The Saline Bank, Bay City Bank & Trust and Manufacturers Bank of Southfield) and established two others (Manufacturers Bank of Livonia and Manufacturers Bank of The Shores).

In 1977, the headquarters of Manufacturers National Corporation were moved to the newly completed Renaissance Center. Manufacturers Bank leases ten floors of office space in

Manufacturers Bank Tower in addition to a full-service branch office opened in March, 1977.

While the modern design of the new offices reflects the bank's dedication to progress, a sense of tradition is also maintained. A carved mahogany fireplace from the former main office is the focal point of the executive offices' reception area.

In 1978, Manufacturers National Corporation announced plans to acquire the State Bank of Michigan, a bank with six offices located in the western part of the state. In addition, the corporation applied for permission to form a new bank, Manufacturers Bank of Novi, in a growing Detroit suburb.

Throughout its 45 years of growth and development, Manufacturers has remained committed to the pledge made by its first president, "The bank pledges itself to be of service in every way that will benefit the citizens."

The fulfillment of that pledge has made thousands of stockholders, employees and customers proud to say, "That's my bank!"

Marsh & McLennan

Worldwide insurance/brokerage program spawned by innovative strides

In hindsight, we can only speculate on what clients or lines of insurance brokerage business led Henry W. Marsh

and Donald R. McLennan to establish operations in Detroit. By May 14, 1914, when Marsh & McLennan was incorpo-

rated in Michigan and licensed by the state, Detroit was already an established commercial center. Certainly the expan-

225

Henry W. Marsh   Donald R. McLennan

It was really their interest in the railway business which brought Henry W. Marsh and Donald R. McLennan together in Chicago in 1904. The firm which became Marsh & McLennan in 1906 was founded there 33 years before — when many new enterprises and ideas rose from the ashes of the great Chicago fire.

sion there was part of the company's plan to serve industry through a network of U.S. offices.

Fire and marine insurance were the principal lines of business, as practiced by the likes of J. S. Fletcher of Detroit, the state representative of the Norwich Union Insurance Company and one of the original directors of Marsh & McLennan's Michigan corporation. Casualty insurance, including boiler, was still young, and life insurance had not received the great impetus which came soon thereafter with the end of World War I. Steel production, however, was underway, the automobile era had just begun, and with it, the need for insurance underwriting markets willing to write auto coverages.

About this time, Marsh secured a binding contract from Lloyd's of London underwriters, authorizing Marsh & McLennan to write up to $20,000 subject to one risk on automobiles. The agreement was significant to the auto industry because, at the time, Boston of Massachusetts was the only company writing automobile insurance in the United States; and it was a giant stride for Marsh & McLennan, marking the company's first Lloyd's contract and first experience in the London market.

In 1927 Marsh & McLennan purchased the agency, S. S. Glass Corporation, which became the company's first full-service operation in Detroit, with its own offices located at the southwest corner of Woodward and Congress. The organization grew to one of the largest in Michigan, with accounts such as Briggs Body & Manufacturing Company (later sold to Chrysler Corporation), J. L. Hudson Company, Hudson Motor Car Company, and others.

Glass was manager until January 1, 1935, when Philip G. Clifton took over. The same year, the office moved to the National Bank Building, where 29 employees occupied approximately 4,400 square feet of space.

During World War II, operations became difficult. Although Detroit was "the arsenal of democracy," the War Labor Board declared insurance "less essential" to the war effort. Therefore, Marsh & McLennan could not hold any employees who wanted to go into war industries, nor could it hire any new employees who were in war work. Several young men whom the Detroit office had recruited from college and had put through an insurance training program were taken into active military service.

In 1945 Clifton retired and F. V. Rudd became the new manager of the Detroit office. Two years later, Marsh & McLennan in Detroit was appointed sole agent by Ford Motor Company, the first time Ford had ever placed its total insurance program with one broker. In part, the decision reflected a new importance which commercial businesses assigned to the insurance function during the post-war era of economic expansion. The emphasis changed from insurance buying to insurance administration and to financial management for risks never envisioned 20 years before.

R. T. Johnstone succeeded Rudd in 1953, and continued as head of the Detroit office until 1968. In those years, a branch office was established in Kalamazoo, Michigan (1960) and the Detroit office was moved again to One Woodward Avenue (sometimes referred to as the Michigan Consolidated Gas Company Building), where it remains today. A Grand Rapids, Michigan office was added in 1970.

For Johnstone and his successors, Thomas O. Mayberry, Albert L. Lund and Vincent F. Johnson, all three of whom are presently serving as senior executives of the company, the maturation of the insurance brokerage business has been enormous.

It has to do with the development of what is known as the risk management process — the protection of corporate assets through loss prevention services and mathematical and financial techniques to determine the most cost-effective means of risk retention and/or of risk transfer for each client situation.

In the Detroit office today, 133 specialists in property, casualty, marine, bonding, boiler and personal lines insurance employ risk management planning as part of their everyday routine. Finding innovative insurance solutions and marketing coverages worldwide for business and industry, individual or group buyers, is what they mean when they say — "I'm from Marsh & McLennan."

Michigan Bell Telephone Company

Starting with a single telephone line, company now serves 3 million customers

The "speaking telephone" made its Michigan debut in Detroit only 16 months after Alexander Graham Bell and his young assistant made history with the famous "Mr. Watson, come here, I want you!" message more than 100 years ago in Boston.

In the fall of 1877, a sign in a Detroit drugstore heralded Michigan's first commercial telephone line by inviting people to "Come in and talk over the amazing long distance telephone. Throw your voice almost two miles."

That first telephone line — a single iron wire strung over the roofs of houses — linked Sterns' drugstore at Woodward and Jefferson to his laboratory at Woodbridge and Sixth.

Despite some skeptics, Detroiters flocked to try the new device and in August, 1878, 53 customers ordered telephone lines connecting them to a central switchboard set up in the Telegraph Block Building at Griswold and Congress Streets...the present site of the Guardian Building.

Messenger boys from the local telegraph office were hired as operators and the following month Detroit's first telephone directory was published. By that time the list of customers had grown to 133, all of whom were listed by name in the directory. In January, 1879, Detroit customers were first in the nation to be assigned phone numbers to facilitate handling calls.

In 1879, Grand Rapids became the second Michigan city to have phone service. Soon after, telephone exchanges were established in Bay City and Saginaw and the Port Huron exchange celebrated its opening on Christmas Day, 1879.

In 1880, the world's first international communications were established with a line linking Detroit and Windsor and the following year, the first long distance line in the state was strung between Detroit and Port Huron.

During this early period, girls began replacing boy operators. Detroit made the switch to women operators late in 1879.

By 1906, the Michigan State Telephone Company — later to become Michigan Bell — had 200 exchanges and nearly 100,000 customers. That same year, the Michigan State Company issued the first directory in the country featuring classified business advertising on yellow pages.

Early in 1915, Michigan hooked up to the first cross-country long distance line and the first Detroit to San Francisco call was made. It took 30 minutes to set up the three-minute call and cost the customer $16.70. Today, with customer direct distance dialing, a similar call would go through in seconds and could cost less than a dollar for three minutes.

Automatic dial service was introduced in Detroit in 1923 permitting customers to dial their own local calls. The first transatlantic call from the state was made to London early in 1927 and later that year television images carried over telephone lines were demonstrated for the first time to the Detroit public.

Early in the 1940s, Michigan Bell topped one million telephones in service and state residents were making more than four million calls a day. Ship-to-shore phone service for Great Lakes vessels was inaugurated in 1942 and mobile car phones in 1946.

During World War II, Michigan Bell helped serve the war effort by installing telecommunications equipment at military bases around the state. More than 3,000 company employees went into the armed forces — 67 of them died in service.

In 1952, Michigan Bell installed its two-millionth phone. A year later Birmingham became the second community in the nation to have direct distance dialing (DDD), enabling customers to dial their own long distance calls direct without operator assistance. DDD came to Detroit in 1960 and today all of the company's nearly three million customers have the service.

Also in the early 1950s, color phones started to become a common sight in homes and offices around the state.

The Princess® telephone made its debut in the state in 1960, followed closely by Bellboy® service. The Speakerphone arrived in 1963 and Touch-Tone® service was introduced the following year. In 1965, the modern Trimline® phone — with its dial in the receiver — made its national debut in Michigan.

In the late '60s, electronic switching systems, able to handle calls a thousand times faster and more economically and efficiently than previous equipment, arrived in the state.

In 1973, Michigan Bell marked another milestone with its five-millionth

With increasing demands for phone service the four-way pole was designed to handle telephone wires from four directions. This giant pole stood in front of a Detroit central office building in the late 1890s.

phone — a white Trimline® installed at Greenfield Village. Also that year, International Direct Distance Dialing permitted customers to begin dialing their own overseas calls direct.

Michigan's last manual phones faded into history in 1974 when electronic switching replaced St. Ignace's old-fashioned "number, please" operator-manned switchboards.

The fourth-largest private employer in the state, Michigan Bell employs some 29,800 people. Serving almost three million customers — with six million telephones — in 73 of the state's 83 counties, the company handles an average of more than 35 million calls a day to points within the state, to other states and throughout the world.

National Bank of Detroit

Born in Depression, bank was leader from the start

National Bank of Detroit has a fascinating history. It started at the top and worked its way up.

From the day it opened it was the largest bank in town. Shortly after its founding in 1933, it became the largest bank in Michigan. Through the years, it has maintained a tradition of leadership with an impressive rate of growth. By its 40th birthday, it had attained the $6 billion mark in assets — the only U.S.

bank ever to have reached that level in such a short period of time. In 1978, at the tender age of 45, its assets stand at more than $8 billion.

NBD's financing came in response to an economic crisis that had gripped the entire country, but which had been especially severe in Detroit. In February 1933, all the banks in Michigan had been closed by proclamation of the governor. When President Franklin D.

Roosevelt was inaugurated a few weeks later, he extended the "banking holiday" to the entire nation.

Without banking services, business activity ground to a halt. It became almost impossible even to cash a check. Detroit's leading businessmen held many meetings trying to find some way of reactivating the stalled economic processes.

Finally, the General Motors Corporation — with many plants and thousands of employees in Detroit — worked out a plan to start a new bank. The auto maker subscribed $12.5 million, providing the entire common stock capital of the bank; the Reconstruction Finance Corporation, a federal government agency, purchased

On the day National Bank of Detroit opened, in 1933, customers stood in long lines to open accounts totaling more than $12 million.

One entrance of National Bank of Detroit's famous Money Museum, located in its new Renaissance Center office.

preferred stock dollar for dollar, thus bringing the initial capitalization of the bank to $25 million. (The bank having become firmly established, GM sold all of its stock to the public by 1945; the RFC's preferred shares were redeemed by 1947.)

Hundreds of thousands of Detroiters were depositors of the two major banks in the city, which never re-opened after the "holiday." The entire city was affected, directly or indirectly, as a result of the business stagnation that followed, with its unemployment, depressed property values and general destruction of public confidence.

Arrangements were completed with extraordinary speed to relieve this situation, and National Bank of Detroit opened its doors on March 24, 1933. A tremendous rush of people swarmed in, carrying bundles of currency and coins wrapped in newspapers, in cigar boxes, suitcases and every imaginable way. So great were the crowds that deposits had

to be crammed into drawers temporarily. In the first hour a total of $2.5 million in new accounts was received. Almost $12 million came in the first day. More than three million pieces of printed matter, such as forms, deposit tickets and signature cards, were needed for opening day. Most of these were produced overnight.

The first head of National Bank of Detroit was a distinguished midwestern banker named Walter S. McLucas, who was brought in from Kansas City, Missouri. After nine months of operation — by the end of 1933 — the bank had more than 96,000 accounts with deposits totaling $189 million. The staff consisted almost entirely of experienced personnel from the closed Detroit banks. For most, it meant starting all over again, but promotion was rapid. There was challenge in every job. And there was a team spirit that continues to this day.

Through the years, NBD has been

fortunate in having a succession of outstanding bankers in its top management. McLucas was followed by Charles T. Fisher, Jr., whose period of leadership was marked by exceptional growth and the planning of the new main office that is now the bank's headquarters — a landmark in Detroit at Woodward and Fort. Upon Fisher's death in 1958, the top duties were taken over by Donald F. Valley, then by Henry T. Bodman. The current chairman of the board and chief executive officer is Robert M. Surdam. Charles T. Fisher III is president and Norman B. Weston is vice chairman of the board.

The establishment in 1972 of a holding company, National Detroit Corporation, has facilitated expansion in both domestic and international activities. At the end of 1977, National Detroit Corporation had 118 domestic banking offices, three overseas branches and numerous subsidiaries and affiliates.

In line with its avowed objective of being a good corporate citizen, National Bank of Detroit has established an urban affairs committee that studies and responds to issues of community concern, special lending programs for minority business enterprises and a policy group that works to insure equal opportunity in hiring and promotion.

NBD served as the lead bank in assembling the construction financing for the magnificent new Renaissance Center project on Detroit's riverfront. Its newest office, along with the bank's famed Money Museum, is located in one of the Renaissancce towers.

Parke-Davis

One of nation's top pharmaceutical companies a legacy of Dr. Duffield's Drug store

"Ether, Sweet Spirit of Nitre, Oil of Wine, Hoffman's Anodyne and Blue Pill Mass." Those were the products that poured from the back of the tiny drugstore that stood at 162 Woodward Avenue. The store's proprietor, Dr. Samuel Duffield, who was both a chemist and a physician, had sunk all of his savings into the business venture that represented the realization of his dream of bringing to the United States some of the chemical manufacturing expertise that he had witnessed in Germany while studying there. The year was 1864.

Duffield's drugstore, which he had purchased two years earlier, stood in the heart of the business district which was then clustered around lower Woodward Avenue. Down the street, the proprietor of the C. R. Mabley clothing store promoted his wares in the style of P. T. Barnum, frequently employing a tightrope walker in gaudy costume, to cross the street, high in the air, from his building to the McMillan Building.

Parke, Davis & Company traces its earliest beginnings to Duffield's struggling enterprise. The company's history actually began on October 26,

1866, when Duffield was joined by Hervey C. Parke. Parke, who had been a teacher, financial manager of a mining company and the owner of a successful mining hardware store, knew little about pharmaceutical manufacturing but he recognized the unlimited opportunity for development and growth. The partnership was one of the first attempts at pharmaceutical manufacturing west of Buffalo.

In the East, Detroit was regarded as a crude backwoods settlement. It was as difficult to find customers as it was to attract investors. What was needed was

228

a supersalesman. Enter George Davis in 1867, a dynamic young man who at 22 had already established himself as having a sales technique that was irresistible.

The year Davis joined the firm, the books, as usual, showed no profit. Nevertheless, in many ways the company was progressing, and new products were being introduced. At the instigation of Davis, advertising was vastly expanded and emphasized "fluid and solid extracts, sugar coated pills, concentrations, elixirs and syrups."

That same year, the business moved to a modest building on Henry Street between Cass and Clifford, where it remained for six years, when it moved its operations to the Detroit riverfront location, its worldwide headquarters for the past 105 years. The combination of Duffield, Parke and Davis brought together scientist, businessman and salesman and formed the needed basic foundation upon which the company has grown and prospered for the past 112 years.

In 1869, Duffield left the business to go into private practice and for two years his position was filled by Dr. A. F. Jennings. In 1871, the name was adopted which was to become a permanent part of the American scene — Parke, Davis & Company.

Hervey Parke and George Davis were contrasting personalities. Parke was a model of the conservative gentleman of his era. Davis was full of ideas for innovation and daring action. Their common meeting ground was their insistence on the highest possible standards for their products.

It is impossible to compress within a page the events and people that have shaped the 112 year history of a company. Parke-Davis' long record in

The courtyard of Parke, Davis and Company's Detroit Laboratory about 1888. Seated in chairs are H. A. Wetzel, George S. Davis, Hervey C. Parke and John Clay.

the industry boasts many "firsts". P-D was the first company to develop a process of standardization by chemical assay which assured medicinal products of uniform strength and potency — a simple process by today's measurements, but nonetheless revolutionary in its time. It was also the first commercial company to erect a research laboratory building. The company's long experience in the manufacture of biologicals dates back to 1903 when Parke-Davis was issued License Number One from the U.S. Government for the production of biological products.

The list of drug products to emerge from the laboratories of Parke-Davis over the past century run the gamut from the early extracts of roots, barks and herbs to today's sophisticated chemically synthesized medicinals. Over the years, Parke-Davis has been a

leader in vitamins, anticonvulsants, hormone products, antihistamines, antibiotics, biologicals and specialty chemicals. P-D has also been one of the world's key suppliers of capsules.

In more recent years, Parke-Davis, now a subsidiary of Warner-Lambert Company, has expanded its product line to include medical-surgical dressings, surgical instruments, and orthopedic devices as well as drug delivery systems.

With its long history of operation in the heart of Detroit's business community, Parke-Davis has had a day-to-day relationship with the people of Detroit and with the affairs of the City. It is not surprising that the company enthusiastically accepted the invitation to participate in Detroit's renaissance as one of 51 corporate partners furnishing financial support to the construction of the Renaissance Center.

R. L. Polk & Company

Directory publisher spans four generations and 108 years downtown

In 1870, a full quarter-century before an automobile was to appear on the city's streets, a former Union Army drummer boy arrived in Detroit with an idea. He was the first Ralph Lane Polk, just 24, and his idea was a directory of businesses along the Detroit and Milwaukee Railroad for traveling salesmen. He set up headquarters in a one-room

office in downtown Detroit, obtained credit from a leading Detroit printer, and soon was publishing a gazetteer and business directory for the entire state of Michigan.

Success in those two ventures led young Polk into the city directory business. Four years later, his firm produced its first Detroit City Directory. There

were then only about 90,000 residents in the city.

The city directory business continued to flourish and by 1878, when the company was the subject of an article in the *Detroit Evening News,* the firm was publishing nine biennial state gazetteers and city directories for Detroit, Indianapolis, Toledo, Grand Rapids, Saginaw, East

Saginaw, Bay City, Jackson, Port Huron, Ft. Wayne, and London, Ontario.

The author of the *Evening News* article was James E. Scripps, the paper's founder and editor and a close friend of young Polk. Their relationship in a way was responsible for Scripps' founding the *News*. While Scripps was editor and manager of the *Advertiser and Tribune,* he had collaborated with Polk on the state gazetteer and business directory. The paper's stockholders objected to this outside activity, so Scripps resigned and organized the new paper, forerunner of today's *Detroit News.*

The firm was soon to outgrow its facilities in the Butterfield Building at 40 West Larned Street for a new home at 431 Howard Street. Originally of two stories, the building was expanded to three floors and then in 1923 six more stories were added. This building, completely remodeled in recent years, still serves as the national headquarters of R. L. Polk & Co.

A second-generation Ralph L. Polk assumed the presidency of the company upon the death of his father, in 1923. He previously had served as assistant to his father and, in fact, had begun his apprenticeship at the age of 10 by making deliveries of city directories to Detroit businesses.

The company's experience and acumen in gathering and compiling city directory information naturally led it into allied fields.

Automobiles still came with hand cranks and side curtains when the company began compiling statistics that reflected new vehicle sales and the number of vehicles in operation. By 1927, the company was able to announce a complete national census of motor vehicles.

Through the years, the automobile industry has utilized this statistical information to better serve its customers through more efficient distribution, more convenient dealer locations, market re-

R. L. Polk & Co. moved into this building in 1913. Originally just two stories tall, a third floor was added in 1920 and then six more stories were added in 1923.

search and future planning.

Another outgrowth of the city directory operation was the firm's Direct Mail Division, established in 1921 and later renamed as the Marketing Services Division. Today, the division furnishes a variety of services to both automotive and non-automotive clients. In addition, this division offers fulfillment services, warehousing, packaging and shipping, and computer, research and creative services.

In 1916, the Polk company acquired the Bankers Encyclopedia, forerunner of today's Polk's World Bank Directory. The directory is published in both North American and International Editions, and the information reported on each bank includes communications data, officers, directors, correspondents and statements of condition. The directory is distributed to subscribers in more than 75 countries.

The company's newest enterprise is the gathering and compiling of urban statistics to furnish detailed information relating to cities' population, housing,

employment and business activity. The information is packaged in Profiles of Change reports, used widely by city and state governments.

Because of the vast amount of information handled in all its operations, the company was one of the pioneers in utilizing computers. Today it operates four computer centers, and among the hardware are two pieces of equipment designed as "the world's first delivered models."

Only one of a handful of Detroit companies to remain under single family ownership for more than 100 years, R. L. Polk & Co. has spanned four generations. Today the founder's grandson, Ralph L. Polk, is chairman of the board of directors, and Ralph L. Polk, Jr. is chief financial officer.

With its downtown Detroit headquarters, the firm also occupies more than a million square feet of office and production space in more than 50 other locations across North America, in Great Britain, Belgium, West Germany, and Australia.

Radisson-Cadillac Hotel

Major center of Detroit hospitality has first-class heritage and grandeur

Guests arriving at Detroit's Radisson Cadillac Hotel follow a proven path to hospitality established by their ancestors seven generations ago. The site, at the hub of downtown activities, has housed a hotel continuously since 1836, with each bigger and better than the one preceding.

This hotel dynasty owes its beginnings to a gregarious veteran of the War of 1812, Nathaniel Champe. With a love for greeting and swapping yarns with travelers, it was natural that he build a 20-room inn on a lot he purchased on the Chicago Road just a block from the rail station. Tiring of the business side of running the inn, he later leased it to a firm which operated it as the Temperance House until Champe sold it in 1851.

New owner, John Blindbury, cleared the site and erected a more spacious four-story brick structure which he ran successfully under his name until 1868. For another 15 years, it was leased for operation as The Antisdel. In 1883, the property came into the hands of Detroit's famed Scripps family and in turn was sold to local tobacco tycoon, Daniel Scotten.

With a growing demand for first class travel accommodations, Scotten bought up adjoining lots and in 1888 built an imposing new structure of 200 rooms which he christened the Cadillac Hotel in honor of the city's founder. Taking advantage of its key location, the plush hotel prospered under a series of leasing companies until the surrounding neighborhood began to show signs of advancing age.

However, the area's potential was not overlooked by the three Book brothers, sons of a leading doctor and grandsons of Francis Palms, a man of prestigious French ancestry and at one time the largest landowner in the state. The brothers dreamed of transforming Washington Boulevard, the street fronting the hotel into "The Fifth Avenue of the Midwest." Their master plan included 10 skyscrapers, apartments, office buildings, and a great hotel.

While their vision never came to full fruition, they left a remarkable heritage of building and leadership that gave the city its impressive avenue and several imposing structures, including one of the world's great hotels.

The Books bought the old Cadillac Hotel in 1917 and spent $60,000 updating it while their plans for the new structure kept growing. Originally planned for 20 stories, it was changed

This 1906 view shows first hotel on site bearing Cadillac name in honor of city's founder. Tree-lined boulevard remained part of "Fifth Avenue of Midwest" as present structure rose in 1924.

Under Radisson banner, Cadillac Hotel enjoyed $6 million renovation to emerge again as one of the world's great hospitality centers.

to 24, then 28 and, when finished in 1924, it emerged as a 32-story tower, the tallest building in the state at the time.

Built over a 17-month period at a cost of $14 million with another $2 million for furnishings, the 1,200-room hotel in its Italian Renaissance mode was a marvel of its age. The floor area covered 11 acres and the magnificent structure included 6,700 tons of structural steel, four million bricks, 85 carloads of stone and terra cotta, 11 million pounds of plaster, a million square feet of gypsum tile, and 40 million square feet of glass set in 2,152 windows.

Guests were greeted by staircases of

Breche Violette marble, beams of solid walnut, Sevres vases, Venetian bronze chandeliers, handcarved furniture covered with Italian velvet and innumerable other marks of lasting beauty. A crowning touch was a two-story Grand Ballroom with gold leaf ceilings, two half-ton crystal chandeliers, an electric fountain and matching rose carpet and draperies.

Through succeeding years, the hotel won fame around the world. It served the city well as the favored headquarters for major conventions and other events in Detroit. In 1951, it was acquired by the Sheraton Corporation as the second largest in its 30-unit chain. Renamed the Sheraton Cadillac, it was given a million dollar refurbishing and its popularity rose to new heights.

Noted names from around the world made the Sheraton Cadillac their Detroit stopping place. Its elegant Presidential Suite was enjoyed by a long procession of American presidents.

Released from the Sheraton chain in 1975, the venerable structure remained open as the Detroit Cadillac for another year while all Detroit pondered its fate. Happily, the announcement soon followed that the hotel would become part of the Radisson collection of hotels.

In October 1976, the hotel was closed to make way for dozens of craftsmen working with carefully conceived plans to restore it in a manner that would exceed its original grandeur. As an indication of the hotel's importance to the city, the $6 million funding for the renovation was supplied by a consortium of six Detroit financial institutions with the loan guaranteed from the Federal Development Administration.

Even while work was still in progress, the doors reopened in April 1978, to help host one of the nation's largest conventions. However, a gala celebration in June 1978 marked the official reopening under the Radisson Cadillac banner. National, state and local dignitaries participating cited it as "truly a historic moment for the city."

Ross Roy, Incorporated

One of America's top agencies is a hometown believer

Ross Roy, Inc., now the only major Detroit-owned advertising agency in the city, was founded by Ross Roy in 1926.

From a beginning of little more in the way of assets than a typewriter, kitchen table and chair, the company

headquarters in nearby downtown Detroit now occupy all or parts of five buildings. Other offices are located in several major U.S. and Canadian cities.

Roy began as an automobile salesman. He compiled detailed product information for his own use based on facts and figures from car literature and ads, convinced that a prospective buyer would decide favorably if he had the right information on his line of cars as well as those of competition. And, more often than not, the better informed customer did buy from him. Noting his success, other salesmen asked for the information he was using, and a business was born, In 1927, the company moved from Janesville, Wisconsin, to Detroit and incorporated. The move to the Motor City brought the new, specialized service company closer to Dodge, its major client of the time. In 1928, the Chrysler Corporation acquired Dodge, and Ross Roy, Inc. was then able to offer the now well-

A 1941 Dodge Truck ad prepared by Ross Roy, Inc. for its first advertising client.

developed sales service to all Chrysler Corporation dealers.

In the 1930s the company moved into new fields of sales training and merchandising, and soon found that other large U.S. corporations could use these selling methods. The company was among the pioneers in the development of visual aids used widely today in industry and in education. Ross Roy, Inc. soon became a leader in the production of sound slidefilms, and at one time was the largest user of 35mm film outside of the motion picture entertainment industry. In the late 1930s, the company found that it was assisting clients in all of the follow-through training and merchandising steps in the sale but other organizations were doing the advertising. The decision was made to seek advertising clients. In 1940, Ross Roy, Inc. became a full-fledged advertising agency with the multi-million-dollar Dodge Truck account.

The war years following 1941 brought an end to automobile advertising and merchandising, and to many agencies associated with the business. Ross Roy, Inc. however, with expertise in

Ross Roy, Inc. headquarters on East Jefferson Avenue in Detroit.

communications met the needs of the armed forces for education and training materials. Early in the war, the company was called upon by the War Production Board to produce the entire educational program for the Controlled Materials Plan in U.S. industry.

At the end of the war, the company resumed its merchandising business and turned full attention to the development of advertising clients. This marked a period of growth that has continued to this day. From a four-million-dollar volume in 1946, the company has grown to a $175-million plus agency serving a long list of clients in widely diversified fields.

The "spirit of service" of the agency has carried over into volunteer support of many of the Detroit area's community activities. The concept of community leadership, first started by Roy, has been continued under the leadership of agency President John S. Pingel. Pingel joined the agency in 1960 through a merger with Brooke, Smith, French and Dorrance. The company client list was enhanced by two additional mergers with old-line Detroit agencies: Zimmer, Keller and Calvert in 1970, and Gray and Kilgore in 1975.

As an advertising agency, Ross Roy, Inc. stands unique in the world today. Its clients are leading names in the retail, automotive and industrial fields. From Bacardi & Company, Chrysler Corporation, Detroit Bank & Trust, Detroit Edison, Federal-Mogul, through divisions of General Electric, K mart, Michigan Bell Telephone Company, Uniroyal, and Ziebart, to name just a few, Ross Roy, Inc. represents people you know. Client services range from in-house art and film animation and award-winning ads and commercials to engineering reports and analyses; in all, services not available from any other single organization. Ross Roy, Inc. is an outstanding example of the opportunities for growth and success in American enterprise.

Fred Sanders

Sweet success began with a barrel of borrowed sugar

On the front page of the June 17, 1875 edition of the Detroit *Free Press,* there appeared this brief notice:

A NEW ESTABLISHMENT — Mr. F. Sanders, late of Philadelphia, will this morning open a confectionery and ice

cream establishment in the new store, No. 166 Woodward Avenue, corner of State street. He is a practical confectioner, has a handsome place, and will devote his entire attention to customers.

For young Frederick Sanders, this date marked the beginning of an enterprise which is now well past the century mark in service to the Detroit area.

Born in Biehl, Baden, Germany in 1848, Frederick was brought to America

The World's Fair fountain bought by Frederick Sanders after the Chicago Fair in 1893

The Palace of Sweets, opened in 1897 by Frederick Sanders (at right)

with his family at the age of three. His father, a baker, settled his family in Peru, Illinois, and it was here that Frederick learned his first baking lessons. But his hopes went beyond baking white bread and rolls, and at 17, he sailed for Germany to learn the secrets of confectionery and catering.

Frederick learned his trade rapidly in Karlsruhe, and within two or three years opened his own small shop on a narrow street in Frankfurt. The shop was successful, but the New World beckoned as it had for Frederick's father. In 1870, he returned to America with his young wife, Rosa, finally selecting Detroit to start anew.

With some misgivings and little capital, he opened his shop on Woodward Avenue, where the J. L. Hudson block was to rise later, and far above the center of business along Jefferson Avenue. With his limited capital drained to outfit his shop, Frederick managed to open only through the kindness of W. H. Edgar, founder of Edgar's Sugar House, who loaned him a barrel of sugar.

The exceptional quality of Sanders confectionery and ice cream was quickly recognized, but alas, the store was too far north to succeed. Within a year, Frederick moved down Woodward toward Michigan Avenue, and here he prospered.

Here, too, in the mid 1870s he was

the first to make a business of the ice cream soda, happening upon the idea one sultry evening when all of his cream, used for the then-popular sweet cream soda, had soured. It was an instant success.

In 1891, Frederick expanded to the corner of Michigan with the construction of the baroque "Pavilion of Sweets", soon to become a social center for the growing city. Here, Frederick Sanders installed one of the first electric motors in the city, but it continually broke down. Faced with the loss of a customer, the electric shop pleaded for one more chance and sent over a young man who fixed the motor so that it stayed fixed. His name was Henry Ford.

The corner of Michigan and Woodward was far too valuable for a single-story building, however, and in 1897, Frederick again moved to make way for the Majestic Building. He opened a new "Palace of Sweets" just a couple of doors north. Across its back wall, with its gleaming flavor taps, was the famous World's Fair Fountain, bought by Frederick Sanders after the Chicago Fair in 1893.

In 1900, Frederick brought his son-in-law, John Miller, into the business, taking him from Colonel Goebel, the brewer. And with this move, the young company's future was charted. Within a few years, Frederick's real love, baking, was added to the candy and ice cream

operation. And in 1913, the year of the founder's death, John Miller bought 100 front feet on Woodward Avenue near Henry Street for $150,000, to build a second store and plant. Concurrently, the business became a partnership of John Miller, Frederick's son, Edwin, and his grandson, Fred W. Sanders.

The company grew rapidly with a burgeoning Detroit. At the approach of World War II, 21 Sanders stores were in neighborhood and downtown shopping areas, served by a new and larger plant, opened in 1941 in Highland Park. In addition to the sale of candy, bakery and ice cream products of the highest quality, these stores were pioneers in fast food service. At the heart of it was the hot fudge sundae, which by then had replaced the ice cream soda as the Sanders trademark.

Diversification followed World War II, as Sanders departments were established in area supermarkets, while many more Sanders stores were being opened across the sprawling metropolitan area.

In its fourth generation of family ownership and direction, the company entered the 1970s with more than 50 stores and 300 supermarket departments, and with the beginnings of a national sales program. The name which first appeared on the little shop on a narrow street in Frankfurt was on its way to becoming known across the United States.

Smith, Hinchman & Grylls Associates, Inc.

SH&G: the nation's oldest, continuous architectural/engineering/planning firm

Three consecutive generations of the Smith family, Sheldon, Mortimer and Fred L. — all self-taught architects —

were the beginning of today's Smith, Hinchman & Grylls Associates, Inc., the oldest continuous architectural firm in

the United States. Sheldon Smith came to Detroit in 1855, after spending his early years in Jamestown, New York, and his first practice in Sandusky, Ohio. His son and grandson came into the profession as they reached manhood, and in 1903, the firm became an architectural-engineering corporation.

The growth story of SH&G matches the physical growth of Detroit, and more than thirty downtown Detroit buildings stand as proof of the firm's influence, including such buildings as the First Federal Savings & Loan, the Guardian, Buhl and Penobscot Buildings, the J.L. Hudson department store, the Patrick V. McNamara Federal Office Building, and the Michigan Bell Telephone Headquarters. Two five-story commercial buildings

The Penobscot Building (now City National Bank Building), as it looked shortly after completion in 1928. It remained the tallest building in the city until the completion of the Detroit Plaza Hotel in 1977.

These two buildings on Monroe Street are the oldest remaining structures designed by Sheldon Smith. They were built in 1859 for a merchant named Williams.

on Monroe Street, dating from 1859, are the oldest remaining examples of Sheldon Smith's work.

Today, SH&G is part of a family of companies that employs more than 700 professionals and support staff, has billings of over $22 million, and is involved with projects having a value exceeding a billion dollars. Headquarters is a five-story glass and aluminum building in downtown Detroit, completely modernized in 1972 from a building originally designed by the firm in 1910. On the roof is a 1,000 square foot solar collector, one of the first privately financed solar installations in the nation.

From its origination as a one-man practice in 1853, SH&G now has offices or associated companies in Ann Arbor, Chicago, Illinois; Louisville, Kentucky; Phoenix, Arizona; Washington, D.C.; Atlanta, Georgia; Toronto, Canada; and Jeddah, Saudi Arabia. Projects have been designed for every continent in the world except Africa, and a long list of awards and citations attest to the high quality of architecture and engineering in the buildings.

Since its incorporation in 1903, SH&G has been closely associated with industrial clients in many fields, including automobiles, utilities, farm equipment, electronic equipment and heavy machinery. Some of these facilities are more than two million square feet in size, and all involve the most sophisticated materials handling systems, manufacturing engineering and waste treatment plants.

Health facilities are another major segment of SH&G billings, and include such outstanding hospitals as Harper-Grace, Crittenton and William Beaumont Hospitals in Detroit, and national

institutions like the National Institutes of Health in Bethesda, Maryland, the Air Force School of Aerospace Medicine, at San Antonio, the Howard University Teaching Hospital in Washington, D.C., the University of Louisville Health Sciences Center and the new University Hospital, and a number of dental schools.

Education and Commerce is another large Division of the firm, which has executed a number of outstanding projects. Among them are the million square foot K mart International Headquarters, at Troy, Michigan, the new Detroit Riverfront Arena, a research and administrative complex for Owens-Corning Fiberglas, at Granville, Ohio, and a major new government office building across the Potomac from Washington, D.C. The Transportation Division is engaged in the design and engineering of Atlanta's new Hartsfield International Airport.

The three founders of the corporation, Fred L. Smith, Theodore Hinchman, Jr., and H. J. Maxwell Grylls died between 1935 and 1941, and since that time, ownership of the firm has been in the hands of the officers and associates and no descendants of the original families are involved today.

Beginning in 1972, SH&G began a program of internal expansion through the provision of additional professional services to their clients, and through the purchase of stock in, and association with, outstanding professional firms in other areas of the country. The first such arrangement was with the outstanding planning and landscape architecture firm of Johnson, Johnson & Roy, in Ann Arbor, Michigan. Later, an entree into the mid-South was made when Ryan, Cooke & Zuern Associates, Inc., of Louisville, Kentucky and became a member of the family of firms. The largest such association came in 1977 with the joining of Chicago's Metz, Train, Olson & Youngren, a fifty-year old architectural/engineering firm.

Ranking in the top dozen of A/E firms in the country, SH&G is constantly expanding its professional base of services. Specialties like interior design, graphics and signage, computer programming, construction management, and project development are examples of fast growing areas of client services. Under the direction of President Philip J. Meathe, FAIA, and board members James R. Livingston, AIA; Merrill M. Bush, PE; Peter P. Petkoff, PE; and Peter C. Darin, PE, SH&G is headed for its ultimate goal "to be the No. 1 A/E firm in the country".

Hiram Walker Incorporated

Hiram Walker's arrival in Detroit heralded new era

Had it not been for adverse legislation in effect in the State of Michigan in 1858, Hiram Walker, the founder of Hiram Walker-Gooderham & Worts Limited, might well have built his distillery in Detroit instead of on the Canadian side of the Detroit river.

Born in East Douglas, Massachusetts on July 4, 1816, Hiram Walker was nine years old when his father Willis died in a smallpox epidemic. Learning to shift for himself, he left the family farm at 20 and, after working in a dry goods store in Boston, he headed west. In 1838 he arrived in Detroit (population 9,000). Failing in several early business ventures, Walker eventually opened up his own grocery on Woodward. He got a good look at the whisky business through the buying and selling of grain and by 1857, he was known throughout the United States and Canada as the leading commissioned merchant in Detroit.

Investing $40,000 in 468 acres of timberland on the Canadian side of the Detroit river, Walker entered the market with flour, feed and whisky in 1858. From his small distillery, he developed a consistent light spirit for sale under his own label, "Club" Whisky, which became an international success. When American competitors persuaded Congress to pass a law requiring the country of origin to be prominently displayed on the label, Walker incorporated the word "Canadian" into his brand name. Thus was born "Canadian Club." When competitors tried to pirate his success,

he fought them with every device known, including injunctions and advertising.

Walker hired a "drummer," John McBride, in 1859 and became the first distiller in the entire area to have a traveling salesman. He took McBride into partnership and the firm became Hiram Walker & Co. In 1867, he lost McBride to a rival distilling company which Walker later bought out. The name changed to Hiram Walker & Sons when he took his eldest sons, Edward Chandler and Franklin Harrington, into the business.

Hiram Walker remained a citizen of the U. S. until his death, January 12, 1899.

The Walker family kept control of the company until 1926 when they sold it to Harry C. Hatch and a group of associates, who united it with the oldest distillery in Canada — Gooderham & Worts Limited, of Toronto. The price was $14 million — $5 million for the physical assets and $9 million for the Canadian Club trademark.

Hatch brought a tremendous surge of expansion to the operation. In 1927, he established Hiram Walker-Gooderham & Worts Limited as the parent company and when Prohibition ended in 1933, construction of the world's largest distillery, Hiram Walker & Sons, Inc., was started at Peoria, Illinois. Next, he turned to the Scotch whisky industry and bought the entire stock of George Ballantine & Son Limited, Glasgow. Two years later, Hiram Walker & Sons

(Scotland) Limited, the largest grain distillery in Europe, went into production. In 1943, the company purchased a distilling company outside Buenos Aires, Argentina. The company was ready for the postwar boom with the building of a bottling plant, now located at Burlingame, California.

Hatch died in 1946 and was succeeded by two presidents (Howard R. Walton, who retired in 1961 and Burdette E. Ford, who retired in 1964) before his son, H. Clifford Hatch, took over. Mr. Hatch currently is president and chief executive officer of the company.

A major expansion program began. Work was started on a program which virtually doubled the production facilities at Walkerville, the largest distillery in Canada, and construction of a new distillery-blending-bottling complex was completed near Winfield, British Columbia. In addition to its distilleries in Canada, the U.S. and South America, the company owns and operates through subsidiary companies eight distilleries in Scotland, the Courvoisier company in France and the Kahlua company in Mexico.

Little did Hiram Walker dream his investment of $40,000 in timberland would one day become the nerve center of an $890 million international operation. Today, the company is the third largest distiller of alcoholic beverages and the only one among the top four not to diversify. There are more than 31,000 shareholders and 7,500 employees world-wide. Sixty percent of the company's products are sold in the U.S., 18 percent in Canada and the remaining 22 percent in Europe and elsewhere. The demand for Canadian Club continues to grow and it is now sold in more than 150 countries.

All the operations were performed by hand in the three Canadian Club bottling lines during the 1800s.

Laden with cartons of Canadian Club on their way to customers, the first truck sold in Windsor in 1911 found the going rough.

235

WJBK-TV

For 30 years, they've seen it all together.

For half of all Metro Detroiters, it would be difficult to imagine life without television. The other half, those over 35, can recall clearly when broadcasting meant only radio. For them, the coming of television ranks as one of the great events in our national life, as something of a miracle — living pictures transmitted instantly through the air.

WJBK-TV2, Detroit — founded, owned and operated by the Storer Broadcasting Company — was among television's earliest pioneers, inaugurating regularly scheduled telecasts on October 24, 1948. At first, TV was a little more than a curiosity, a tremendous corporate gamble, a venture of faith. It was a time of unpredictable live programming and scratchy movies, of fuzzy kinescopes and frequent "technical difficulties," of scarce and tiny-screened home receivers.

But early telecasters and their audience quickly realized the infant medium's limitless potential, with program schedules expanding rapidly from the initial few hours in the evening. Viewers marveled at TV2's first live telecast of Detroit Lions football. They watched, fascinated, as Harry Truman and G. Mennen Williams came out on top in 1948 in Michigan's first live TV election returns, on TV2. They were there a year later when TV2 presented Detroit's live, local television newscast. No one knew it at the time, but they were seeing the new medium take its first tentative steps toward becoming the number one source of information and entertainment for most Americans that it is today.

Technological developments came quickly. The network "cable" reached the Motor City, bringing with it a live galaxy of stars on the CBS Television Network, with WJBK-TV2 a charter affiliate. Meantime, the station continued to pile up an impressive list of additional "firsts," including the first local television newsfilm, taking Metro Detroiters inside their city halls and school board meetings, to ballgames and parades, to scenes of triumph and tragedy.

TV2 Eyewitness News and its team concept of electronic journalism evolved rapidly. In 1952, the station took its viewers on television tours of eight schools in just seven days — live. Today, of course, it is common to see three or more live reports in a single half-hour newscast. Ten TV2 remote crews, equipped with electronic "mini-cams" and both videotape and instantaneous microwave transmission facilities, range through every corner of Southeastern Michigan, in addition to widespread coverage by new, lightweight film cameras.

Twice in its three decades, WJBK-TV outgrew its studios — moving in 1956 from its first cramped quarters in Detroit's Masonic Temple to its own, entirely new building in the city's New Center area. Then, in 1971, Storer Broadcasting created one of the nation's major broadcast centers at TV2's transmitter site on Nine Mile Road in suburban Southfield, bequeathing the old New Center facility to Public Television's WTVS.

All the while, the station continued following its destiny to be "first" — first in Michigan with total color capability (beginning with live color previews of Detroit's prime product, the new cars) and first in Michigan with a complete videotape installation in 1957.

But even as the station led the way in technical innovation, it remained close to the community, to the people it was

WJBK-TV2 became Michigan's first television station with full color capabilities in 1956. Cameras were cumbersome but technology quickly advanced to the "mini-cam" and instantaneous videotape images.

pledged from the start to serve. Nowhere was electronic progress coupled with the human touch more evident than in still another TV2 "first" — the first live telecast of the birth of a baby and the first Eyewitness visit to a hospital emergency room. They were dramatic early examples of the concern for people and people's needs that has distinguished WJBK-TV2 through all of its 30 years.

In 1962, the station initiated Michigan's first television editorial — not so much to champion particular points of view as to stimulate viewers to form and act on their *own* opinions. The traditional tagline of TV2 editorial Viewpoints — "What do *you* think?" — has become a watchword for positive and constructive community action.

During the critical period of urban unrest in the late '60s and early '70s, TV2 originated, hosted and continuously sponsored annual spring tours of Metro Detroit by the entire state legislature, an opportunity to view Michigan's metropolis and its problems first hand — for many lawmakers, for the first time.

During overheated big city summers, TV2's 6 roving "Swimmobiles" — the "ol' swimming hole" materializing on teeming urban streets — have become an annual treat for tens of thousands of Detroit kids.

WJBK-TV2 conceived and maintains learn-by-doing trainee and internship programs for students interested in broadcast or electronics careers. It has sponsored numerous college scholarships for promising young people, notably through another traditional TV2 community event — TV2 Editorial Writing Awards for Detroit high school seniors.

But, beyond these behind-the-scenes efforts to be a close and faithful friend of the community, WJBK-TV2's major contribution to Metro Detroit has been on the air, as a broadcaster reaching a potential audience of more than four million. Nor has it been a one-way street of communication. Through continuous audience research, surveys, and person-to-person interviews with both community leaders and citizens, the people have reached and impressed the station with their problems, their needs, their aspirations.

Certainly, TV2 exists to inform, educate and entertain.

But over 30 years, TV2 and its viewers have formed in a very real sense, an active and successful partnership. For three decades, they've seen it all together.

Arthur Young & Company

Continuing the practice of service and trust to clients

In 1894, a youthful Scottish-trained accountant began an accounting firm in Chicago. Nine years later, the accountant, Arthur Young, was joined in his ambitious undertaking by his brother, Stanley, and William Sutherland, and the firm became known as Arthur Young & Company. The three partners soon had offices in Chicago and Kansas City; the headquarters of the firm later moved to New York City where it remained.

Today, the nationally recognized Arthur Young & Company serves more than 1,500 clients in the State of Michigan alone. Its roots in Michigan go back to a merger with a Toledo-based firm in 1950 — Wideman, Madden & Dolan — and that Company's history is traced to a 1938 merger with Simeon Janes & Company, a Detroit firm.

Simeon Janes was a University of Detroit accounting instructor in the mid-1920s when he began to realize one of his cherished hopes. He opened his own accounting firm, Simeon Janes & Company, and continued attending classes at the University in the morning while he took care of h8s business in the afternoons. Accounting was strictly a wintertime business in those days — revolving around the arrival of March 15 and the end of the tax season (then the deadline for tax returns). Janes, striving for a year-round practice, put many of his University students to work in his firm, and also employed friends from the Detroit College of Law where he had obtained his law degree.

In 1960, Arthur Young & Company was joined in partnership by the firm of Shaw & Olsen. Shaw & Olsen, which began on May 16, 1946, employed several partners in its service years in Michigan. Donald Schweitzer and Lawrence Handren joined the firm some time after its start in the '40s, and, later, Grace Dimmer became a partner in the company. Dimmer was the first woman in Michigan to win a Certified Public Accountant designation.

From the beginning the firm had clients covering every part of Michigan's economy. One particularly vivid memory is of the United Auto Workers' Local 600 and their elections which Shaw, Olsen & Dimmer supervised. Some 45,000 UAW members belonged

William R. Shaw, Edward G. Olsen, Lawrence E. Handren and Donald L. Schweitzer at the 1960 entry of their practice with Arthur Young.

to Local 600, making it one of the largest units in the world. To provide each member the opportunity to vote, the polls were open for five days, 12 hours a day, and the auditing firm had to be present at all times. Since 15 to 20 candidates normally ran for offices, more than 70,000 ballots would be cast. The Shaw, Olsen & Dimmer auditors then spent Friday night and all day Saturday tabulating the vote.

By the time the firm merged with Arthur Young & Company in 1960, Dimmer had retired. Shaw became managing partner in 1962 and served in that capacity until 1972. He was president of the Michigan Association of CPAs in 1965-66 and won the Association's Distinguished Service Award in 1967. Olsen continued the Arthur Young tradition of professional responsibility by serving as MACPA president in 1974-75. He was awarded a life membership in 1978.

In 1965, Arthur Young & Company merged with the firm of White, Bower & Prevo. Harry Prevo, who served as president of the Michigan Association of CPAs in the mid-1940s, began WBP in 1933 along with Edwin H. Bower and Hugh A. White.

Although the firm's beginnings were in a time when the nation was experiencing the throes of the Great Depression, its business developed steadily. White, Bower & Prevo was formed in response to the insistence for open reporting to shareholders of a company's business position. Within a few years WBP was auditor for the large

This early Burroughs adding machine was standard equipment for turn-of-the-century accountants.

brokerage houses in Michigan, as well as the Detroit and Chicago stock exchanges.

A major spur to the firm's growth was the re-establishment of breweries with the 1933 repeal of the Volstead Act. City Brewing Company (since absorbed by larger breweries) was the first public stock offering in which WBP acted as the independent auditor.

Today, Arthur Young & Company's offices in Detroit and Lansing, Michigan provide a full range of business, tax and advisory services. The firm has grown to 4,500 professionals in its United States offices, with another 6,500 professionals in 51 countries, a practice conducted by member firms of Arthur Young International.

Peter H. Burgher is managing partner of Arthur Young's Michigan practice. He leads eight partners who share responsibility for continuing the firm's tradition of trust and service to clients.

Around 1900 the corner of Michigan and Trumbull shows the south side of Michigan across the street from the haymarket, above. Sifting the past: Archaeologists screen soil searching for clues to Detroit's 19th century heritage at the construction site of the Renaissance Center.

238

Detroit Savings Bank Building (formerly the Chamber of Commerce Building), at Griswold and State. This was the main office of the Detroit Savings Bank (later the Detroit Bank) from 1921 to 1963.

Epilogue

etroit has had, by North American standards at least, a long history — often colorful and exciting, at times disheartening and discouraging, and on occasion even dangerous. Most importantly, it has been the story of people.

Detroit is the story of Cadillac landing with a party of French soldiers and Canadian woodsmen, building a small log fort and establishing an outpost to control the Great Lakes fur trade. It is the saga of siege and confrontation between the Ottawa Chief Pontiac and the British Major Gladwin. It is the story of surrender, occupation and famine, of General Hull and General Brock.

Detroit is the story of Lewis Cass, Father Richard and Judge Woodward, and families from New England coming to settle in the wilderness of the Old Northwest. It is townspeople on the frontier facing the dreaded cholera. It is a growing mercantile center and a busy waterfront.

Detroit is the story of the conflicts of abolition and slavery, the Underground Railroad and the Civil War. It is Eber Ward producing the first steel by the Bessemer process, Jeremiah Dwyer manufacturing stoves, James Vernor brewing a barrel of his ginger ale, and Elijah McCoy perfecting his railroad car lubricating cup. It is the story of copper and iron and lumber, and, of course, the horseless carriage.

Detroit is Charles King driving along Jefferson Avenue, Henry Ford at work in his Bagley Street garage, Ransom Olds building his curved-dash runabout. It is $5-a-day and crowds at factory gates, and workers from Poland and Armenia and Hungary and Belgium. It is the story of World War and the growth of an industry — the Huppmobile, the Brush, the Maxwell, the Krit, the Saxon, and the most famous of them all, the Model T.

Detroit is the empty stomachs of people faced with the reality of no work, closed banks and breadlines. It is the story of hard times, hunger marches and union protests — bathtub gin, blind pigs, bootleg whiskey and gangland murder. It is Ty Cobb, Gar Wood and Joe Louis. It is Pearl Harbor and men and women building tanks, bombers and gun sights, ambulances, ball bearings and cannon shells.

Detroit is the story of freeways, urban renewal and Paradise Valley. It is books and paintings and theater, the Lone Ranger and the sound of Motown. It is the story of marching and rioting and New Detroit, of people struggling and people working together.

Detroit is the story of the *Abend-Post* and Greektown, of strawberry festivals and "pysanky." It is the people from a hundred different countries — neighborhoods and children, the Eastern Market and Belle Isle, sailing on Lake St. Clair and 1000-foot ore boats.

And, on the bank of *le Détroit*, the great towers of the Renaissance Center.

As Detroit enters the last decades of the 20th century, the story is of a city faced, as are most of America's urban centers, with the problems that some say are unsolvable: the problems of inner-city decay, a shinking tax base, racial tension, air and water pollution, street crime, the financing of municipal services.

But Detroit today is being provided a new life and times because people who are in leadership positions or who are moving into those positions see Detroit's future not as insufferable but as a challenge than can, in reality, be met head on. The problems that are there are solvable; as some say, they just have to be, no matter their nature.

Detroit has magnificent presence and potential for mastering the art of urban livability and economic success — a necessary duality for existence. Its population of nearly five million is as productive as it is diverse in its cultural heritage. Backing that population is one of the world's great industrial complexes. Detroit's strong and practical minded business community has an increasing unity and awareness of the city's current and future needs. The ethnic leadership is strong, capable and motivated toward the resolution of historic conflicts and the commitment of structuring a more dynamic and livable community.

This book has portrayed Detroit in all its important yesterdays and foretold of a new era arising out of the ashes of its existence. And through the sound of muted pessimists can be heard the ever increasing roar of optimism. The surge toward the new Detroit: American Urban Renaissance, is there.

Coleman A. Young, first black mayor of Detroit.

Credits

Anyone who is interested in studying the history of Detroit will, before long, find themselves in the reading room of the Burton Historical Collection at the Detroit Public Library. Here will be found in books, newspapers, photographs, maps, letters, diaries and other manuscripts, the story of this great city.

I spent many hours in the Burton Collection and owe a sincere debt of gratitude to Alice Dalligan, Chief of the Collection, and her staff: to Noel Van Gorden, First Assistant; to Margaret Ward, Field Archivist, who helped dig out many of the details of Detroit's black community; to Gloria Birkenmeier, Reference Librarian, who expertly guided me in my search through hundreds of photographs; and to Joseph Oldenburg, Curator of Manuscripts, a fine researcher and knowledgable historian.

I would also like to express my thanks to Agatha Kalkanis, Chief, Music and Performing Arts Department, Detroit Public Library, and to her staff: Jean Currie, Curator, E. Azalia Hackley Collection, and to Terence Gahman, Department First Assistant, who often turned up answers to difficult reference questions.

Thanks also to James Bradley, Chief, National Automotive History Collection, Detroit Public Library, for his expert help and advice; to Richard Maciejewski, Chief, Municipal Reference Library; and to James Dance, Coordinator of Public Relations, Detroit Public Library.

My heartiest thanks to Solon Weeks, Director of the Detroit Historical Museum, and his staff — Sylvia Williams, Curator of Urban History, and James E. Conway, Curator of Architectural History, who was always prompt in helping with my frequent requests. Thanks also to Robert E. Lee, Curator, and Maurice Jackson, Museum Preparator, Dossin Great Lakes Museum; and to Dr. William Phenix, Curator, Fort Wayne Military Museum.

For the selection of material and photographs on Detroit's labor movement, I had the help of Dr. Philip P. Mason, Director, and Margery S. Long, Audio Visual Curator, Archives of Labor and Urban Affairs, Wayne State University.

In Dearborn I received assistance and guidance from Douglas A. Bakken, Director, and David R. Crippen, Reference Archivist, Ford Archives/Henry Ford Museum; from David Glick, Vice President in charge of Education, Greenfield Village; and from Robert Ritter, Director, and David E. Wojack, Office of Public Relations, Greenfield Village and Henry Ford Museum.

I would also like to mention several individuals who deserve a very special thank you. It was indeed a pleasure to work with Nemo Warr, an outstanding photographer. Always ready to help, he often produced photographs of documents and paintings superior to the original. Thanks to my friends Glen and Elaine Moon. Elaine was most generous in sharing her research of Detroit and its history. Thank you to Harry Wolf, who welcomed me into his home and let me borrow freely from his fine collections of photographs.

And, there were so many many others who helped, including: Michael H. Fritz, Administrator, Harper Hospital; Ruth Lee of Belle Isle; Michelle Kapecky, Head Librarian, and Tony Spina, Chief Photographer, *Detroit Free Press*; Susan Cherry, Money Museum, National Bank of Detroit; Dr. James Anderson, Director, University of Michigan Ethnic Heritage Center; William Rauhauser and Carla Anderson, Center for Creative Studies; James Wren, Librarian, and Bernice Huffman, Motor Vehicle Manufacturers Association; Charles H. Martinez of Detroit; Joseph Wiedelman, Photographic Department, and Edward Becker and Sharon Martin, Reference Library, *Detroit News;* Hal Middlesworth, Director of Public Relations, Detroit Tigers; Herman Allen, St. Clair Shores Historical Commission; Clarence C. Woodard of Grosse Pointe Woods; Robin Bahr, Coordinator of Social/Cultural/Recreational Events, International Institute; Thelma Young of Detroit; Sherry Bird, Public Relations Director, Trizec Development, Inc.; Connie Ruohomacki, News Bureau Manager, University of Detroit; Joseph P. Giumette, Senior Vice-President, Anthony M. Franco, Inc; Diane Edgecomb, Central Business District Association; Barbara Lewis, Public Relations Associate, Jewish Welfare Federation of Detroit; James Hillman, Director, and Rose Silvey, Detroit American Indian Center; Dr. Robert Sinclair, Department of Geography, Wayne State University; Frederick Osten of Detroit; William Bostick of Detroit; Janet Langois, Director, Folklore Archives, Wayne State University; Leon L. Carr, Director of Communications, Detroit Urban League; Richard Kinney, Associate Director, Wayne State University Press; Leon Buyse, Editor, Belgian Publishing Company; Walter Steyskal of Highland Park; Berthold Vogt, Editor, *Detroiter Abend-Post*; Ferruccio P. De Conti, President, Sokol Detroit; Marlene Baker, *The Italian Tribune;* Mitchell Lewandowski of Hamtramck; Stanley Krajewski, Editor-in-Chief, *Polish Daily News*; Henry Garcia, Director, H.O.P.E.; David A. Armour, Assistant Superintendent, Mackinac Island State Park Commission; James P. Gallagher, Director of Public Affairs, Smith, Hinchman & Grylls Associates, Inc; Dr. John Dann, Director, and Dr. Douglas Marshall, Curator of Maps, William L. Clements Library, University of Michigan; George Booth, CIT Photo Services, Wayne State University; Edward C. Weber, Head, Labadie Collection, University of Michigan; Jean A. Brooking, Publications Division, Minnesota Historical Society; and Joel L. Samuels, Director of Library Services, The Newberry Library, Chicago.

Finally, to all those people who were kind enough to stop and ask, "How is the book coming?" To you — thanks.

Arthur M. Woodford

The editors and publishers of *Detroit: American Urban Renaissance* are indebted to a number of people and organizations who, over the many months of production, believed as we did that Detroit citizens and visitors to Detroit should have available an entertaining and pictorially oriented history.

Our special thanks, in addition to those extended by Arthur Woodford, go to:

The staff and volunteer leadership of the Greater Detroit Chamber of Commerce for their continuing support and assistance, including John R. Hamann, Chairman of the Board; John S. Pingel, Immediate Past Chairman; Frank E. Smith, CCE, President; Dwight Havens, CCE, Immediate Past President; Charles A. Muer, Board Vice Chairman, Communication & Member Services Division; Robert L. Sweany, CCE, Senior Vice President, Administration/Operations; Robert Stockton, J. E. "Bud" Stedman, Susan M. Halwachs, Donald A. Booth, Donald M. Paget, and to Marian Belman for her good natured and consistent efficiency.

We extend our heartfelt thanks to the Detroit History Editorial Advisory Board, Greater Detroit Chamber of Commerce, especially to Chairman William E. Stevenson. Members of the special board included John H. Burdakin, Mrs. Esther G. Edwards, Tom Jones, Patti Knox, Benson Manlove, Charles A. Muer, Alberto Pulido, Ms. Khadejah Shelby, Saul J. Waldman, Mrs. Pat Walker, and Solan Weeks.

From the technical side, we want to give our own pat on the back to Detroit photographer Nemo Warr, who provided excellent copies of historical pictures.

Others who contributed to the success of *Detroit: American Urban Renaissance* and who deserve a special note of thanks include Dale Ware, Miller Williams, John Williams, Jr., Burch Williams, Tom Warren, Joseph H. Williams, Jack McMichael, Jr., David York, Richard Sullivan, Clyde C. Cole, Marvin Wynn, Carolotta Brandon of The Type House, Inc., J. R. Jones and Scott Yandell of Lightshed Studios, David Wadley, Hobart and Sue Hammond, Ed and Mary Brett, Peggi Ridgway, Brian Ridgway, Pat Briggs, and, of course, Caroline Johnson, Mary Rounds and Glenda Silvey.

Concept and design by Continental Heritage Press, Tulsa.
Printed and bound by Von Hoffmann Press, Saint Louis.
Type set in Souvenir by The Type House, Inc., Tulsa.
Text sheets are Warren Payflo by S. D. Warren Company.
Endleaves are Antique Multicolor Oatmeal
by Process Materials.
Cover is 10 point Lexotone print by Holliston Mills.

Sources of photographs, maps and art appearing in this book are noted here in alphabetical order and by page number (numbers in parentheses indicate multiple pictures provided by source on one page). Those photographs appearing in the chapter *Partners in Detroit's Economy,* pages 198 through 237, were provided by the represented firms.

Anderson, Carla: 150(2).
Archives of Labor and Urban Affairs, Wayne State University: 58, 88, 90-91, 90(2), 93, 96, 97, 106, 121, 128(2), 130(4), 131(3), 132(3), 134-135, 136(3), 137, 138(2), 142-143.
Ayer, Edward E. Collection, The Newberry Library, Chicago: 14.
Baker Family: 166.
Bonaldi Family: 166
Bass, Robert R., ***Early Bench and Bar of Detroit,*** **(Detroit, 1907):** 29.
Bruce, Eleanor: 192
Burton Historical Collection, Detroit Public Library: 12-13, 16(2), 21, 22, 23(2), 24, 26-27, 27, 29(2), 30, 32-33, 34, 35, 36(3), 39, 40, 41, 42(3), 43, 44(2), 45(2), 46(3), 47(2), 49, 50, 52(2), 53(2), 54, 55, 56(2), 57, 58, 59, 60(3), 61(2), 62-63, 66(3), 67, 68(2), 69(3), 70(2), 71, 72(3), 73(2), 74(2), 75, 76, 79(2), 80(3), 81(2), 82(3), 83(4), 84(2), 85, 86, 87, 91, 94, 95(3), 97, 99(2), 100, 102(2), 105(2), 106, 108, 109(2), 110, 113, 116(3), 117(2), 119(2), 122, 124(3), 138(3), 139(3), 141(3), 148(3), 154-155, 155, 156(2), 157(2), 172(2), 173(3), 180(2), 181(3), 238.
Buyse, Leon: 161, 162(3), 163(2).
Clements, William L. Library, University of Michigan: 18, 19, 20, 22, 24, 25, 28, 29.
DeConti, Ferruccio P.: 164, 165.
Detroit American Indian Center: 168(2).
Detroit Bank & Trust: 75, 239.
Detroit, City of, Department of Public Information: 182-183, 195, 197, 239.
Detroit Free Press: 28, 126, 127(2), 141, 146, 147, 149, 158(3), 159(2), 167, 168.
Detroit Historical Museum: 15(2), 54(3), 71(2), 72(2), 77, 101, 105, 110, 150(3).
Detroit Institute of Arts: 20, 49, 176(2).
Detroit Medical Center: 191.
Detroit News: 11, 74(2), 112, 112-113, 114(3), 115, 116, 118(3), 119, 121(2), 122(3), 123(4), 125(4), 126(5), 127, 140(2), 144(2), 146, 147, 149(3), 177, 184(4).
Detroit Pistons: 127.
Detroit Police Department Photo Lab: 179, 188(2).
Detroit Public Library: 17, 21, 173(2), 183.
Detroit Tigers: 125, 127.
Dossin, Great Lakes Museum: 38, 39, 104(3).
Finnish Cultural Center: 165(2).
Ford Archives/Henry Ford Museum: 100, 103(2), 107(2), 142, 189.
Ford Motor Company: 103, 108, 140.
Fort Wayne Military Museum: 190.
Giglio Family: 166.
Goslow, Alice: 170, 182, 196(2), 197.
Grant, G. M.: ***Ocean to Ocean: Sanford Fleming's Expedition Through Canada in 1872,*** **(London, 1873):** 18.
Greater Detroit Chamber of Commerce: 169, 190.
Greenfield Village & Henry Ford Museum: 189.
Hackley, E. Azalia Collection, Detroit Public Library: 172.
Halstead, Alan: 170-171.
Italian Tribune: 166.
Jewish Welfare Federation of Detroit: 168.
Labadie Collection, University of Michigan: 129(2).
LaBarge, David: 193.
Lee, Ruth: 171, 187.
Lewandowski, Mitchell: 167(4).
McDonald, Edward J.: 187.
Mackinac Island State Park Commission: 17, 20(2), 25, 26, 35(2).
Martinez, Charles H.: 238.
Mason, Philip P., ***Detroit, Fort Lernoult, And The American Revolution,*** **(Detroit, 1964):** 25.
Michigan Bell Telephone Company: 2-3, 4-5, 6-7, 10-11, 14, 30-31, 37, 48, 50-51, 64(2), 65.
Mickelson, Keith: 170, 178-179, 179, 188, 191, 194(2), 195, 197, 198.
Money Museum, The, National Bank of Detroit: 17, 19(2), 75(3).
Moon, Glen: 196.
Motor Vehicle Manufacturers Association: 8-9, 86-87, 87, 88, 89, 92(2), 93, 94 (4), 96-97, 99, 103, 134, 136.
Motown Record Corporation: 174, 175(5).
National Automotive History Collection, Detroit Public Library: 88, 89, 91, 92, 93, 96, 108.
North American Fur Trade Conference, ***Aspects of the Fur Trade,*** **(St. Paul, 1967):** 15.
Pospeshil, M. F.: 179, 182, 187.
Rauhauser, William C.: 76, 169.
Sanders, Fred: 1.
Simmons, William J., ***Men of Mark, Eminent and Rising,*** **(Cleveland, 1887):** 77.
Sinclair, Leni: 174(2).
Sinclair, Robert and Bryan Thompson, ***Metropolitan Detroit: An Anatomy of Social Chance,*** **Association of American Geographers, Ballinger Publishing Co., 1977:** 145, 163.
Sokol Detroit: 164, 165.
Spina, Tony: 154.
St. Clair Historical Commission:116.
Steyskal Family: 160-161.
Stuart, R. L.: 197.
Trizec Developments, Inc.: 110.
University of Detroit: 185(3).
Vogt, Berthold: 165.
Warr, Nemo: dust jacket.
Warren, Francis H., Comp., ***Michigan Manual of Freedmen's Progress,*** **(Detroit, 1915):** 78(4).
Wayne State University, CIT Photo Service: 186(3).
Wayne State University Press: 12.
Williams, Ronald G.: 121(2).
Wolf, Harry: 110(2), 111(2), 133, 187, 190, 192(3), 193(2), 194-195, 196.
Woodard, Clarence C.: 65, 98(3), 108, 180.
Woodford, Arthur M.: 120, 160(6).
Young, Mrs. Thelma: 151(3), 152(4), 153.